The Emergence
of State Government

The Emergence of State Government

Parties and New Jersey Politics, 1950–2000

Jeffrey M. Stonecash
with Mary P. McGuire

Madison • Teaneck
Fairleigh Dickinson University Press
London: Associated University Presses

Associated University Presses
2010 Eastpark Boulevard
Cranbury, NJ 08512

Associated University Presses
16 Barter Street
London WC1A 2AH, England

Associated University Presses
P.O. Box 338, Port Credit
Mississauga, Ontario
Canada L5G 4L8

The paper used in this publication meets the requirements of the American National Standard for Permanence of Paper for Printed Library Materials Z39.48-1984.

Library of Congress Cataloging-in-Publication Data

Stonecash, Jeffrey M.
    The emergence of state government : parties and New Jersey politics, 1950–2000 / Jeffrey M. Stonecash with Mary P. McGuire.
        p. cm.
    Includes bibliographical references and index.
    ISBN 0-8386-3953-4
    1. Political parties—New Jersey. 2. Political planning—New Jersey. 3. New Jersey—Politics and government—1951– I. McGuire, Mary P. II. Title.

JK2295.N6 S76 2003
320.9749'09'045—dc21

                                                                2002190213

Contents

The idea of equality, once loosed, is not easily contained.

—Source unknown

The goal of a thorough and efficient system of free public schools shall be to provide to all children in New Jersey, regardless of socioeconomic status or geographic location, the educational opportunity which will prepare them to function politically, economically and socially in a democratic society.

—New Jersey Statutes Annotated, 18A:7A-5

This [increase in income tax rates on the affluent] won't affect most people in Democratic districts. The median income in Newark is $13,000. In Camden, it's $11,000, and in Perth Amboy it's $16,000. Where the tax will have an impact is in Alpine, where the median family income is $78,000, and in Bedminister, where it's $60,000. And there are no Democrats representing those districts.

   —Democratic Speaker of the Assembly Alan Karcher
      in 1982, urging increasing the income tax rate on
      those making more than $50,000

.nine of ten of the people in this state have more in common with the guy in the city on an economic basis than they have with Steve Forbes [wealthy publisher of Forbes Magazine].

   —Jim Florio, former governor of New Jersey, in 1996,
      in commenting on why Democrats should be able to
      convince most people in New Jersey that they should
      rely on the Democratic Party

We're not going to try to allocate money away from the middle-income school districts in order to achieve the court's decision. I want to make it very, very clear that I will not approve a single additional dollar to be spent in these districts [the twenty-eight low-income special needs districts] without assurance that these dollars can be spent efficiently.

   —Republican Governor Christie Whitman announcing
      her opposition to a May 1997 New Jersey State Su-
      preme Court decision that the state had to spend more
      within low income districts.

Preface

State governments have changed. In the last fifty years they have steadily taken on more responsibilities. They impose higher taxes, manage more programs, and distribute far more aid to local governments than was the case in 1950. As a consequence, the state political process has emerged as a primary arena for making significant political choices, and there is less reliance on decisions made by a multitude of local governments.

Some see this emergence as reflecting a relatively recent resurgence of the states.[1] With declining faith in the federal government,[2] and greater confidence in state government capabilities,[3] the presumption is that members of Congress trust states more and are willing to turn more responsibilities back to them.[4] The increased role of state governments, however, is not really a product of recent events. Their role has grown steadily over the last century. In the early 1900s states raised far less in taxes than local governments did, but during the early decades of the century states steadily increased their role in raising taxes and providing services. During the Great Depression states enacted many new taxes and increased state aid to localities.[5] By the end of the 1930s many states were raising more in taxes than local governments.[6] By 1950 states on average raised as much in taxes as local governments did. Since the 1950s there have continued to be steady and significant increases in state roles. During the 1960s there was a decisive shift, with state taxes becoming much higher than local taxes.[7] A greater state role is not just a product of declining faith in the federal government in the last decade or so. The role of state governments has grown steadily during the last century. It is that steady growth which we need to understand.

Efforts to increase the role of state governments prompt major political battles and reveal fundamental divisions in American politics. A greater state role redistributes power between levels of government, and among groups within society. When a greater state role is proposed, the impetus to pursue change is often the issue of whether decentralized, autonomous, local outcomes should prevail. Should local communities, with varying wealth bases, pursue their own policies using their own revenues?[8] Or,

7

should state taxes be imposed to create greater state revenues that might be redistributed across communities? Should progressive state taxes be imposed, which tax some individuals and communities more, or should taxation be decentralized? The affluent cluster in suburban communities and use zoning practices to shape the composition of their populations, while central cities face declining tax bases. That results in vast differences between local governments in tax bases and in abilities to support schools and other programs.[9] The immediate political issue is whether state government should impose taxes and use state revenues to distribute greater revenues to areas with poorer tax bases. But the much larger question is whether the inequality in tax bases across communities is simply a natural result of market forces or a product of people exploiting government powers to zone municipalities to create inequality. Should we take from those who have achieved to distribute to those who have not? Should we encourage centralized government or rely on decentralized responses? Given the depth of conflict over these issues, the battles are intense, and change is not easy.

These battles over the role of state government inevitably involve issues of taxes, since state government needs resources to act on many policy issues. As expressed by others:

> Politics generally comes down, over the long run, to a conflict between those who have and those who have less. In state politics the crucial issues tend to turn around taxation and expenditure.[10]

> The evolution of state taxing and spending [is] a metaphor for the contest between state and local forces.[11]

These issues are also central to national and state politics. In recent decades we have witnessed emotional and protracted arguments about whether the national government should intervene in state affairs about civil rights, air and water pollution, open housing, and welfare. Much of the national debate in recent elections has been about whether the national government should do more or less.[12] While those national conflicts have consumed our attention, the same concern about accepting diversity of outcomes has played out at the state level regarding state-local relations. States have faced continual battles about whether state taxes should be increased or decreased and whether state governments should do more or less for their local governments.

New Jersey is a state where the role of state government has increased significantly since the 1950s, and the issue of state obligations has been central to political disputes. New Jersey provides an opportunity to understand how and why state government comes to play a greater role. The central concern of this study is how such changes occur. How does the issue of change get on the agenda? How do political parties react to these issues and what role do they play in advocating or opposing change? Does change occur incrementally or is it a product of major confrontations over future directions?

The conclusions of this analysis tell us much about how these issues emerge and are resolved in state politics. Efforts to change the role of state government are unpredictable. Politicians, and particularly legislators, are often reluctant to address them. Parties play a very significant role, with Democrats often differing from Republicans in their inclination to push issues of inequality. Perhaps most important, these partisan battles, which so disturb much of the public, do matter. Change occurs and parties play a major role in enacting and preserving change. But how parties play a role is complicated. Understanding their role in enacting change is best understood by following the path of change in New Jersey. This story tells us much about how issues of equity and government obligation are handled within the democratic process. It also tells us much about what role politicians and parties play in the process. I hope readers find the story of change as interesting as I have found it.

The Emergence
of State Government

Part I:
Introduction

1

The Role of the State

STATE GOVERNMENT IN NEW JERSEY PLAYED A MINIMAL ROLE IN STATE-LOCAL affairs in 1950. There was no state sales tax or income tax. The state generated little revenue for providing aid to municipalities, counties, and school districts. Of all tax revenues raised by state and local governments, state government raised less than 25 percent. Local governments relied heavily on the local property tax and received little state aid. State government was not a major actor in affecting policy within the state. Indeed, the governor was proud that per capita state taxes in New Jersey were less than in any other state.

By 1999 dramatic changes had occurred. The state had enacted a sales tax and raised it several times. It had enacted an income tax and raised it several times. The state raised over 55 percent of all tax revenue within the state and provided considerable aid to local governments. State government was involved in a broad array of issues. It was a major actor, and attention was focused on the state capital as the place where many important decisions were made.

The concerns of this book are how and why these changes happened. The decision to enact state taxes, to have the state provide more aid, and to have the state play a greater role in policy decisions constitutes a major reallocation of government authority. How do such changes come about? Does change occur incrementally through the accumulation of many relatively small decisions, or does change come about through major, highly visible decisions that involve major debates about the obligations of state government? Do Democrats and Republicans play major roles in structuring the debates over these issues? Do changes reflect a broad consensus or are changes enacted as partisan, political acts despite the fundamental opposition of other groups?

The analysis involves a case study, structured by specific theoretical concerns, to try to understand change. New Jersey is the focus because the state represents an important case of change. A state that played a limited role changed to one playing a significant role. Understanding how such change occurred in a state so decentralized in the 1950s should provide some insight into how changes of such magnitude can come about. The change has been accompanied by major partisan battles over whether taxes and the state role should increase and over how benefits should be distributed. Understanding how these issues emerge and why some politicians respond to them are important concerns. New Jersey is of interest not because it is typical—we don't know what the typical pattern of change in the nation is at this point—but because it represents an example of significant change. Subsequent studies in other states will indicate if the arguments made here have broader generality.

The Political Issues

Increasing the role of the state is a contentious political issue. An enduring question in state-local relations is how much the state will shape local policy. Will diverse outcomes be accepted or will the state intervene and override local preferences? Will the state redistribute authority and resources?

State involvement with local governments takes many forms. States create local governments, establish their responsibilities and legal powers, and determine their taxation and debt limitations.[1] Local governments inevitably develop different populations, tax bases, and policies. State government is then faced with the issue of whether to accept these variations, or see them as embodying unacceptable inequalities. If the latter is the judgment, the state can intrude in several ways, each of which generates controversy. The state can mandate that local governments must follow specific practices or provide specific programs at some minimal level. The state can provide intergovernmental aid to help local governments provide services that might otherwise not be provided. Finally, the state can go so far as to assume direct responsibility for local functions.[2]

The inequalities in tax bases and resources that develop among communities are a continual basis of pleas for more state involvement. Low-income groups want access to better housing opportunities and want state government to require local governments to change their zoning laws so affordable housing can be built in more jurisdictions. Low-income groups want the standards of eligibility for welfare to be uniform across the state.[3] Communities with less-affluent tax bases want more state aid for their schools. Individuals who feel their property is assessed at a higher level than that of others want uniform assessing practices so owners of similar properties will pay equal taxes. Communities with lesser tax bases want state aid so that they can spend the same on schools as wealthy districts.

State involvement in these issues brings out fundamental divisions in society. Liberals support these changes because they think there should be more fairness and equality in individual opportunities and in the policies that affect people. Liberals think the state should provide more state aid to low-income school districts so that there will be greater equality of resources. Conservatives oppose such changes because they fear the growth of state government power as potentially intrusive and oppressive. They do not want higher taxes. They do not want their assessments controlled by the state. They think those who have succeeded economically should be free from state intrusion so that they can enjoy the benefits of their position. Many affluent people have spent considerable effort to achieve and locate themselves in suburban communities with people of similar incomes.[4] They do not want their tax dollars used to support welfare in central cities. They also do not want state government to support building low-income housing in their communities. They strongly oppose the state dictating who will live in their communities.[5] They argue that local policy administration is the best way to keep government close to the people.

If state government is take actions on these issues, it needs more revenues, which means higher state taxes. Adopting state taxes invariably involves the issue of the redistribution of wealth among individuals and communities. Low-income groups and communities want more education aid distributed to low-income districts. They argue that access to tax resources is central to providing equality of opportunity. A state sales tax or income tax will provide the state with resources to distribute more money to low- income districts. Even if the state tax is regressive and higher-income individuals pay a smaller percentage of their income in taxes, redistribution occurs if more revenues come out of expenditures from more-affluent communities and the state in turn distributes much of these tax resources to lower-income individuals and communities.[6]

Suburban constituents are far less supportive of state taxation, particularly when redistribution is explicitly involved. If most services remain funded and provided by local governments, redistribution among communities is largely prevented. Many of the affluent oppose state taxation in general because it takes their money. If state taxes create a steady flow of revenues to state politicians, it creates continuing possibilities for redistribution. The affluent stress the importance of self-reliance and worry about money being spent on people who the affluent think should exert more individual effort.[7] They are much more supportive of local funding of schools.

In other policy areas the issue is whether the state should assume direct responsibility for programs. Low-income groups argue that welfare eligibility and benefits should not be dependent on where someone lives, and that the state should provide welfare. As an alternative, they want the state to impose regulations and provide more aid. Affluent communities do not want to provide welfare and would be glad to have the state assume responsibility. But they do not want to pay the taxes that are likely to be necessary for a uniform statewide welfare program.

Taxation is central to the ability of the state to play a greater role. The conflicts about state aid and state fiscal responsibilities inevitably lead to tax battles. As we shall see, tax issues have been central to New Jersey politics. Since 1950 state government in New Jersey has changed from playing a minor role to playing a significant role. Politicians have responded to ongoing debates about whether the state should play a role by making decisions to have the state play a greater role than it did. In most cases their response has involved imposing taxes. The question is why politicians would impose taxes, which are so disliked and could hurt politicians' reelection prospects.

DEMOCRACY AND CHANGE

Battles over the state role are contentious and protracted. As arguments drag on and on, there are doubts about the abilities of politicians to resolve conflict. Critics and editorials suggest that the political process is failing to handle conflict. Politicians are regularly portrayed as seeking to avoid conflict for fear of alienating constituencies. Politicians are characterized as having myopic concerns with the next election, and as being afraid to engage in discussions about fundamental issues such as equality of opportunity and the obligations of government.[8] Political parties, which we often presume will play a role in debating and resolving such broad issues, struggle to organize coherent debates about such issues. Politicians are seen as parochial, worrying more about their own districts and reelections rather than about larger party positions. This "individualism" has presumably increased in recent years as campaigns have become more candidate-centered.[9] Commitments to parties have declined among the public and among politicians. Politicians think of themselves first, and their ability to form party positions and collectively adopt policies that might create change becomes that much harder. Faced with conflict, politicians are seen as preferring to avoid it.

The ability of politicians to respond to policy problems is further limited by the perpetual changes that buffet them. A party may struggle to form a consensus around some policy they will pursue in the next year, only to find they must postpone its pursuit because of the intrusion of more pressing problems. Recessions erode state tax revenues and change the focus from new programs (and taxes to support them) to the question of which existing programs might have to be cut, or what taxes might have to be raised just to preserve existing programs. Federal aid may be cut, forcing a decision about whether to use state funds to continue a program. Long-term shifts in jobs from one region of the country to another can force politicians to reconsider whether they want to impose additional burdens on business.

Individualistic politicians, faced with a continual flow of unanticipated events, find it hard to sustain focus on coherent policy agendas. Every proposal for change is opposed by a vast array of groups arguing that change will be detrimental to society. The status quo prevails, and inequities persist. The state does not take on any more responsibilities, and the inequities that emerge from local fragmentation of tax bases persist.

CHANGES IN PUBLIC POLICY AND THE ROLE OF THE STATE

For all these reasons, change is difficult. Yet, while change seems so difficult, change has occurred across the nation and in New Jersey in recent decades. State governments now play a greater role in many ways. Since the 1940s state governments have steadily taken on new program responsibilities. In 1942 state governments were responsible for 61 percent of direct expenditure for state and local public welfare.[10] By 1991 this was over 80 percent. In 1960 state governments, on average, provided 39 percent of the funding for local schools.[11] They now provide almost 50 percent nationwide. Many states did not have extensive higher education systems in 1950, but all now provide large amounts of money to support higher education. Welfare has moved from being a locally administered program to a state-managed function in most states.

To take on more responsibilities and provide more aid states have had to impose taxes. Figure 1.1 presents state and local tax effort for all state and local governments in the United States since 1950.[12] Tax effort is defined as the percent of personal income taken in taxes (mostly income, sales, and property). Over time state governments have increased their tax effort from around 3.5 percent of income to over 6 percent, while local governments have been fairly stable in their tax effort. State tax effort increased steadily during the 1950s, and then major increases occurred in the 1960s, with another significant increase occurring in the early 1980s.

With greater tax revenues, states have increased their role in a broad array of policy areas. This greater role shows up clearly in fiscal indicators. One indicator of the state's role is the proportion of all state-local tax revenue raised at the state level.[13] This is determined by dividing all state taxes by total state and local taxes. This proportion has steadily risen since 1950.

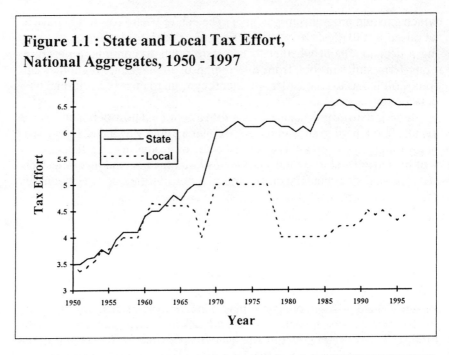

Figure 1.1 : State and Local Tax Effort, National Aggregates, 1950 - 1997

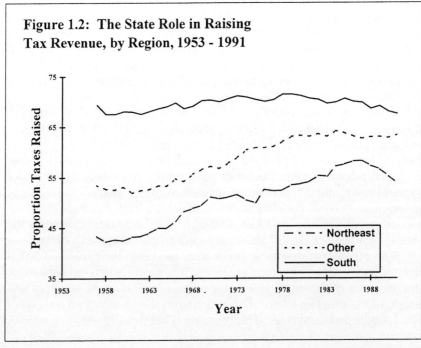

Figure 1.2: The State Role in Raising Tax Revenue, by Region, 1953 - 1991

The proportion of all state and local direct general expenditure spent directly by state governments has also increased, as has the proportion of all local general revenue that is derived from state aid to local governments.

These broad national changes, while significant, mask considerable variation in patterns of change by region.[14] The greatest increases in the role of the state have occurred outside the South. States in the Northeast and West were relatively decentralized at midcentury. Since the early 1950s these states have experienced a steadily growing state role. Figure 1.2 presents trends since 1953 in the state role for the indicator of the proportion of taxes raised by state government.

CHANGE IN NEW JERSEY

The greatest increases in the role of the state have occurred in Northeast states. New Jersey presents a significant example of these changes. In 1950 local tax effort was considerably higher than state tax effort. State tax effort, as shown in figure 1.3, began to rise in the mid 1960s, and by the late 1970s state tax effort was greater than local tax effort. State tax effort

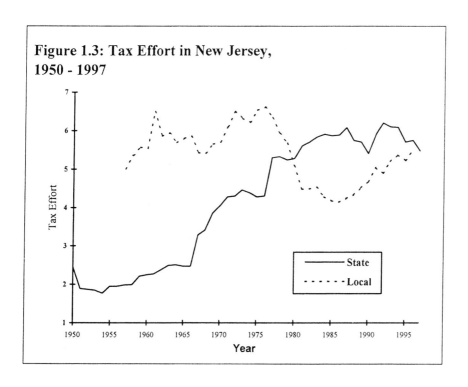

Figure 1.3: Tax Effort in New Jersey, 1950 - 1997

continued to be higher than local taxes through the 1980s, though local tax effort began to rise by the end of the 1980s. There was an increase in state tax effort in the early 1990s followed by a decline as the decade drew to an end. Though there has been some fluctuation in state tax effort over the last decade, state government has taken on a greater role in raising tax revenues, and is now the major actor in raising state-local tax revenues. As a consequence, the proportion of all state-local tax revenues raised by state government in New Jersey is now considerably higher than in the 1950s. In the 1950s state government raise only about 25 percent of all tax revenues. By the 1990s this had increased to over 50 percent.

SHIFTING POLICY RESPONSIBILITIES

The role of state government increased because it assumed new responsibilities. Little was spent on public welfare in the 1950s by either the state or by local governments. The delivery was largely decentralized, with most spending done by local governments. The state also provided little state aid to local governments. Figure 1.4 indicates how much change has

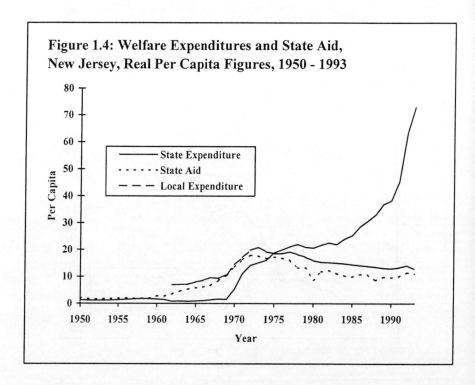

Figure 1.4: Welfare Expenditures and State Aid, New Jersey, Real Per Capita Figures, 1950 - 1993

occurred since then. State aid in real dollars (adjusted for inflation, 1990 = 100) rose until the mid 1970s and then declined because the state assumed more responsibility for the direct delivery of welfare. Per capita spending, again in real dollars, increased significantly beginning around 1970, while local per capita expenditure began to decline around that time.

As a result of these shifts the state's role in delivering public welfare has steadily increased. Figure 1.5 indicates the percentage of all public welfare spent directly by the state since 1950. Since the early 1960s the state proportion of spending on welfare has increased from 10 percent to over 85 percent. The state is now the primary deliverer of welfare services.

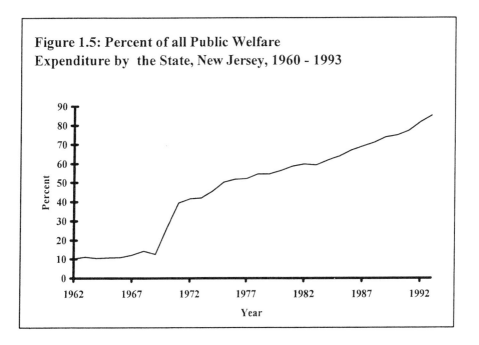

**Figure 1.5: Percent of all Public Welfare
Expenditure by the State, New Jersey, 1960 - 1993**

The state's role in local education has also changed significantly. Figure 1.6 indicates the trend of state aid for local schools, expressed in real dollars (adjusted for inflation, 1990 = 100) per capita. There has been a steady rise in real state support. The state is now a primary source of funding for local education spending. Figure 1.7 indicates the proportion of local education spending derived from state aid. In the early 1950s almost no support was provided by the state. By 1993 state aid was providing approximately 45 percent of the revenues for local spending on education.

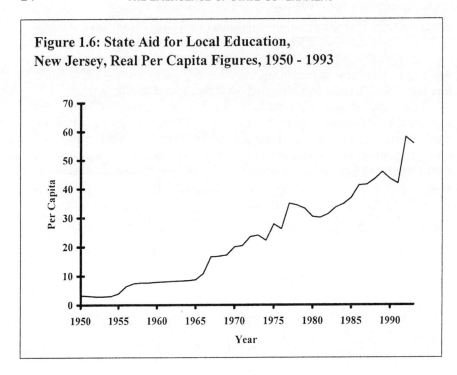

Figure 1.6: State Aid for Local Education,
New Jersey, Real Per Capita Figures, 1950 - 1993

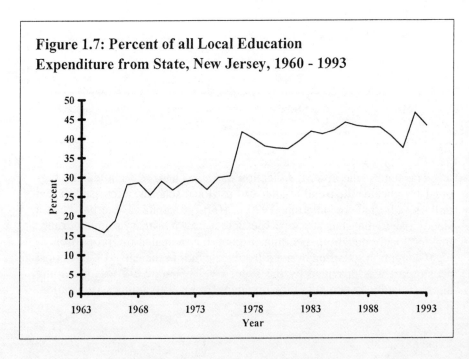

Figure 1.7: Percent of all Local Education
Expenditure from State, New Jersey, 1960 - 1993

THE NATURE OF CHANGE

State government in New Jersey now plays a major role in public policy. Did this change occur in steady and gradual increments, or was it a product of explicit and major decisions to increase the state's role? The former implies that state government in New Jersey drifted into its current position without any explicit decisions to change that role. The latter implies that change came about because major, visible political decisions were made. The difference is important. If the latter is how change came about, then it is important to focus on decisions involving large changes and why those decisions were made.[15]

The major changes in the role of the state, to be discussed in later chapters, have involved contentious tax decisions. State politicians chose to impose statewide, general taxes and then to raise those taxes to give the state more revenue. From 1955 until 1997 several changes in statewide taxes occurred. Each change was accompanied by considerable public controversy and difficult legislative negotiations. Table 1 presents the major tax changes since 1950.

Table 1. State Tax Changes in New Jersey, 1950–98

| | Tax Changes | |
Year	Increases	Decreases
1966	First sales, 3%	
1970	Increase sales from 3 to 5%	
1976	First income tax	
1982	Increase sales from 5 to 6% Increase income	
1992		Decrease sales from 7 to 6%
1994		Decrease income
1995		Decrease income

Each tax increase produced several significant boosts in state tax effort. Figure 1.8 indicates the year-to-year changes in tax effort (the change in tax effort from the prior year) since 1950. Major increases occurred in 1967, 1977, and 1991. Greater state revenues also came about because of increased state fees, such as drivers' licenses, motor vehicle registration, hunting licenses, marriage licenses, and tuition at state universities. But the major increases in state revenue came from enacting broad-based tax increases. Since the last major increase in 1991, the major changes have involved tax cuts.

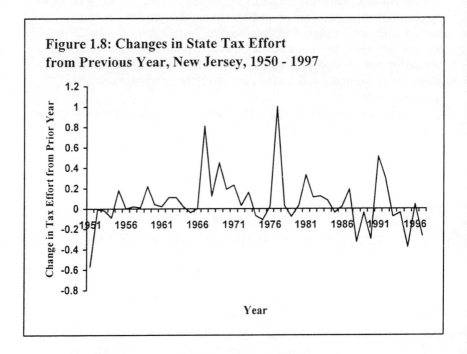

Figure 1.8: Changes in State Tax Effort from Previous Year, New Jersey, 1950 - 1997

Change did not just happen, but occurred because politicians decided to enact taxes and expand the role of the state. These decisions were accompanied by debates about the role of the state and about redistribution. Each change was accompanied by sustained debates about whether state government should do more. The question to be pursued here is why politicians decide to enact such changes.

APPROACH ISSUES: COMPARISON VERSUS A CASE STUDY?

How to analyze change so as to understand what creates it is a continuing dilemma of research. The two primary approaches are multiple-state comparison or a case study involving just one case. In state political analyses, the former approach has dominated, with studies including all fifty states and employing either a cross-sectional or time-series approach. These analyses proceed by creating a measure of state policy change, measures of relevant causal state conditions, and assessing the patterns of association between presumed causes and policy change.[16] It may be, for example, that change is strongly associated with vigorous party competition between two parties that represent very different sets of constituents. Or it may be that economic development creates social problems or complexities that prompt government intervention. The virtues of this comparative approach are that hypotheses are proposed, uniform indicators are collected in a standard fashion across multiple units, and some rigor of assessing hypotheses prevails.

Despite the presumed rigor of this approach, there are serious problems with executing the approach, and there are inherent limits in what the approach can tell us. First, the very virtue of the approach—examining multiple units for greater generality of findings—presents difficulties in gathering the requisite information. It is very difficult to create indicators for all states that we can presume are valid, or accurately capture the specific conditions of importance in states. For example, one crucial political condition that is likely to affect the battle over whether state government should do more is whether political parties have class differences in their electoral bases. V. O. Key argued that when parties have clear and enduring class differences in their electoral bases, the party representing the "have-nots" is more likely to serve as an advocate of programs to help their constituents. They are more likely to support efforts to enact taxes to fund those programs. Sustained support from this party for taxes and programs, he argued, will lead to a greater state effort in this regard, and presumably a greater state role.[17]

Given this argument, to conduct a fifty-state comparative analysis, it is necessary to have information on parties in each state that indicates the electoral bases of each party and the durability of electoral divisions across candidates and across time, along with the positions of party candidates at any one time and across some span of time.[18] It is a very demanding—indeed, perhaps overwhelming—challenge to acquire the detailed information necessary to portray these state conditions.[19] Scholars have made some progress over time in moving from very crude to more refined efforts to measure party competition, but our indicators are still fairly crude. Many initial efforts to measure party competition just assumed that parties have different electoral bases, and focused on the percentage of votes or seats each party held.[20] Later efforts merged public opinion surveys from a number of years to measure the association between income and party identification,[21] and assessed whether states with different divisions at the aggregate level varied in their policy.[22] Despite this progress, the indicators created

still only capture a very limited portion of the phenomena of interest—
enduring class electoral divisions and unified and enduring differences between sets of party candidates in policy concerns. It may well be that the
demands of such studies are simply too great, given the resources available
to students of state politics.

> Scholars of state politics may have to face the fact that it is next to impos-
> sible to study the impacts of political parties on public policies in either
> longitudinal [over time] or cross-sectional [across states at one time] quan-
> titative research that relies on the standard measures [using just the infor-
> mation] of which party controls the various institutions of government.
> The detailed information necessary to understand the nature of the party or
> parties that control a state's government may not be feasible to collect in
> any large sample.[23]

The result is that efforts to pursue analyses of change by assessing all
states inevitably run into the problem of constructing valid indicators. While
studies do proceed and find patterns of covariation across states or within
states over time, the limits of the indicators make it difficult to have great
faith in the meaning of the results. While a comparative approach to analysis is in preferable in the abstract, it is simply too difficult to execute prop-
erly in practice.

Equally important, the comparative approach can never really inform
us about some aspects of change. Why politicians actually enacted change
in one state and not in another is difficult to determine when multiple-state
analyses are conducted. The approach makes it difficult to capture the role
of political context, how politicians saw the situation, the dynamics of in-
teractions between the parties, and the timing and impact of unique events.[24]
The actors, their philosophies, their reading of the political environment,
and their strategy versus their opponents as factors in change get lost. In
short, the political process—"the intervening process, the causal nexus"—
is difficult to incorporate in such analyses.[25]

The alternative is to conduct a case study and assess change in one
political unit over time.[26] A case study allows inclusion of aspects of the
political process difficult to measure across states. It allows inclusion of
the perspectives of the actors, and the dynamics of how situations unfold.
It allows for the detection of the role of unexpected but theoretically important factors.[27] Case studies have a long history as an alternative means
to study state politics.[28]

Despite these presumed advantages, there are also clear anxieties about
using case studies. The common criticism of case studies is that they often
lack rigor, with analysts incorporating situations and events with no apparent plan or logic.[29] Theory often plays only a marginal role in case studies.

Further, whatever effort is made to be analytical is marred by the reality that, for any single case over a short period of time, there are multiple factors or variables that might reasonably explain the dependent variable of interest for the case.[30] Assessing the evidence about what explains a situation is often subjective and very subject to dispute. Analysts may be inclined to see one factor as having primary significance and, without standards of evidence, choose to emphasize that factor in their presentation.

While case studies can be plagued by these problems, these difficulties can be overcome. Case studies can begin with a clear theoretical focus, both in terms of the dependent variable of interest and possible explanations of the dependent variable. In the case of New Jersey the dependent variable is the growth of the relative role of state government. Battles to raise state taxes, as a means to give state government more resources to play a role in state and local issues, are particularly important as decision junctures in which the dependent variable was changed.

With regard to explanation, it is possible to rigorously structure a case study by proposing explicit theories of the sources of change. These theories can then be used to guide the collection of the information deemed relevant, and the evidence can be assessed against the expectations of theory.[31] Chapter 2 will review theories focusing on the role of social change, parties with different electoral bases, federal pressures, and the impact of diffusion. Each theory must be considered for what it suggests we should see occurring if this theory is a plausible explanation of change. Theory can be used to guide the gathering of information and to discipline the review of that information.

While theory can be used to guide analysis in a case study, there is still the persistent criticism that generally only one incident or situation is involved, and what is judged as explaining change is still a subjective matter. A case study covers a lengthy time period, however, such that multiple incidents of change are involved, and the case can provide multiple "tests" of the theories involved. In the case of New Jersey, the "case study" tracks change in just one government unit, but it involves multiple situations of change. State tax levels were altered several times. Party control changed numerous times. Numerous federal programs were introduced. Theories about parties and federal pressures suggest factors that should accompany tax changes if each theory is a plausible explanation of change. If party control is relevant, then tax changes should be associated with changes in party control, and specifically with Democrats gaining control. If federal pressures are relevant, then tax changes should be associated with greater federal pressures or inducements to participate in programs. A case study, then can reduce the dispute about how to interpret one situation by assessing multiple incidents, and engaging in multiple tests.[32]

CASE STUDIES AND THE SIGNIFICANCE OF NEW JERSEY

Case studies can be selected on the basis of two very different criteria. First, we may have a well-developed theory that suggests that if specific conditions prevail, then a specific situation or outcome should also occur. In this case we have clear notions of how the causes or independent variables affect some dependent variable. We might also have relatively precise information about the status of independent variables in a specific setting. We might then presume that given these conditions in a specific setting of interest, a specific outcome, or level of the dependent variable, should prevail. These situations are often seen as "crucial case" analyses.[33] Theory suggests that under certain conditions, an outcome should occur. The case of interest has the conditions, so if the expected outcome does not occur in a situation where the theory clearly suggests an effect should occur, the theory is suspect.

Alternatively, the certainty may not be in the theory or presence of causes, but in the outcome. We know that, in the New Jersey situation, change occurred. There are several plausible theories of why change occurred, and our interest is in assessing the evidence for these theories. The New Jersey situation is of this second type. The dependent variable is known, and has changed. Unlike a crucial case, where the issue is whether change occurred, change has occurred and it is the theoretical explanation that is unknown. New Jersey is a state in the Northeast, where change has been extensive in recent decades. Exploring the sources of change in this state allows a preliminary test of possible theories of change before seeking to understand change in other states. This is also a case in which the change has been over recent decades, unlike other states; the relative role of state governments in the South, for example, grew abruptly during the Great Depression but has changed little since then.[34] Public records for New Jersey should be more available for recent decades and a fuller analysis should be possible. If the case provides evidence about the conditions that lead to change, then explorations of change in other states and in earlier eras can focus on these factors to assess the theory that seems appropriate as an explanation of change. The presence or absence of these conditions should explain why changes have or have not occurred in other states.

APPROACH, METHODS, AND SOURCES

There is also the crucial issue of what approach to gathering information is appropriate for a case study. The general approach used here is twofold. The first step is to find those events in which the issue of the role of the state was prominent along with the decision made. The next step is to draw upon the theoretical framework presented in chapter 2 as a guide to the relevant conditions to research. For example, the electoral bases of political parties and the differences in bases between the two parties are presumed to be important. Therefore, it is necessary to have information on these matters in New Jersey over time, and particularly when issues emerged on the agenda. In the broad sense, the approach of this analysis is to propose a theoretical framework to explain change, and then assess whether the proposed conditions are relevant as explanations of the changes that occur or do not occur.

As for information gathering and the actual analysis, case studies are not shaped by any single technique. In a study that seeks to track change over almost fifty years, it is necessary to know social, economic, and political conditions. It is necessary to know what issues got on the agenda and how. It is necessary to know the electoral bases of parties, and the apparent strategies and logic of parties. It is necessary to know something about the information that was available to politicians. Finally, it is necessary to know what policies were proposed, how party members voted, and what impacts policies had.

The information used in this analysis is equally broad. I draw on government reports and documents, printed legislation, and press releases; existing studies on New Jersey; information on the socioeconomic composition of districts and the party winning seats; public opinion polls and exit polls on gubernatorial campaigns; fiscal data published by the Census of Governments and the state of New Jersey; interviews with public officials; and newspaper accounts of the evolution of issues. The information used is by no means exhaustive, and is not intended to be. The goal is to find information relevant to explaining change, whatever that source may be.

The Contribution of This Study

While considerable history in New Jersey will be reviewed, this is *not* an attempt to provide an historical or contemporary portrait of politics in New Jersey. There are already excellent studies that provide comprehensive overviews of New Jersey politics.[35] The intent here is a much more focused analysis of change in the role of state government over almost fifty years. The goal is to track events associated with the state government's increasing of its role, and to draw on various materials surrounding these events to try to explain change. The plan is to present a narrative of change and explanation, while assessing a theoretical argument.

As noted above, in assessing the relevance of the theoretical argument (for example, that parties and their electoral bases structure the debates about the role of government and changes in that role) the goal is also to use the results of the study to suggest what might explain change , or the lack thereof, in other states. The goal is to understand change in New Jersey, but also to suggest what should be examined in studies of other states. If this study finds that certain conditions in New Jersey appear to lead to increases in the role of state government, then the presence of these same conditions in other states should lead to a greater state role in those states. Likewise, their absence should be associated with little change in the state's role. Only other case studies will indicate if these conditions do cause change. The value in this study is in suggesting what conditions to assess in trying to understand change in other states.

THE PLAN OF THE BOOK

The next chapter will outline a theoretical framework to guide the subsequent analysis of events in New Jersey. The focus is on the role of political parties as organizers of interests and the short and long-term consequences of parties as organizers of constituencies and issues. The subsequent chapters will then use that framework to examine the sequence of changes from 1950 to now. This time period in New Jersey was characterized by a repeated cycle of Republican dominance followed by a short period of Democratic control. Those cycles produced significant change in the state's role and the chapters will follow that cycle to examine how parties played a role in change. A final chapter will offer a more general theory of the sources of change and the role of parties in that change.

2

Policy Change and
the Role of Parties

OVER A FIFTY-YEAR TIME PERIOD STATE GOVERNMENT IN NEW JERSEY TOOK ON greater responsibilities. It provided more state aid to local schools and it assumed a much greater role in providing higher education. It assumed more responsibility for welfare assistance. It enacted new state taxes to provide the state with the revenue to fund these programs. Enacting these changes, and particularly the taxes to support programs, generates significant opposition. If we are to understand why change occurred, the central question to be addressed is why the governor and state legislators would risk electoral rejection by enacting more taxes and fundamentally reallocating power in state-local relations.

For some reason politicians developed a sense that the role of state government should be altered. What makes a majority of state politicians conclude that an existing level of state influence is now in need of change? The argument of this analysis is that change is likely when a specific combination of political context and party situation occurs. Context shapes the pressure to act, and the party situation creates the inclination to act. When the context changes such that the status quo is called into question, there is greater pressure to act. When a party acquires power with a sense that it has a constituency that will benefit from change, and perceives a payoff from acting, change is more likely. When these two combine—the political context suggests a problem exists and a party with the appropriate electoral base acquires power—the probability of change is the greatest.

The chapter will first briefly summarize this argument, and then develop it in greater detail. The role of context and the changes in New Jersey that created more pressure to act will then be reviewed. The role of the party situation and under what conditions a party is likely to be inclined to take action will then be discussed. Finally, the value of this case study as a means for assessing these theoretical arguments will be reviewed.

Context and Pressures to Act

Politicians are the actors who ultimately enact change. As elected officials, they are attentive to their context. To understand change we need to know the context within which they operate. Context is defined here to include the social and economic conditions within the state, belief systems and political pressures that shape the legitimacy of these conditions, and the inducements and pressures that originate from the federal government regarding federal programs for constituents and their problems within the state. These contextual conditions may change significantly over time and alter the inclination of politicians to enact change.

There are many reasons such a shift in context may occur, but the three just reviewed are particularly important when the issue is changing the role of state government. First, the conditions of society—the actual extent of inequality in the distribution of wealth and opportunities—may change to such a degree that the issue emerges of whether the new state of affairs is fair. Second, public beliefs about the legitimacy of inequality and the obligations of government may shift, resulting in a new consensus about the presumed causes of inequality and the proper responsibilities of state government in response to inequalities. Third, the federal government may take a more active role in adopting national policies, such that states are offered new programs and accompanying federal aid. This in turn creates pressure on the state to consider adopting the programs or to assume responsibilities now handled by localities. Each of these changes—social conditions, beliefs, adoption by surrounding states, and federal pressures—alters the context of politicians. Changes in three of these played some role in New Jersey.

Parties and Politicians

While these contextual effects are obviously important, they are only potential stimuli to enact change. Contextual changes do not enact change.[1] Decisions to increase the role of state government are ultimately made by politicians. The governor and the legislature have to reach political agreement to enact change. These decisions to enact change are political in that they alter the distribution of authority between the state and local governments. They are political in that they often redistribute wealth and opportunities, and they often become partisan decisions. In New Jersey Democrats and Republicans generally did disagree on what should be done. The major tax increases were essentially the result of Democratic action, while Republicans, with some notable exceptions to be discussed, resisted tax increases.

Changes in party control do not, however, inevitably and invariably result in change. The central proposition of this analysis is that the impact of changes in party control are conditional upon whether parties have clearly different constituency bases and perceive an electoral advantage from making change. This proposition will be elaborated later in this chapter, but a brief overview may help at this point. In American politics a greater state role generally involves providing more benefits for those less affluent. As V. O. Key argued, "Politics generally comes down, over the long run, to a conflict between those who have and those who have less. In state politics the crucial issues tend to turn around taxation and expenditure."[2] State political battles are generally over whether to provide more state aid to central cities, whether to provide more state aid to less-affluent school districts, and whether to support more Medicaid and welfare assistance. These programs are invariably of greater benefit to the less affluent than the more affluent. If Democrats have a constituency that is less affluent than that of Republicans, then their constituency will benefit from efforts to have the state play a greater role. If Democrats also perceive that their general electoral fortunes will be improved by addressing problems of inequality, they are likely to enact change when they acquire power.

The Combination

Each of these conditions is important, and the presence of either of them—a context creating pressures for change, and a Democratic Party with a base among less-affluent to middle-income constituents—might be sufficient to increase the probability of a greater state role. When they are both present, however, the likelihood of change should increase significantly. While this provides the main argument, it is important to elaborate on it before exploring the narrative of events that occurred in New Jersey over time.

ECONOMIC AND SOCIAL CHANGE

The first contextual condition of importance is the actual degree of inequality in society. American society in general has experienced continual change since World War II. Inequality in the distribution of income, after declining through the 1950s and 1960s, has steadily increased since roughly 1970.[3] That trend has made the issue of inequality more prominent than it was during the 1950s and created pressure on government to somehow respond.[4]

Perhaps more important for state-local relationships has been how change has affected the distribution of populations and income across municipalities. Since the 1950s people have steadily shifted from central cities to suburbs. The more-affluent are more likely to make this move, resulting in greater differences between city and suburb tax bases. These differences lead to questions about the fairness of the distribution of opportunity and wealth and whether government should assume a greater role to try to respond to that change. The redistribution of income and wealth, in particular, is likely to prompt a debate about state government action. In an individualistic society, which prizes equal opportunity for all, greater inequality of wealth among areas alters the distribution of housing, schooling, and employment opportunities, and is certain to prompt arguments that there is less equality of opportunity and that government should do something to respond.[5] Many, of course, will resist pleas for a redistributive response, but advocates of a response will seek to push the issue of the state's obligation to respond onto the agenda.

New Jersey, like other states, has experienced a considerable relocation of the population as suburbanization has occurred. It was never a state with a high concentration of its population in a few large central cities, but much of its population through much of the twentieth century was clustered around a string of metropolitan areas. In 1950 much of the state's population was clustered in the northeast counties around New York City and in the counties immediately east of Philadelphia. After World War II, a significant move to the suburbs began around the country.[6] New Jersey experienced a similar movement, with its population dispersing across the state. It became one of the most suburban states in the country.[7] As the population grew and people moved to the suburbs, the counties elsewhere in the state grew significantly. The major central cities—Camden, Elizabeth, Jersey City, Newark, Paterson, and Trenton—experienced declining populations.

Table 2.1 summarizes population shifts in New Jersey over the forty years from 1950 to 1990. Newark's population declined from 438,776 to 275,221. Camden declined from 124,555 to 82,492. The counties to the west and south of the northeast corner of the state grew steadily. As a consequence, the northeast corner declined from 43 percent of the state's population to 28 percent. Within the northeast corner, only Bergen County experienced growth. Most of the growth in the state occurred in the central and southern counties.

In 1950 almost all local activities were funded by the property tax, with county tax bases varying. The right side of table 2.1 presents the per

Table 2.1. The Shifting Distribution of Population and
Wealth in New Jersey, 1950s–1990s
(Using County and City Data)

Area	Population				Value of Assessed Property	
	1950		1990		1955	1995
	Number	% state	Number	% state	per capita	
Northeast		43.2		27.9		
Bergen	539,139	11.1	842,380	10.8	32,780	89,476
Essex	905,949	18.7	778,206	10.0	18,703	48,154
Newark City	438,776	9.1	275,221	3.5		
Hudson	647,437	13.4	553,099	7.1	12,197	37,590
Northwest		23.4		25.2		
Union, Morris, and Passaic	899,602	18.6	1,370,643	17.6	26,636	71,019
Sussex, Warren, Hunterdon, and Somerset	230,052	4.8	591,003	7.6	27,298	79,265
Central		23.7		27.5		
Middlesex, Mercer, and Monmouth	719,980	14.9	1,550,728	19.9	26,326	65,174
Camden	300,743	6.2	506,585	6.5	19,514	38,902
Camden City	124,555	2.6	82,492	1.1		
Southern Burlington, Ocean, Atlantic, Salem, Gloucester, Cumberland, and Cape May	591,894	12.2	1,581,114	20.3	27,212	63,039
Total	4,835,329		7,773,584			

Population figures for this table for 1955 were taken from the U. S. Department of Commerce, U. S. Bureau of the Census, *City and County Data Book* (Washington, D.C.: Government Printing Office, 1957 and 1992).

capita property tax wealth for each county or grouping of counties for 1955[8] and 1994.[9] The property values are adjusted for inflation so that the 1955 property values are expressed in 1994 dollars, which allows a comparison with 1994 property values.[10] All counties experienced a significant increase in their real per capita property wealth over time. The distribution of property wealth, at the county level, was unequal in 1955, and suburbanization did not change that. Bergen County had more taxable wealth per person in 1955, and it continued to have more taxable wealth in 1994. Camden and Hudson Counties had less property wealth per person than other counties in 1955 and they had less per person than other counties in 1994.

These broad shifts of population and property wealth across counties are important, but conceal the more important changes that occurred in the numerous small municipalities in the state. Counties in New Jersey have not been and are not now the major deliverers of public services. New Jersey has over 566 municipalities and over 600 school districts, most of which are coterminous with municipalities. The issue of inequality emerges because of how property wealth is distributed across these municipalities and school districts. As table 2.1 indicates, the major cities in New Jersey lost population and property wealth. But how was wealth distributed across the multitude of municipalities—small cities, townships, and boroughs? This distribution is particularly important because inequalities in municipal tax bases translate into inequalities of locally generated funding for schools. Inequality of school funding is seen as important, because schools they are seen by many as vehicles of equality of opportunity, and inequality of school resources leads to broad charges of a lack of opportunity.[11]

As suburbs grew, many of them, but not all, became pockets of the more affluent. As the process of change played out, there were clear efforts to shape how specific suburbs developed. The more affluent sought to live in communities with similar and homogeneous populations. They sought to shape who ended up in what suburbs on the premise that community homogeneity would lead to more stable communities and higher property values.[12] State-authorized zoning laws allow communities to shape the size and expense of housing. Suburbs that adopt large minimum lot sizes and large minimums on house floor space end up excluding low-income housing and create communities with more wealth per person. Many communities also engaged in efforts to exclude minorities. The process of creating enclaves of wealth was probably accentuated in New Jersey by the enormous number of municipalities of limited population and geographical size. Many municipalities have less than ten thousand people. As the population spread across the state, some municipalities emerged with wealthy homes and highly valued commercial properties, while others had properties valued much lower. This same process occurred all across the country.[13]

Did the suburbanization process really significantly change the distribution of tax bases and public resources? To try to assess that, a random sample of sixty New Jersey school districts was drawn to compare over time.[14] These sixty districts were drawn from the list of all districts in existence in 1994. Data were then collected on the assessed value of wealth,[15] population, and property tax rate for these districts for 1952, 1969, and 1994. The property wealth per person or per student was determined by dividing the property tax base by the total resident population and the total number of students enrolled. The concern is not the average or absolute tax base or tax rate per district in any year, but the diversity among districts and how that has changed over time.

Measuring the diversity of tax bases might be done several ways. The range (the difference between the highest and lowest numbers) might be used, but that does not indicate the diversity of all districts. The variance is a commonly used indicator of diversity. It is calculated by first finding the mean of all districts, and then subtracting the mean from the score for each municipality to determine the deviation from the mean. These deviations are then squared (to eliminate positive and negative scores), and these squared terms are summed to equal the variance around the mean. The square root of this sum is the standard deviation, which measures variation or dispersion around the mean.

While valuable, the standard deviation makes it difficult to compare dispersion over time if the average value of the measure changes considerably over time. If average values increase over time but the dispersion does not change, the standard deviation will be greater just because the deviations will have greater absolute values. In New Jersey, the average real value of local tax bases has increased significantly over time, and using the standard deviation will lead to a potentially misleading conclusion that there is greater dispersion.

To correct for the general increase in mean values, the usual approach is to divide the standard deviation by the mean for each year. This gives the coefficient of variation, which measures the extent of dispersion relative to the average value for the set of scores for that year.[16] The higher the coefficient, the greater the relative dispersion around any particular mean. In this case, the concern is inequality. These calculations are done for the average real[17] assessed property per student and the total (local government plus schools) municipal tax rate per $100. In the case of the municipal tax rate, the average tax rate has declined over time, so any calculation of dispersion is around a lower average.

Figure 2.1 presents the coefficient of variation for school tax bases and municipal tax rates. The coefficient of variation increased from 1952 to 1994 for the assessed value per student and for the total tax rate for municipalities. Over time, the degree of inequality among municipalities in tax bases and tax rates has increased.

Changes among municipalities can also be seen by comparing tax rates across time by the wealth levels of municipalities. Figure 2.2 groups municipalities by quintiles of wealth levels and presents the average municipal tax rate by group over time. The sixty districts are grouped into fifths, ranging from the set with the lowest average per student tax base to the group with the highest average per student tax base.[18]

In 1952 districts with the least-affluent tax bases imposed higher tax rates than the more affluent fifth, but the differences in tax rates between the two groups were not major. By 1994 the differences in tax rates imposed by the groups of districts had become much more pronounced. By 1994 districts with wealthier tax bases were able to impose much lower tax rates than districts with less-affluent tax bases. The increased inequality of tax rates over time was largely because poorer districts were not able to lower their tax rates over time, while more affluent districts were able to do so.

These changes in tax bases have significant consequences. Communities with lower tax bases, even while taxing their residents at a higher rate, have fewer resources for schools, libraries, and public recreation facilities. Poorer communities have more crime and needy populations and need money to respond to these problems. Communities with highly valued property tax bases can tax their residents at lower levels and still generate more tax revenues per person. They also have fewer social problems, allowing them to devote more of their resources to fund schools and to have better public facilities.

As we shall see, these changes also became part of the political discourse within the state. Advocates of addressing inequality of school finance called attention to these changes, published reports focusing on change, and lobbied politicians to respond. The increase in inequality and the efforts to make it an issue created pressure on politicians to act to address the issue.

CHANGING VIEWS OF SOCIAL OBLIGATIONS AND GOVERNMENT

While the distribution of wealth among municipalities in New Jersey shifted over time, that becomes a political "problem" only if the public perceives it as such. Public support for a government response to this is shaped by general perceptions of what is, what should be, and how far apart these two are. Notions of what government should do can change significantly as views of the sources of inequality change. If individualism,

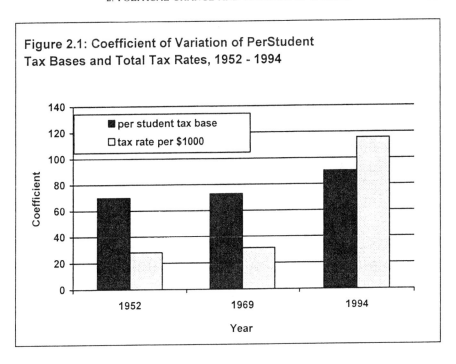

Figure 2.1: Coefficient of Variation of PerStudent Tax Bases and Total Tax Rates, 1952 - 1994

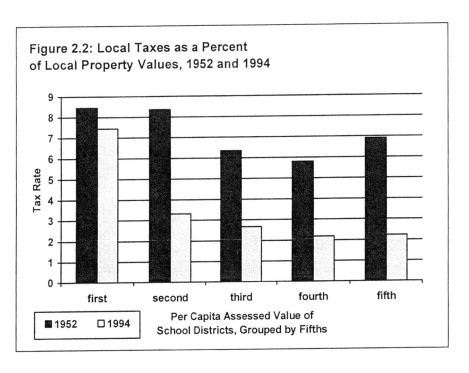

Figure 2.2: Local Taxes as a Percent of Local Property Values, 1952 and 1994

the belief that all individuals are responsible for their own fate, prevails, then inequality is likely to be not only tolerated but endorsed as a legitimate outcome of a merit-driven market process. If it is presumed that individuals are greatly affected by their environment—their family, neighborhood, and schools—then inequalities between communities become less acceptable and legitimate. If more of the public presumes that the "environment" affects people, there is likely to be greater support for government action to redress these inequalities.[19]

The time period from 1950 to the 1990s produced significant shifts in public support for government activity. In broad (and considerably simplified) terms, this time period saw a shift from limited support for government activity (the 1950s) to a significant increase in support for government efforts to respond to social problems (the 1960s and early 1970s) to a considerable ambivalence about the role government should play (the 1980s and 1990s).[20]

During the 1950s the economy grew, and there was a widespread belief that problems such as unemployment and poverty would decline and that extensive government programs were not necessary.[21] There were few, if any, lawsuits about matters such as inequalities of school finance. This faith that social conditions were not a problem, however, faded with the rise of the civil rights movement,[22] the rediscovery of poverty,[23] and the emergence of the "urban crisis."[24] There was an increase in the perception that problems existed and a sense that government should address race and class inequalities. The belief grew that individuals were affected by systemic, societal inequalities. As these beliefs grew, they undermined the legitimacy of existing inequalities. The result was a significant increase in government programs and expenditures in the 1960s to respond to these problems.[25]

The increased support for government programs did not last, however. The Vietnam War and Watergate undermined public confidence in government.[26] Expenditures on public welfare increased, and critics attacked the system, arguing that it undermined self-sufficiency and encouraged people to stay on welfare. Welfare was increasingly characterized as a failure,[27] and many turned against government on the grounds that it was no longer trying to remedy problems but had become too involved in providing unfair advantages to specific groups, such as women and minorities.[28] The conservative movement mobilized supporters and was able to make an articulate case for why government action was ineffective, and why individuals and local communities should be relied upon.[29] The consequence was a general decline in support for government action to address problems. In the space of fifty years government roughly moved from being not part of the solution to being a possibly positive actor, to being part of the problem to many people. These shifts occurred nationally and at state and local levels. If these changes played out in New Jersey, we would see a gradual rise in support for more government activity, and then an erosion in that support.

FEDERAL PRESSURES

The actions of the federal government are also part of the context of state political actors. The federal government can create pressure on state politicians in two ways. It can enact new programs and offer states federal aid as an inducement to participate in the programs. The federal government generally offers to pay a substantial proportion of the costs associated with a program.[30] National programs have focused on responding to problems in diverse policy areas, such as welfare, civil rights efforts, and environmental protection. Since federal programs provide benefits to state constituents, state officials feel some pressure to adopt the state programs so they can respond to constituent needs and be able to claim credit for providing the benefit. Responding to these inducements, however, does not come without a cost to state officials. If states are to adopt new programs, they have to provide some matching revenues, which means there are pressures to raise taxes or fees, or to divert funds from other programs.

State engagement in these federal programs in turn creates additional pressures on state politicians, as the federal government seeks to regulate how state and local governments execute federal programs.[31] Federal officials often seek to have states adopt uniform policies and practices within each state. Many social policies—welfare, assistance to the elderly who lacked money, aid to the blind and disabled—began at the local level, with widely varying practices of administration, eligibility determination, and benefit levels.[32] When the federal government enacted the Social Security Act in 1935 and began to provide federal aid to states, the issue emerged of whether states should be required to have uniform practices across areas within states. Local control over these decisions inevitably resulted in differences (inequalities) in how people are treated by locale.[33] These differences resulted in considerable federal pressure to have states create more uniformity in practices and policies, largely by having states require uniform policies or by having the state assume direct responsibility for the programs.[34]

If state governments respond with mandates on local governments that require local revenues, this in turn creates more pressures for state support of local governments. Local officials then pressure state officials to either provide more state aid to pay for the program, or to have the state assume responsibility for the program.[35]

This dynamic played out in New Jersey. Like many eastern states, the state was very decentralized in the 1940s and 1950s, and programs were generally locally delivered with locally generated revenues. As new federal programs (such as Medicaid) were enacted during the 1960s, state officials had to decide whether they would adopt the new programs and pay the associated costs. As existing programs (AFDC, or welfare), which were locally delivered, were expanded beginning in the 1960s and 1970s, states had to decide how much state aid they would provide for increased benefits. The states experienced new pressures about their commitment to federal programs when federal aid to the states began to decline during the 1980s.[36] Thus, over the time period this study covers, states faced two significant pressures. The first was whether to respond to federal programs during the 1960s and 1970s. The second was whether to maintain support levels when federal aid began to decline and then stabilized.

POLITICAL PARTIES AS PROTAGONISTS IN EXPLAINING CHANGE

All these factors—growing inequalities, changing beliefs, and federal actions—create pressures for state action, but they are not deterministic. While "social forces" are important stimuli to change, they do not enact change. State politicians have to decide to respond to changes in the distribution of wealth, shifting concerns about inequality, and federal pressures, if change is to result. They are inevitably partisans, and their reactions to social change are filtered through partisan perspectives. Parties, then, affect whether there is a reaction to change and events, and the nature of any debate that follows.

The factors that affect whether parties react to these pressures are complicated, but important. We often begin our attempts to understand parties with idealized expectations about their role. A fundamental presumption is that broad conflicts are persistent in society. We have mentioned V. O. Key's statement that "Politics generally comes down, over the long run, to a conflict between those who have and those who have less. In state politics the crucial issues tend to turn around taxation and expenditure."[37] The important questions are whether government does more or less, and more or less for whom. Some want government to intervene in society to enhance equality of opportunity and equality, while others want government to accept the outcomes of the workings of the private sector as legitimate.

Given these presumed broad differences, the important issue is how to make those broad differences the focus of political debates, so the public feels that their differing concerns are being represented. Parties can contribute to this process in several ways.[38] Parties can derive their support from different sets of constituents. On a national basis, Democrats draw their constituents primarily from individuals with middle to low income, while Republicans draw their constituents primarily from individuals with middle to high income.[39] As a result of whom they represent, each party is likely to focus on the concerns of its primary constituents and advocate policies beneficial to their constituents. They can present differing policy options to the public during campaigns and argue for the virtues of their respective policy proposals. The expression of differing views gives the public a means to distinguish among party candidates, and helps the public make choices. After elections, whichever party gains control of the legislature and the governorship can then interpret victory as support for their proposals, and use their political control of government to enact changes. The public can judge whatever policy choices are made, and accept or reject the party by voting for or against the party label. In this way parties contribute to getting concerns on the agenda, to serving as a means to get changes enacted or not enacted, and to giving the public an identifiable group to reward or punish for actions taken.

If all these conditions and practices exist, parties can become the vehicle for focusing attention on issues about the role of state government. Will the state rely on local tax bases (which may vary dramatically) to fund local elementary and secondary schools, with the consequence that well-to-do families have better schools?[40] Will the state tax individuals through state income and sales taxes and distribute state aid to local districts in a way that reduces differences in local education funds? Will the state impose higher taxes to pay higher welfare and unemployment compensation benefits? And who will pay such taxes? Will the state subsidize tuition at state universities or provide grants to enhance equal opportunities in higher education? Or will the state expect students to find their own sources of money or borrow to pay for education? If Democrats militate for more redistributive programs, while Republicans plead for restraint in state taxes and a state role, then the parties contribute to organizing public debates about these issues.

Democrats are more likely to react to pressures to address inequality, while Republicans are less likely to respond to such pressures with programs. Democrats are more likely to support a greater state role as a means to respond to problems. They are also likely to criticize Republicans for not responding to pressures or addressing problems. Democrats, then, are the likely vehicle for enacting change. But they are likely to pursue change only if the right combination of conditions exists. Table 2.2 presents the combinations of importance and the accompanying likelihood of change. If inequality has increased, social thought defines this as a problem, and the Democrats rely on an electoral base of those most likely to be affected by inequality, change is most likely. Under other conditions, it is less likely.

Table 2.2. Conditions Likely to Result in Increased
State Role When Democrats Acquire Power

	Democratic Party Reliance on Lower-to-Moderate Income for Electoral Base and Difference from Republican Party Base	
Contextual Conditions	Low	High
• Stable inequality • Social thought relatively accepting of inequality • Stable federal programs and inducements	Change Unlikely	Change Somewhat Likely
• Increasing inequality • Social thought relatively critical of inequality • Increased federal programs and inducements	Change Somewhat Likely	Change Likely

PARTIES IN NEW JERSEY

These expectations, which presume important matters about electoral bases and their continuity, and about political debates, may well have relevance for understanding change in New Jersey. Table 2.3 indicates which party was in power when various tax changes occurred between 1950 and 1995. Democratic control was a major factor in the major tax changes in New Jersey during that period. Democrats gained control of the legislature and the governorship in the 1965 elections and enacted a sales tax in the 1966 session. They gained control of both branches after the 1973 elections and enacted an income tax in 1976. They won control of both branches again in the 1989 elections and enacted major increases in sales and income tax rates in 1990. In each case Republicans opposed the change. Democrats were the party that enacted taxes that led to a greater state role, and Republicans were the party trying to restrain the growth of state government. Partisanship mattered, and it mattered as we might expect.

But there are also significant deviations from our expectations about parties. When Republicans won office in 1969 they did not cut taxes. Instead, they enacted an increase in the sales tax from 3 to 5 percent. After

Republicans won the governorship in 1981, the Republican governor agreed to increases in the sales and income tax in 1982, and the increases were supported with Republican votes in the legislature. Only in the 1990s did Republicans use their political control to enact tax decreases that cut back the ability of the state to raise revenue.

Furthermore, the behavior of parties is even less clear than this brief review indicates. Democrats in the 1965 campaign did not advocate a state-wide tax. The Democratic legislature in 1966 rejected a gubernatorial proposal to enact an income tax. They enacted a sales tax only *very* reluctantly. Legislative Democrats did not run in 1973 or 1975 pledging to enact an income tax. They enacted one in 1976 only after there was extraordinary pressure from the courts to address inequalities in school finances. Democrats in the 1989 campaign again did not campaign on a promise to enact taxes.

Table 2.3. Major State Tax Changes in New Jersey, 1950–95

| Year | Tax Changes | | Party Control |
	Increases	Decreases	
1966	First sales, 3%		Democrats
1970	Increase sales from 3 to 5%		Republicans
1976	First income		Democrats
1982	Increase sales from 5 to 6% Increase income		Divided
1990	Increase sales from 6 to 7% Increase income		Democrats
1992		Decrease sales from 7 to 6% Decrease income	Republican
1994		Decrease income	Republicans
1995		Decrease income	Republicans

The gubernatorial candidate largely avoided the issue when asked about taxes during the campaign, and Democratic legislative candidates did not discuss it all. Democrats were not at all eager to enact taxes once in office. There is an expectation that Democrats are advocates of tax increases and a greater role of the state, but the events in New Jersey do not provide much support for that expectation. Democrats enacted change, but only with great reluctance.

The process of change in New Jersey presents a puzzle about change and about the behavior of political parties. Democrats did play the role of enacting a greater state role, but the role was played reluctantly. Republicans sometimes supported taxes, other times opposed them, and other times cut taxes. Is there, therefore, any clarity to the role of parties? Do parties act like the theoretical ideal just reviewed? Does the New Jersey situation help us understand parties, or just suggest that their behavior is simply erratic?

These discrepancies between our idealized expectations of parties and their actual behavior are not confined just to New Jersey. There is considerable evidence that the conditions often do not exist within states for the ideal of parties just reviewed, and that parties often do not behave as we might expect. First, party bases often do not differ as we might presume. In some states parties differ in their attraction of liberals or conservatives, while in other cases they do not.[41] In some states, Democratic success is not at all connected to the average family income of state legislative districts, while in other states it is.[42] Second, many parties do not propose party policy platforms.[43] Campaigns are candidate-centered, with each candidate running his or her own campaign and defining his or her themes.[44] If any policy platform does emerge, it generally reflects the preferences of the gubernatorial candidate, and legislative candidates do not feel bound by it. Third, the media generally does not provide extensive coverage of state politics, and often neglects to explain the policy differences behind partisan battles that occur during legislative sessions.[45] The result is that "party" positions often do not exist, or those that do exist are not reported to the electorate. Finally, the public also does not meet our expectations. Most people do not follow politics extensively, and more than half do not vote in state elections.[46] Awareness of what parties have proposed or done in the past is often very inaccurate. Attachment to parties in the electorate has steadily declined over time.[47] The conditions for coherent party action and for a clear connection between parties and constituents often do not exist.

Not surprisingly, the evidence from the states also indicates that party control over the gubernatorial and legislative branches often results in no changes. In some states change occurs, but in other states there is no impact as party control changes.[48] The findings almost seem to match the perception of the public that partisan squabbles are meaningless posturing by parties and detract from a focus on major issues.[49] Regardless, it is clear that we have much to understand about how parties approach policy and why their policy impact is erratic. Parties clearly do not behave in the consistent fashion that a simple model might suggest.

This seeming conformance of parties in New Jersey to expected patterns, but the clear reluctance of Democrats to enact change with any enthusiasm, provides an opportunity. We can use the repeated cases of change in party control and policy changes to assess how combinations of contextual pressures and party electoral bases produce changes in the role of state government.[50] A case study allows us to explore the issue of why party members were clearly reluctant to engage in the behavior that did occur, and in so doing, develop a theory about the political conditions that are necessary for party control to have consequences.[51] Repeated cases of the situation of interest within one state allow us to replicate our assessment of whether a general pattern prevails.

Before reviewing the actual events of change, however, we need to know what information to gather as we seek to understand change. Case studies do not simply involve gathering information. We must have some theoretical presumptions about what information is relevant to gather.[52] With that goal in mind, we need to develop preliminary theoretical notions of what specific conditions are important in shaping whether a party is likely to be inclined to change.

FORMING EXPECTATIONS OF PARTIES

Our problem in forming theories about the role of parties and understanding their impact may stem from our models. We may in some sense be trapped by expectations derived from ideal models. Initial efforts to assess the role of parties included several questionable assumptions derived from a relatively simple model of parties. Parties are often presumed to be differentiated, unitary, and invariant in their behavior. That is, it is presumed that parties within states differ from each other, that they act as cohesive sets of actors, and that their policy goals and behavior are essentially the same across time.[53] To exaggerate, in ideal models a party is seen as an army of unified ideologues, differing from another army of differing ideologues; and this army acquires power and acts upon its ideology without reacting to any variations in the political context over time.

Practically, many analyses assume, in the course of the quantitative tests of the impact of party control, that all party members are the same. Democrats are presumed to always want more programs and always raise taxes to fund the programs.[54] Republicans are presumed to always want to cut back on government and to cut taxes. Such presumptions are in many ways appealing, for we know that, on average, Republican and Democratic candidates and elected officials differ from each other.[55] But this focus on the average sidesteps the issue of diversity within parties, the consequences of diversity, and the issues of how politicians react to context.

The presumption of party unity has led to conducting tests to assess whether parties meet these expectations, and stopping with that assessment. We have neglected the questions of why parties deviate (or don't deviate) from the expectations.[56] To understand parties we need to move away from models or idealized expectations and explore how parties actually operate—the situations parties face and how they react to those situations. The existence and behavior of "parties" tends to be much more ad hoc and conditional than our ideals, and to understand how they affect policy we need to incorporate that reality.

In this study, the primary concern is with the party of elected officials. It is they who must make political decisions about whether to increase the role of state government. The relationship of these elected officials to the electorate is clearly crucial, and that relationship will be given considerable attention in the analyses to follow, but the primary focus here is with the behaviors and perceptions of elected party candidates. They constitute an apparent party in the sense that they share the same party label. Whether this commonality means anything and has any policy implications is a matter that must be established rather than merely assumed.

The crucial question to pursue in trying to understand the nature of a party is to ask under what conditions its members might act like a "party." The argument here is that the emergence of "party" is likely to be conditional.[57] Whether there is any commonality of policy among party members is conditional on the commonalities of the constituencies and interests of party members in office, and on how similarly they see the immediate political context. The interpretations of party members of their commonalities determine whether any clear policy agenda emerges and there is a coalition to enact it. We can form an expectation of what parties are likely to do with power, if we presume that a few factors shape the behavior of parties. What follows is not so much a precise theory of party behavior as it is a review of the important conditions that affect the formation of a "party" and "party policy." It is assumed that campaigns and policy voting tend to be candidate-centered. That is, candidates focus on *their* own political situation and worry about how *their* positions and voting will affect *their* standing with *their* constituency, whether that constituency is statewide or within a legislative district. From those individualistic perspectives flow numerous dynamics.

Candidate-Centered Campaigns

Political campaigns in American politics are decentralized and candidate-centered. Candidates generally run their own campaigns and form their own themes. They focus on and operate within the context they face as they try to win. A Democratic legislative candidate who runs in a conservative, suburban district will take more conservative positions than a Democrat running in a liberal, urban district. A Republican legislative candidate running in a liberal, urban district will take more liberal positions than a Republican running in a conservative, rural district. Ideological positions vary with the context. Candidates facing varying constituencies operate independently and may not even want a state party platform. They may not want to be constrained by or identified with a statewide set of policy positions.

In some cases, ideological or policy positioning may not even be relevant to a campaign.[58] Some candidates, particularly incumbents, try to shift the focus of the campaign to questions of qualifications and character to downplay the role of policy positions in their campaigns. The candidate may do this because he or she is running in a district where support for the other party is generally high, and the candidate wishes to avoid a strong party vote driven by policy differences between voters. The candidate may also take this approach because both candidates' positions are similar and accord with the district, and the incumbent wishes to make other criteria the focus of the election to gain an advantage during the campaign.

The same principles apply to gubernatorial elections. Candidates choose the campaign theme they wish to pursue, and how they wish the campaign to be conducted. Much of this will depend on their own record, that of their opponent, and the current political context. If the economy is growing and the general trend in the country is liberal, then a Democrat is likely to stress liberal themes, and a Republican candidate may also be relatively liberal. If the country is drifting to the right, then a Democrat is likely to emphasize more conservative themes. Since gubernatorial and legislative candidates are all elected separately, there may be little connection among their campaigns.

For all these reasons, campaigns are unlikely to revolve around party themes presented to the electorate. The question has been put: "Do parties propose policies to get elected, or do they get elected to propose policies?"[59] The answer is really neither of these. There is not a "party" presenting policies, nor is there a "party" trying to get elected. There are multiple candidates getting elected. Candidates simply try to get elected, and employ multiple strategies to do so. Sometimes they campaign together, but most of the time they campaign alone. This does not mean that candidates do not care about the party, but the first concern of candidates is to get elected.

It is after the election that the entity of "party" as we so often conceive of it (a collective working together for some policy purposes) *may* emerge. Those who are elected begin the process of exploring their commonalties to discover if "party" positions can be negotiated and whether there will be much cohesion around them. In large part (with qualifications to be discussed) the party position will be a product of the composition of constituencies that party politicians represent. The essential matter is that parties take differing positions when their constituencies differ. It should not be presumed that parties always have clearly defined constituencies, or that the constituencies of parties differ. These are matters to establish by examination.

Political Constituencies and Ambitions of the Governor

Governors traditionally take the initiative in proposing policies. Legislatures generally wait to see what a governor proposes, and then form a response. The agenda that a governor proposes depends on the electoral base of the governor and his or her future ambitions.[60] A governor whose primary success was in suburban and rural areas will have to focus on responding to those constituencies. A governor with a largely urban electoral base will give urban concerns more attention.

But governors cannot focus only on the past. Most governors can run for reelection, and each must decide if his or her previous electoral base is sufficient to win reelection or if it is necessary and possible to expand the appeal to a broader constituency. Does a Republican governor with a suburban and rural focus need to do better in urban areas to ward off a strong Democratic challenger?[61] Does a Democratic governor have a largely urban constituency, and need to do better in suburban areas? There is no way to predict how a governor will assess such a situation. Each governor will make his or her own judgments about what must be done to ensure reelection, and those judgments are likely to differ.

Political Constituencies in the Legislative Party

Elected officials *within* a party almost always have differing constituencies. Within a legislature some Democrats represent urban minority areas. Other Democrats represent suburban and rural areas. Republicans also have diversity among party members. The crucial issue for a legislative party is the distribution of constituencies for those elected members of the party. A legislative party in the majority with a governor of the same party must also decide how well its constituencies match those of the governor.

There are many possible variations on legislative party constituencies. Table 2.4 indicates two possible variations for just one house. Assume there are one hundred legislators in a house. In State A, the Democratic Party does well in urban areas and these legislators form a substantial proportion of the legislative party. The Democratic Party does not do well in rural areas, and these legislators are a small part of the party. If Democrats from urban areas have liberal agendas (more social services, more state aid for schools, more public housing), then the party is likely to lean toward that agenda because of the dominance of the urban group within the party. The composition of the party is primarily urban-based, and the party leans toward those concerns.

But deriving a party position and deciding to enact change is never that simple. It is not just the dominant group within the party that determines party policy. In our example, the Democrats in urban areas do not constitute a majority within the house. To assemble a majority of votes within the house, the party must also have the support of legislators from suburban or rural areas. These legislators provide the votes to keep the party in the majority, and they are very unlikely to vote for a strictly urban agenda. The less likely these legislators are to agree with urban interests, the less cohesion the party will have and the less likely the party will be able to act in a simple unified way to enact change.

Table 2.4. Political Constituencies for Two Legislative Parties

Area/Number		State A		State B	
		Dem	Rep	Dem	Rep
Urban	(50)	80/40	20/10	60/30	40/20
Suburban	(30)	60/18	40/12	50/15	50/15
Rural	(20)	30/6	70/14	40/8	60/12
Totals	64	36	53	47	

Note: For each cell the numbers are the proportion of seats won in an area and the number of legislators from that area.

The difficult issue for the suburban and rural legislators is whether they can risk voting for policies that may identify them with urban interests. Suburban districts are often seen as "swing" districts, or ones where partisan support may switch from one party to another across elections. Suburban areas have many independents, who tend to switch their votes easily from one party to another across elections. Suburban interests are also sometimes compatible with urban interests (more school aid), but sometimes not (opposition to the income tax), and suburban legislators must carefully judge whether their votes with their own urban majority will help or harm them.

The formation of a party position is a product of the negotiations among these different wings of a party. A dominant group, such as urban legislators, may have considerable clout, but that clout is reduced to the extent that the party's majority party status is based on the election of legislators from other areas of the state. The total number of seats a party has in the legislature is not a good indicator of the likelihood of a party taking decisive policy action. It is the relative composition of the party that is crucial, and legislators from swing districts are likely to have the greatest impact in the process of forming policy. Legislators representing solidly Democratic or Republican areas are generally "safe." While these legislators may speak with great confidence for the party, it is legislators from swing districts who often put a party in power. It is these legislators who are most vulnerable to electoral volatility, and who can make the argument that the party must listen to their needs if the party is to stay in power.

In State B, the differences in party success by area are less. The Democrats are still the majority party, but their overall margin of control is less and their constituency base is different. Urban legislators comprise a smaller proportion of the party, and will have less impact. In this situation, the legislators from suburban districts become even more influential because they comprise a larger proportion of the party. Moreover, it will be even more difficult for the party to form and enact a clear policy change.

There are, of course, an infinite variety of party compositions that may exist for a majority party, and state legislative parties vary considerably in the party cleavages that define them.[62] The policy that will emerge must be assessed for each party based on the set of districts held by the majority within each house. The same logic applies regardless of whether Democrats or Republicans hold power.

Compatibility of Gubernatorial and Legislative Constituencies.

For any party that has acquired control of government, there are at least three "party" constituencies that much be dealt with to reach some policy agreement. The governor and both houses of the legislature must agree, and each house may have a different electoral base and a different sense of what policies the party should enact to remain in office.

Interpreting Elections and Reading the Prevailing Winds.

Politicians respond to their environment, and they are continually faced with the need to interpret changing conditions. When party control shifts as a result of an election, it is necessary to decide what that shift means. In 1964, the Republicans nominated Barry Goldwater, a conservative, for president. The electorate saw him as too conservative, and there was a national movement to the Democratic Party. In 1973 and 1974 Republicans were plagued by the Watergate scandal of Richard Nixon, which resulted in another significant movement to the Democratic Party. In each case, these national shifts also put Democrats in power in New Jersey. Politicians had to decide whether shifts in party control were a positive endorsement of Democratic policies, a rejection of Republicans, or just a reaction to a particular candidate or situation. There are usually widely divergent views within the party about what these shifts mean. Politicians discuss and must decide what the shift means as they form policies. In 1966 Democrats in New Jersey acquired control of both houses of the legislature and had to decide whether their election was an endorsement of "Democrats," whatever that meant, or an electoral fluke in response to Barry Goldwater.

Politicians must also deal with long-term shifts in public opinion. These shifts are also subject to interpretation by politicians. During the late 1960s the country was seen as drifting to the left, while in the early 1980s it was seen as drifting to the right. Politicians need to decide if these trends really exist, if the trend is occurring in their state, and whether it is relevant to their district.

Events

Finally, the decision-making process is often jolted by events over which politicians have no control and to which they must simply react. The economy may slow down and create a shortfall in state revenue. Previous policy plans may have to be abandoned as the decision shifts to whether to cut state services and state aid or to raise taxes and fees as a way to increase revenues. The economy may grow, generate more state tax revenues, and erase the need for a confrontation over what programs must be cut. The federal government may change its program and aid options, and force decisions that state politicians would otherwise avoid. The courts may issue decisions about state policies that require state political decisions. A large part of the life of a politician consists of reacting to such events and adjusting his or her plans accordingly.

THE CONDITIONS OF PARTY ACTION

Changes in party control create the potential for change to occur. Whether change occurs is contingent on the presence of several conditions.[63] At a minimum, the following conditions must prevail. At any stage of this process the prospects for change can cease because one of these conditions does not occur.

- Trends culminate in recognition of a "problem" and there is a sense that the problem should be addressed, or an event occurs to place an issue on the agenda of politicians.

- Both the governor and a coalition in the legislature share a sense that a different public policy should be adopted.

- The legislative coalition has a cohesive majority party and can muster a majority of votes in each house. This coalition shares a perception that enacting change will not result in loss of offices and loss of control of government.

The role of state government in New Jersey has changed from 1950 to now, and the major changes have occurred when Democrats were in power. The concern of the following analysis is how these conditions came together to alter the role of government.

PARTIES AND LONG-TERM POLICY CHANGE

Much of our focus in political studies is on the short-term impact of parties. The primary question has tended to be what do parties do with power. The drama of specific policy debates and decisions lead us to adopt such a short-term focus. There is also a long-run battle, however, which while less dramatic, is perhaps much more important. A series of tax increases and greater state aid to local governments may or may not lead to a long-term increase in the role of state government. Republicans may acquire power following Democratic control, see their election as justification for reversing change, and repeal the actions of Democrats. If parties alternate control over government and each responds to differing constituencies, the net effect of party actions over the years might be no change. Cumulative change, however, did occur in New Jersey. The process did not result in policies alternating around some constant level of state activity. The level of state activity continually rose. Again, the question is why. Republicans could have reversed the policies of Democrats, but generally did not choose to do so.

Parties are again perhaps relevant in trying to understand the connection between short- and long-term change. Parties can structure political debates and affect the pressures each party experiences. To return to the arguments of V. O. Key, the enduring issues revolve around "have-nots" versus "haves." Will the state do more to respond to problems of inequality of opportunity or will the workings of private actions and markets determine outcomes? The crucial matter in exchanges between the parties over public policy is the role of the Democrats. Key argued that if the Democrats have a clear "have-not" constituency and they engage in sustained advocacy of their constituency's needs, it keeps their concerns on the agenda. They can seek to make policy debates focus on issues of inequality. Their role can be crucial when Republicans consider whether to repeal the policy changes of Democrats. Democrats can seek to portray Republicans as uncaring about the situations of those less well-off, and as catering to the rich.

Democratic attacks about a lack of concern will have an impact only if Republicans feel uneasy about criticisms that they are insensitive to equality of opportunity issues. They may well not feel uneasy. The culture of American society emphasizes individual effort and achievement and the right of individuals to keep what they have earned. If individualism was completely dominant in American society, then pleas to address opportunity issues would have little impact. Political debates might focus only on individual responsibility and how policy could make conditions favorable to individual entrepreneurs in business. But there is also concern in American society with equality of opportunity and individuals having the opportunity to achieve.[64] To the extent that there is emphasis in our culture on equality of opportunity, claims about insensitivity will have an impact.

If the concerns of the have-nots are to be a regular part of the agenda, Democrats can play the role of creating pressure on Republicans to worry about looking like they do not care about equality of opportunity. If Democrats continually call attention to policy changes that may diminish opportunity, they can make Republicans uneasy about acquiring an image of appearing to be unconcerned about equality of opportunity.[65] These criticisms may make Republicans hesitant to repeal changes. Making opportunity and inequality issues is crucial in enacting change, but it is also crucial in defending enacted changes when Republicans acquire power. To understand long-term changes, we also need to know what New Jersey Democrats did when they were not in power, and how Republicans reacted to whatever criticisms Democrats made. Did Democrats defend prior policy enactments? Did Republicans consider repealing tax and aid increases? And how did they react to Democratic criticisms?

The fundamental concern of this analysis is the dynamics of political and policy changes that changed the role of state government. The actions of parties and the exchanges between them are of fundamental interest. Tax increases are not desired by the public, but several tax increases were enacted over this time period. The questions to be pursued here are why would a party enact such changes, how did the electorate react, and how did the opposing party respond? How is it that the democratic process brings about change?

Part II:
The State Becomes
an Actor

3

The Emergence of Democrats and the State, 1950–67

In the early 1950s state government in New Jersey played a relatively limited role. A review of fiscal data for 1953, in inflation adjusted dollars,[1] indicates how little the state did. Per capita state taxes in 1953 were $19.70, and state direct general expenditure (money actually spent by the state government, not counting funds transferred to local governments for their uses) was $31.15. In contrast, local governments raised $56.40 per capita in taxes, over twice as much as the state government. Their direct general expenditure per capita was $38.14.[2] Most tax revenue was raised by local governments, and the state had neither a sales tax or income tax. By 1970, again using inflation-adjusted figures, the state's role had changed. It raised $69.20 per capita and spent $68.06 per capita. Local governments raised $97.40 and spent $105.70 per capita. State taxes per capita had tripled, while local taxes per capita had increased by about 100 percent. The state had adopted a sales tax, and the percent of state-local tax revenue raised by the state had increased from 25.9 percent in 1953 to 41.5 in 1970. State aid to local governments had increased from $7.00 per capita in 1953 to $37.70 per capita.

Political change had also occurred. Throughout the 1950s Democrats were the minority party in New Jersey. They held neither house of the legislature nor the governorship. By 1970 they had held the governorship twelve years. From 1966 to 1967 the Democrats had unified control of state government, with Richard Hughes as the Democratic governor. They lost the 1967 legislative elections and returned to minority status in the legislature. Republicans also regained control of the governor's office in the 1969 gubernatorial elections.

The position of the state and of Democrats changed over time. The question to be pursued here is the connection between these changes. Were

Democrats the source of change in the role of state government, and, if so, why did they pursue these changes? By what political logic did they see it as worthwhile to tackle the difficult issue of state taxes? And, when Republicans regained control, did they use this power to reverse any of the changes that occurred over time?

STATE GOVERNMENT IN THE EARLY 1950S

The limited state role in New Jersey in 1950 was a product of the long tradition of localism, with local governments raising most revenues and delivering most services.[3] There was no state sales or income tax. State revenues came from taxes on alcohol, cigarettes, gasoline, railroads, the granting of corporate franchises, and inheritances and estates. The state also taxed employee payrolls to pay for unemployment compensation, and imposed fees for registering cars and obtaining a driver's license. State tax revenues were considerably less than those raised by local governments, which raised almost all their funds from the property tax.[4] As noted by one state commission study, the state had achieved "the record of the lowest per capita state tax collections of any state in the nation."[5]

This pattern of decentralized financing, however, had not resulted in lower overall taxes within the state. Total state and local taxes paid per person or as a percentage of income in New Jersey were about the same as states in the surrounding region.[6] The difference was that local governments bore the burden of funding many services. The situation with education illustrates this.

> New Jersey is near the bottom of the list in the rank of states measured by per pupil state aid, but New Jersey is at the top of the list in having the highest average expenditure per pupil in average daily attendance. The difference is a matter not so much of educational policy as it is of tax policy.[7]

The state had traditionally played a limited role and there did not appear to be much support for imposing new taxes that would change the role of the state. As a state commission concluded: "There is considerable evidence indicating that the present temper of public thinking is entirely unsuited to any large-scale tax adjustments involving the creation of new tax bases."[8]

This limited state role was accompanied by little focus on "state" politics. The state was not seen as a source of solutions. Issues did not emerge as "state" issues and most people did not pay much attention to state politics. Much of this was due to the absence of attention to New Jersey issues in the media. The dominant newspaper dailies within the state came out of

Philadelphia and New York City, and their focus was primarily on their own states and not New Jersey. Television coverage of political events was only beginning, and what little existed also came from and focused on Philadelphia and New York City.[9]

Political parties might have presented differing views of state obligations. While the parties drew their electoral bases from different areas and constituents, neither party advocated increasing the state role by changing the tax system. Republicans drew their strongest support from rural and suburban areas in the northwest part of the state and from southern counties along the shore. Democrats were strongest in urban counties running roughly from Newark in the northeast down to Trenton.[10]

These constituency differences did not, however, result in significant policy differences between the parties. In the 1947 gubernatorial campaign, the Republican platform read as follows:

- "We are against a personal income tax."
- "We are against a general sales tax."
- "We are against a 100 percent assessment of real property."

The Democrats differed only slightly. Their platform read as follows:

> We are against and will continue to oppose the imposition of any general sales and personal income tax. The Democratic party will continue its opposition to unfair, discriminatory taxation. Furthermore there should be no basic change in the tax structure without a referendum.[11]

Politicians in both parties saw danger in taxes. During the Great Depression, faced with rising municipal bankruptcies, the state had passed a sales tax. The tax generated so much voter hostility that the legislature repealed it four months later. After that experience, "the entire New Jersey political establishment concluded 'that endorsement of new taxes constitutes political suicide'."[12]

The early 1950s produced little change in the inclination of parties to advocate change. County organizations and localism dominated the state, and county organizations found it advantageous to continue raising taxes at the local level to maintain the tradition of home rule and the importance of the county organizations.[13] Representation in the legislature perpetuated the county focus. Legislators were elected by county, with one senator and one or more assembly members per county. The rural population was heavily overrepresented. Eleven counties, with 18 percent of the state's population, had a majority in the senate.[14] These rural conservative counties were not in favor of change. In the early 1950s Republicans held both houses of the legislature and the governorship, and the governor was not interested in the state playing a greater role. Republican governor Alfred Driscoll proposed that the state get out of the business of handling unemployment relief, and transfer the responsibility from the state to municipalities.[15] He regularly attacked the centralizing and spending tendencies of the national government[16] and proposed budgets with no increases or cuts. He boasted of the low state taxes and wanted constrained budgets so that "the state may continue to have the lowest per capita tax collection in the nation."[17] Republican legislative leaders agreed.[18] The party platforms for the 1953 gubernatorial race for both parties reiterated opposition to new state taxes.[19] The only indication of willingness to consider tax issues was that both parties supported a state commission to study the state's tax system.[20]

INITIAL BATTLES OVER THE ROLE OF THE STATE

While there was little desire for a general increase in the role of the state, there were occasions during the 1950s in which the role of the state did emerge as an issue. Twice there was a concerted effort to raise state taxes. In each case the proposals were initiated by a Democrat. A controversy about local assessment practices and inequalities of local tax obligations also raised the issue of what role state government should play in local affairs. Partisanship played a role in the tax increases but not with the assessment issue. This is important for what it says about why issues become party issues.

The efforts to raise taxes in the 1950s originated with policy goals. Democrats in New Jersey did not want to raise taxes, but they did want to provide more state aid for schools and they wanted revenues to maintain state services. Those goals affected the role they played on the issue of whether the state should do more in the area of education.

From 1950 to 1954 the governorship and the legislature were controlled by Republicans. Democrats, as the minority party, opposed the Republican budget in 1951 and 1952 for not providing enough school aid.[21] As the minority party in the legislature, their proposal was ignored. The issue persisted, and became relevant during the next administration.

Robert Meyner was the Democratic nominee in the 1953 election, which he won. He provided a glimpse of his views about taxes during the 1953 party convention. Amidst a discussion about continuing a "no new taxes" pledge in the party platform, he took the floor and said:

> This business of no new taxes is the greatest bit of nonsense I have ever heard in the state of New Jersey. Let us be frank. The people are not stupid and they are not supporting any candidate merely because he says I am against

new taxes. I personally am in favor of economy in government but it is impossible to forecast what taxes we may or may not need in the future.[22]

Meyner's inclination to at least consider new taxes distinguished him from Republican governor Driscoll, who sought to maintain New Jersey's low taxes. Meyner also differed in the kinds of concerns and goals he articulated. In his inaugural address he stressed the need for the state to do more to help schools without raising local property taxes and raised the issue of "whether the burden [of taxation] should be distributed more fairly and equitably."[23] His different disposition became relevant when a state commission studying the state tax system released a report in his first year. The commission recommended that the state raise taxes for schools and other purposes. Meyner embraced the report and submitted a supplemental budget to the legislature that year asking for $89,500,000 in new taxes.[24] Republicans in the legislature, unwilling to accept a tax increase that large, accepted an increase in the gas tax of one cent, and mandated that all funds be dedicated to school aid. The consequence of Meyner's actions was a significant increase in state aid to local schools. As figure 3.1 indicates, state aid more than doubled from 1954 to 1956, when the aid increases took full effect.

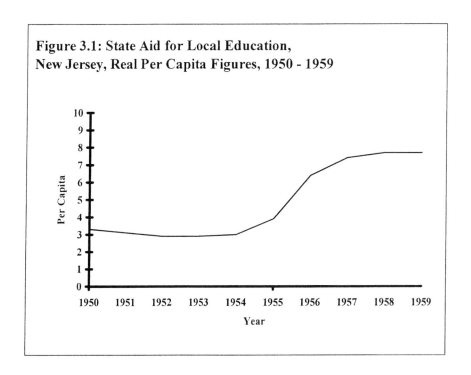

Figure 3.1: State Aid for Local Education, New Jersey, Real Per Capita Figures, 1950 - 1959

Meyner's disposition about how to react to fiscal issues was again relevant in his second term, when another state tax increase became an issue. Following the gas tax increase of 1954, state revenues increased fairly steadily, helped along by a strong economy. Meyner, who regularly mentioned the importance of the state helping schools, was able to increase state aid and expenditures for the 1955–56 budget without asking for another tax increase.[25] In his 1956 address to the legislature, however, Meyner asked for another one-cent gas tax increase.[26] The revenues would be used to provide matching funds for the new federal highway program. The Republican-controlled legislature cut his budget and turned down his tax-increase request.[27] In 1957 he again indicated he would seek a gas-tax increase but ultimately decided not to seek the increase. Republicans indicated they would use this request against him in his reelection bid, and that may have led him to not make the proposal.[28] With a growing economy, state revenue yields continued to increase, providing sufficient funds to do more while avoiding battles over tax increases.

The 1958 session, however, involved a different political situation and policy outcome. Meyner ran for reelection in 1957 and won with 55 percent of the vote. Democrats made significant gains in the assembly and took control of that house for the first time since 1937. They picked up 20 seats to have 42 of 60, their largest margin since 1913. The seats gained by Democrats were in Essex County, where Republicans generally did well. The senate remained Republican, with Republicans winning 13 of 21 seats.[29] Meyner began the 1958 session with several proposals to increase the role of the state. He sought greater state support of schools and higher education, and requested more funds to finance a scholarship program and road construction.[30] These programs were to be paid for by a one-cent increase in the gas tax and a tax on corporate net income.[31]

The assembly passed his proposals, but Republicans in the senate responded with cuts in his budget, a smaller corporate income tax, and no gas tax.[32] After extensive negotiations and some budget cuts, the Senate agreed to the gas tax and a reduced corporation income tax.[33]

Meyner was able to increase the state role through two separate tax increases. Compared to tax and funding increases that would occur in later years, the increases were relatively small, but they were still increases. Meyner served as an advocate of more state aid for schools and of state activism in building roads and taking advantage of the federal highway program. He also supported more state support of higher education.

Partisanship clearly played a role. As a Democrat, Meyner differed from Driscoll in that he did not cite the state's low taxation as something to be proud of, but focused on needs and problems. He emphasized the need to support local and state schools, which would help the traditional Democratic constituencies of low-income, urban residents, but would also help middle-class districts. He supported building roads, which in the 1950s was not seen as helping one class over another, so support was widespread. He was also able to take advantage of his party's success in winning the assembly to create more pressure on Republicans to go along with his proposals. The effect of his administration was an increase in state tax effort and greater state aid for local schools. These increases are shown in figure 3.2.

While Meyner, as a Democrat, did bring about modest tax increases, it is important to note that, in campaigning, he did not raise the issue of taxes or advocate them. He had a predisposition to be more receptive to taxes, and he was inclined to advocate programs that suggested he was going to need more revenue. But he did not campaign on the need for taxes. The pattern is important. A Democratic governor ended up being an advocate for taxes after being elected, and was successful in securing some of what he wanted. The electoral process, however, was not a simple referendum on taxes. This Democrat fit the expectations that Democrats are more likely to enact taxes once in office. But he began with a concern for state government playing a role on policy issues, and that led him to support state taxes. It is a pattern to remember when reviewing subsequent events.

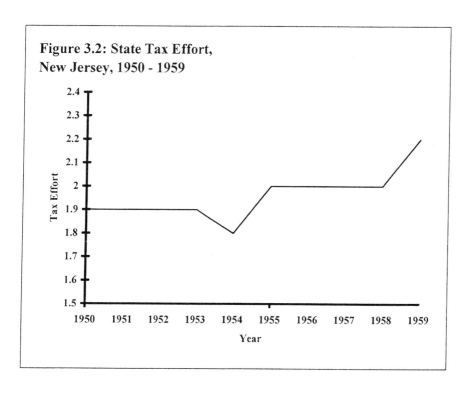

Figure 3.2: State Tax Effort, New Jersey, 1950 - 1959

State Involvement in Local Assessment

With fiscal responsibilities highly decentralized in the 1950s, the heavy reliance on local property taxes combined with the emergence of state aid created a situation with enormous potential to prompt state involvement. Property assessment and the imposition of property taxes were done locally and huge inequities in assessment rates and taxes prevailed, raising the question of whether the state should intervene. Perhaps more important, state aid was distributed on the basis of local wealth, measured by assessed value. The state found itself in a situation where aid distributions were being affected by questionable local practices, prompting the question of whether the state should intervene to secure valid local estimates.

Local property taxes are raised by determining the value of local properties, determining how much tax revenue is needed, and then applying a tax rate to each property to obtain the necessary revenue. The process of establishing the value of properties is called assessment, and it was done entirely locally in New Jersey in 1950. Each municipality had its own assessor who assigned values to properties.

These local practices were conducted under state authority. State involvement began with the constitution and state law. The constitution specified:

> Property shall be assessed for taxation under general laws and by uniform rules. All real property assessed and taxed locally or by the state for allotment and payment to taxing districts shall be assessed according to the same standard of value. . . .[34]

The state had responded to this clause by specifying that:

> All property real and personal within the jurisdiction of this state not expressly exempted from taxation . . . shall be subject to taxation annually . . . at its true value, and shall be valued by the assessors of the respective taxing districts.[35]

The state had also created regulations about the selection of assessors, the timing of assessments, and the coordination of assessments within counties. Local assessors were elected. They were required to submit assessments annually, and to meet regularly with county boards, supported by the state, to make sure assessments were fairly uniform within the county. These rules, however, had not created a uniform process. Assessors varied enormously in background. Some had staffs and others had virtually none. There was no agreement as to what "true value" meant. There was great resistance to using the current sale price of properties, because this would require regularly raising assessment values, which elected assessors wanted to avoid. Properties were not regularly reassessed, and some had not been reassessed for years. There was little coordination of practices within counties, the state did little to prompt such efforts,[36] and funding for county boards was very inadequate.[37]

The assessment process determines the taxes property owners pay, and the process in New Jersey had resulted in two serious problems. There were enormous inequities *within* municipalities in the assessment rates and taxes paid for individual properties.[38] Some inequities were because the system was incapable of regular reassessments as change occurred, but there were also charges of political favoritism in how assessment rates were set. There were continual complaints about these inequities.

The other problem was that the average assessment rate of municipalities varied considerably. Most properties were assessed at a fraction of their estimated market values. In 1950 the estimated assessment ratio was 28—that is, assessed values were 28 percent of the estimated market values. This average was deceptive, however, because local township assessment rates varied from 6 to 98 percent.[39] The most troubling accusation was that some municipalities were reducing their apparent tax base to make the municipality more attractive as a candidate for state aid. Since state aid formulas gave more aid to municipalities that had lower property tax bases, lower assessments could result in more aid than a municipality would otherwise receive.[40]

This situation had enormous potential to draw in the state. The state constitution and statutes made references to using uniform valuation, however vaguely defined, but there did not appear to be much uniformity in practice. The state had created a system of tax assessment that was largely being ignored. State law was being violated, and the inequities in actual taxes paid angered many taxpayers. As state aid increased during the 1950s, based on local wealth estimates, state politicians were aware that the distribution of state aid was being influenced by a very suspect local assessment process. It was a process amenable to manipulation by local officials to exploit the state aid system.

Despite these problems, there was enormous anxiety about changing the assessment system. After years of underassessment, property owners feared that any reassessment would result in higher property taxes. The uncertainty of the impact of change led to a general reluctance to do anything systematic. The public was not asking for a systematic reassessment of properties, and there were few politicians who saw any gain from advocating change on this issue.

The reliance on local assessments created more problems as suburban-ization proceeded. Local governments already varied tremendously in tax bases and in their generation of revenue to support local government services such as police, parks, and schools.[41] As suburban sprawl began, differences in tax bases increased. The goal of the state aid system was to respond somewhat to this problem, and there was concern that the local assessment process might reduce the ability to distribute aid equitably. These issues had existed for some time. The important political matter was whether any of them would become political issues that politicians would focus on and try to change.

THE STATE IS DRAWN IN:
COPING WITH DIFFERENCES BETWEEN MUNICIPALITIES

The increase in state aid to local governments and schools after World War II led to more concern with the problem of differences in assessment rates among municipalities. State politicians were aware that municipali-ties assessed property at different rates, and that this affected how state aid was distributed.

To try to remedy the problem of varying municipal assessments, the state took a step toward involvement in local affairs. It was recognized that the system was not working as expected. The state responded by creating an equalization board within the Division of Taxation.[42] The intent was to compile data at the state level on the market value of local properties and use that information to estimate the value of property within municipalities so that the distribution of aid would be based on the actual property wealth of communities.

Equalization is done as follows. Data are collected on the sale prices or estimated values of properties. These values are compared to the assessed values, and an assessment ratio is derived. If property is estimated to be worth $10,000,000, but is assessed at $2,000,000, the assessment ratio is .20. Property is then estimated to be worth five times more than the values recorded on the assessment rolls. To derive an estimate of actual values, the state first derives an assessment ratio for each municipality. This is the assessed value of all property divided by the market value for all property. For each municipality the total of assessed values (on the assessor's rolls) are divided by this equalization ratio, or .20 in this example. Once this is done for all municipalities, the state can estimate the actual value of prop-erty for each municipality. It then allows the state to distribute state aid on the basis of actual property wealth in communities rather than on the as-sessed values that local assessors might report.

The creation of this board and its processes represented an important but limited intrusion of the state into local affairs. The move involved rejection of some local diversity, but acceptance of other kinds. For an equalization board to operate it had to collect information on the sale prices of local properties or estimates of their value. This moved the state into a position of implicitly rejecting the estimates of local assessors and gave the state some power, because a state agency now had its own information base. The practice of deriving municipal assessment ratios also deprives local assessors of the power to set their own rates in a way that might affect state aid. The intrusion was limited, however, in that the state did not affect variations in assessment ratios *within* municipalities. The state was concerned only with the average assessment ratio within a municipality and making sure that differences between municipal practices were adjusted before state aid was distributed. The acquisition of information on properties within a municipality might allow the state to become involved in estimating and addressing inequities within a municipality, but that was not the purpose of the state equalization board.

The creation of a state equalization board was an incremental change in the role of the state. It allowed the state to circumvent the problem of the diversity created by local assessors, but it did not involve challenging the practice of inequities within municipalities.

THE COURTS AND ASSESSMENT PRACTICES

While politicians were not inclined to address the issue of inequalities in assessments and taxes for similar properties, individual citizens could pursue these issues through the courts. Assessments became one of the first local issues that individuals, using the courts, made a state politics issue. Individuals can sue in the courts if they feel that their treatment by local officials is unfair, and if they think state government should correct the treatment. In the case of assessments, the disparities in assessment rates among properties provided grounds for the filing of lawsuits.

The responses by the courts indicate much about how ideas and issues evolve over time, and how ideas have an impact. The essential argument of those filing suits was that they were being treated unequally. The intriguing matter is how ideas of equality changed over time. In this case, the norm that equality of treatment should play a role evolved very gradually.

The state constitution stated that property should be assessed "by the same standard of value." The state statute said that the standard should be "true value." These principles were established because of a general belief that consistency should prevail. Individuals who felt their property was assessed unfairly (usually meaning that an assessment was higher than similar properties) could first appeal to the local assessor to adjust their assessment. If the appeal was denied, a suit could be filed to require an adjustment. In principle, the norm of equality had been stated and a procedure was in place to ensure that equality would prevail in practice. The important political question was what happens when there is clear evidence of a significant discrepancy between the ideal and reality.

Court cases became the means of pursuing that discrepancy. The first major case involving assessment was *Royal Manufacturing Co. v. Board of Equalization of Taxes of New Jersey, et al.* in 1908. The plaintiff was assessed at a higher rate than others in the same area, and argued that this was unfair. The court concluded that the assessment was acceptable, and the inequity was ignored by the court. Since the law required assessment at true value, and the assessor had assessed this particular property at or under true value, the court found that the plaintiff was not overassessed. The court noted that the plaintiff could not receive a reduction, but could ask that the assessment of others be raised.[43] The U.S. Supreme Court had ruled in 1923 that such practices were unacceptable, but New Jersey did not find its practices of unequal assessments challenged until 1946 when a federal court ruled against such practices in New Jersey.[44]

In a series of rulings from 1949 to 1951, the state courts acknowledged that properties were generally assessed at less than true value, and indicated that "The constitutional mandate to assess at full value must yield to the even more fundamental requirement of relative equality."[45] The courts were willing to accept assessments at less than true value, as long as they were equal. The court did not specify what was relative equality, recognizing that assessments varied enormously within local governments. The courts had moved from accepting inequality to rejecting it.[46] The difficulty was in coming up with a standard of equality to rely upon that would be accepted in practice. Given the enormous disparities in existence at that time across the state, it would be very difficult to get equality of assessment accepted and enforced.

Finally, the court made the transition to addressing the equality issue involving assessment. The state supreme court, in *Switz v. Middletown Twp.* in 1956, took on the issue of variations within local governments in assessment rates. The court, with several dissents being filed, ruled in March 1957 that equal properties had to be treated alike. Much as with politicians, however, the members of the court (some of whom had been elected officials) were not eager to be too intrusive into state policy. The logic of cases considered over the years may have carried the court to the point where they had come to see the need for equality of treatment of similar properties, but they also were reluctant to make public policy in such a politically sensitive area. The court decided that the present set of practices was illegal, but indicated that the court ruling would not take effect for two years, beginning in 1959. The hope of the court was that the legislature would deal with the problem before that, either by changing the law or by adopting legislation to create local compliance with the court ruling.[47]

The issue of inequality of assessments had taken several decades to work its way through the courts, and the idea of equal treatment had been embraced with considerable reluctance. The crucial matter was that the general principle of equality had been placed in the constitution and statute law. The discrepancy between the law and practice became too obvious to ignore. The evolution of cases and decisions led the courts to eventually acknowledge the discrepancy between the law and reality and to rule that the discrepancy should be eliminated. There is no political inevitability to the recognition of the inequality issue, but in this case the progression resulted in the courts recognizing the issue. The practice of local diversity and the state's acceptance of that practice had now become a state issue. The question was how the political process would respond.

POLITICAL AVOIDANCE

When the court ruling was announced in March 1957, legislators were besieged by expressions of opposition to change and fear of its consequences. Some opposed change because they were sure it would mean higher taxes. Others were simply concerned that change, after decades of partial and unequal assessments, would create chaos.[48] Legislators were also not eager to institute change.

Legislators had reacted before the court issued its *Switz* ruling in an attempt to eliminate the issue. The legislature sought to replace the constitutional provision that required assessment at true value. The legislature sponsored a concurrent resolution of both houses that would allow each municipality to assess at a ratio below 100 percent, but would require that the ratio within each municipality would be uniformly applied. This would make it legal for municipalities to have different assessment ratios from other municipalities. The resolution would become an article or part of the state constitution if passed by voters in a referendum in the November 1956 elections. The proposal prompted considerable opposition from newspapers and groups across the state who argued that the inequality issue should be dealt with. The vote went against the proposition by a 2 to 1 margin, and the legislature had to start over in seeking a solution.[49]

The next response of the legislature was to request a commission study of the situation. In December 1956 the legislature directed the State Tax Commission to review the situation and suggest proposals. The commission reported in February 1958, and recommended uniform statewide assessment at 40 percent of full value.[50]

The assembly responded with a bill repealing all references to true value and inserting language that would sanction considerable discretion in decision-making by local assessors. The legislation would have made legal the status quo of unequal assessments and taxes. This bill failed in the senate because it was not seen as a solution. The senate then tried to formulate a proposal that would assess property at a percentage of full value. That legislation also failed because there were numerous groups with very conflicting goals who opposed equal assessments. Farmers wanted special treatment, as did veterans. Some local governments and labor saw the situation as an opportunity to shift the tax burden from property to the sales tax or income tax, which might be more progressive. The political parties in the legislature were not interested in using the situation as an excuse to enact a statewide tax, since they had pledged opposition to that.[51] It was not possible to develop a consensus, and the legislature failed to meet the deadline set by the courts.

In this case the issue did not develop into one in which the parties represented different issues, largely because there was no clear division of interests that coincided with party divisions. Interests were fragmented and diverse, and unease about change was widespread among the public. Neither party found itself in a situation where they had a dominant set of constituents in favor of a single type of change. The parties found no reason to participate in creating a greater state role.

The issue, however, did not go away. While the governor and the legislature failed to meet the 1959 deadline, subsequent pressures from the courts led the state to take a more active role in monitoring local assessments and to push local governments to raise their overall assessment ratios. This led to gradual increases in average county assessment ratios over the next several decades. By the early 1990s the average assessment ratio for counties had climbed to 78.[52] By the late 1980s there were again strong complaints about inequities in assessments and taxes paid across counties and municipalities.[53]

The issue of inequality of taxation of property had existed for decades. It took a change in court rulings to make it an issue that state politicians had to address. While the political process addressed the issue grudgingly and slowly, the state did gradually assume a greater role over time and did have some effect on equality of treatment, and the variation in assessment practices declined somewhat by the 1990s. The process was slow, but the logic of equality of treatment had become difficult to resist.

EMERGING ISSUES AND A CHANGING POLITICAL CLIMATE

The 1950s were a time of sustained economic growth and population movement nationally and in New Jersey. There was a steady growth of suburbs in the state. This movement of population created service expectations, because each new suburb needed roads, sewers, police, and schools. There was a tremendous increase in the number of students who wanted to attend college. These new services required government revenues. Despite these increased needs, however, by the end of the 1950s the state ranked last in per capita total state expenditures.[54] The state continued to provide limited aid, because it had no statewide general taxes that could generate significant amounts of revenue.

As was happening elsewhere in the country, perceptions of the seriousness of problems and expectations of government began to change in the early 1960s. The movement out of cities led to significant population declines in urban areas. Racial segregation was increasing at the same time that awareness of and concern about racial inequities were increasing.[55] Poverty was discovered.[56] Not everyone, of course, saw these changes as problems and many strongly opposed state taxes and a greater state role. Despite continued opposition, however, there was an increase in the sense of the possible positive contributions of government from 1950 to the early 1960s. The question was whether this might translate into a political response.

THE EMERGENCE OF DEMOCRATS

In the early 1950s the Republicans dominated New Jersey politics. Democrats had not been in control of all branches of state government at one time since 1917. Even that brief control was largely a result of a short-term division within the Republican Party.[57] In the 1955 assembly elections, for example, Republicans won 24 of 35 seats in rural and suburban counties,[58] and they even won 16 of 25 seats in the urban counties of Essex, Hudson, and Union.[59] Overall, two-thirds of assembly seats in the legislature were held by Republicans. They controlled the governor's office, though the Republican governor, Alfred Driscoll, won with only 47.1 percent in 1949.

By the late 1950s, the situation of the Democrats began to change. All throughout the Northeast Democrats were gradually gaining more seats, and this was happening in New Jersey, too.[60] In 1957 Democrats took advantage of a short-term national movement away from Republicans, and the Democratic Party went from 20 of 60 assembly seats to 42 of 60. Their gains came largely in the urban counties. The senate remained Republican in 1957. In 1959 Democrats lost some of these gains in the assembly, but still won 31 of 60 seats. In the senate they picked up two seats to control 47.6 percent of the seats in that house. A comparison of 1955 to 1959 (two years without national political tides intruding) indicates how the Democrats' electoral base was changing. In 1955 in urban areas, Democrats won 9 of 25, while in 1959 they won 14 of 25. In suburban areas in 1955 they won 9 of 29, while in 1959 they won 15 of 29.[61] They were acquiring more of an urban-suburban electoral base. By the 1961 elections Democrats had risen from a party of limited impact to one with a chance of taking control of the legislature. After the 1961 elections, Democrats held 37 of 60 seats in the assembly and 10 of 21 seats in the senate, and the Democratic candidate Richard Hughes had won the gubernatorial race. Figure 3.3 indicates this increase in their electoral success.

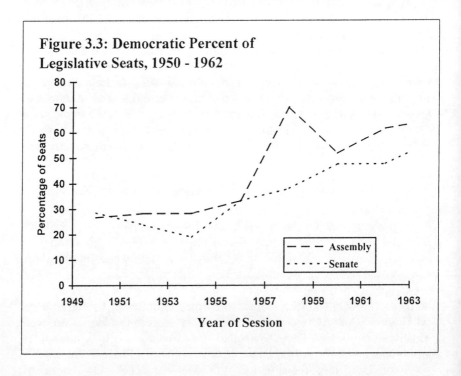

Figure 3.3: Democratic Percent of Legislative Seats, 1950 - 1962

STATE POLICY DEBATES AND POLITICAL MANDATES

Democrats were increasing their seats in the legislature, but it would be difficult to interpret that gain as reflecting a positive public reaction to an articulated party program by the Democrats. Some crucial conditions were lacking for that to occur. First, there was still little sense of a coherent "state" politics, in which statewide issues were discussed and served as the basis for electoral decisions. Much of the population lived around metropolitan areas (New York and Philadelphia), in which the focus of newspapers was events in New York and Pennsylvania, respectively.[62]

Second, there were not cohesive statewide parties presenting policy options to which the electorate could react. Parties were built around strong county organizations.[63] These organizations focused on local concerns and did not coordinate their efforts with other county organizations to adopt statewide policy positions. Frank Hague, for example, led the urban Hudson County Democratic Party organization. His concern was maintaining the dominance of his county, and he did little to build up the Democratic Party outside his county. He did little to develop ties with organized labor. Instead, he focused on maintaining the dominance of his county organization as the dominant Democratic organization.[64] Other county leaders also focused on serving county needs.[65] The legacy of localism, decentralization, and a limited state role also contributed to this lack of a sense that the state should be seen as the means for addressing major policy issues.

The apportionment of representation in the legislature contributed to this lack of interest in expanding the state's role. The constitution specified that each county was entitled to one senator, regardless of population size. The allocation of assembly members was also done by county, with some counties having more members than others because of greater population. The effect of using counties as the basis of representation, however, had led to significant overrepresentation of rural areas and underrepresentation of urban areas. The population in urban and suburban areas was growing, but each county still received one senator and at least one assembly member. The allocation of districts was not changed even though census data indicated that population distributions were changing.[66] The overrepresentation of rural areas had a powerful effect in the senate, where a cohesive caucus of rural Republicans could block any legislation not in their interest. These rural legislators were primarily preoccupied with preserving local organizations, and approached legislative proposals with that concern.[67]

The inclination of legislators to focus on county concerns and solutions rather than statewide policies was made more pronounced by the presence of strong county organizations and leaders and the practice of "rotation" in office. Many legislators were nominated by their local party as reward for service or loyalty to the local organization. They went to Trenton and stayed for one or two terms, and were then replaced by a new party nominee.[68] This practice inhibited the development of a set of legislators who might be concerned with a statewide party and differing policy proposals.

The idealized role that parties might have played in structuring debates, discussed in chapter 2, was not taking place. There were some advocates for change within the Democratic Party, but they were not dominant.

Finally, these conditions—a lack of a state focus, a history of localism, strong county organizations, and malapportionment—had led to the formation of a dominating legislative political coalition that stifled the emergence of parties as meaningful and differing policy entities. For many years the legislature had been dominated by a coalition of the powerful Hudson County Democratic machine led by Frank Hague, who was willing to bargain with county leaders from the rural Republican counties.[69] Together these counties controlled enough votes to make sure that legislation favorable to their local concerns was passed, but statewide approaches to policy concerns were thwarted. This bipartisan coalition and its preference for local response to local problems stifled the emergence of significant statewide policy proposals, and the development of alternative statewide proposals from parties. These organizations and their dominance persisted through much of the 1960s.

The election of Richard Hughes in 1961 and Democratic control of the assembly did not lead to changes in the role of the state. While he was inclined to be an activist, Hughes was faced with a Republican senate unwilling to consider change, and a Democratic assembly not much more interested. Hughes spent most of his first term in office not able to change much.[70]

Hughes did pursue and achieve some expansion of the state's role in higher education and an increase in the opportunities to pursue higher education within the state. State government had made limited steps in the 1940s and 1950s to increase its role in higher education. In the early 1940s the only state higher education system was a collection of nine normal colleges, largely devoted to preparing teachers. In 1945 legislation was passed that placed those schools under the authority of the state board of education, and designated Rutgers University, previously a private school, as "The State University."[71] In 1956 the state assumed full responsibility for Rutgers University. These limited efforts, however, did not produce enough spots to accommodate all state residents who wanted to attend a state public college, and parents regularly complained about the lack of spaces.[72] In the mid 1960s 55 percent of New Jersey residents who went to college went out of state to college, the highest percent in the nation.[73] The inclination to focus on the higher education system was limited, because the developing state system had been assigned in 1945 to the state board of education, which was responsible for elementary and secondary education. Those in the state board were not inclined to promote higher education over elementary and secondary education.

Hughes was able to change this system in two ways. During his first term, he significantly expanded education opportunities through a system of county community colleges. After taking office in 1961 Hughes introduced legislation to establish a system of community colleges, with the state authorized to pay as much as 50 percent of all costs associated with the system. The state would have the power to approve construction plans, degree programs, and general accreditation.[74] This change was particularly important for those who could not afford to attend four-year private or public colleges. The legislation establishing the system had been proposed prior to 1962, but had been bottled up within the Republican-dominated legislature. Hughes's accomplishment was that he made it an issue and forced it out of committee for a vote by the legislature, where it passed without opposition.[75]

He also led an effort to increase the autonomy of the higher education system so it could manage its own development. In 1963 he appointed a commission to study the higher education system. That commission recommended that a Governor's Advisory Board on Higher Education be appointed, but the education bureaucracy resisted. In 1965 he again appointed a commission, which recommended that a separate department of higher education be created. That was also resisted. It would take the election of a Democratic legislature before he could achieve change in 1966.

THE 1965 ELECTIONS

The four years from 1961 to 1965 saw considerable change in the national political climate, which was reflected in the behavior of New Jersey's parties. The national concern with social and urban problems increased. John Kennedy articulated many idealistic goals. When Lyndon Johnson became president in 1963, he advocated a broad array of liberal legislation—the Great Society agenda—to respond to these concerns. Congress responded and passed laws providing expanded benefits in many areas, and raising the level of government involvement in attempts to solve many newly recognized social problems.

The general increase in the willingness to use government to address problems was reflected in the party platforms of the New Jersey parties. By the early 1960s both parties had removed the antitax pledges from their platforms.[76]

The question was whether the greater willingness to use government to address problems evidenced at the national level would also occur in New Jersey. The 1965 elections, accompanied by some unique events, put the Democrats in power, and created the potential for change. One of the crucial factors was that the structure of representation was changed prior to the 1965 elections. A series of court cases led to a court decision that counties could not serve as the basis for legislative representation because of their enormous differences in population size. The court ruled that representation had to be based on "one man, one vote," which meant that urban and suburban areas had to receive more legislative seats. New Jersey complied grudgingly, and went through several reapportionments, each of them representing a partial discarding of using counties as the basis for legislative districts. The initial efforts at compliance, for example, attempted to retain counties, but to add more seats to those with a greater population. Eventually county boundaries were abandoned entirely.

The first reapportionment, which increased the size of the Senate and gave urban areas more seats in that house, took place in time for the 1965 elections.[77] That was also the year after Republicans ran Barry Goldwater, a conservative, as their presidential candidate. The national electorate reacted very negatively to his candidacy and the image of the Republican Party, and voted heavily for Democrats. That carried over to the 1965 New Jersey elections, and Democrats took the legislature with a 41–19 margin in the assembly and a 19-10 margin in the senate. The gradual climb of Democrats to majority status since the 1950s is shown in figure 3.4.

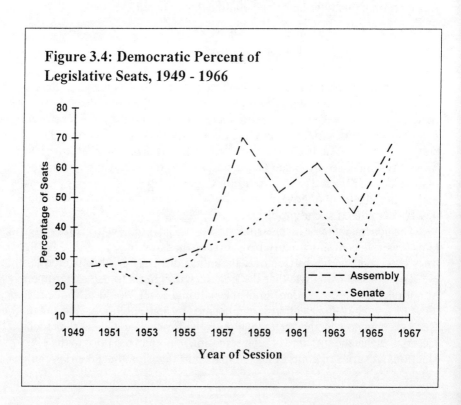

Figure 3.4: Democratic Percent of Legislative Seats, 1949 - 1966

The crucial matter when a party becomes a majority is where it gains seats, for that determines its electoral base. Table 3.1 compares election results for 1963 and 1965. In 1963 in the assembly Democrats did not do well in rural areas. In areas they might have done well in—urban areas— they got only a little more than one-half of the seats, or 59 percent. In the suburban counties the Democrats also won only about 50 percent of the seats. In the senate, the record of Democrats was somewhat worse. Of the total of 21 seats in 1963, 13 of 21 were in rural areas, and Democrats did poorly there. They were left with eight seats in suburban and urban areas, and Democrats won only four of those.

The 1965 elections produced a dramatic change for Democrats. They gained all across the state, but their most significant gains were in the sub-urban areas once held by Republicans.[78] In the urban and suburban counties Democrats won over 80 percent of the assembly seats. In the senate, the number of seats in urban and suburban counties increased and Demo-crats won almost all of the seats in these areas. In both houses, Democrats still did poorly in rural counties. The 1965 elections left Democrats with a strong urban-suburban base. Hughes, the Democratic incumbent governor, also won with a large proportion of the vote, 58 percent.

The party now had control of the governorship and both houses of the legislature for the first time since 1917. The first question for the party was what to make of this control over state government. Did the emergence of Democrats reflect electoral support for a set of Democratic principles and a mandate for Democrats to pursue a clear policy agenda? In particular, was there any mandate for increasing the role of the state by having the state raise more revenue? The ensuing evaluation process indicates how diffi-cult it is for parties to read the meaning of elections and take appropriate action.

Hughes interpreted the Democratic victory as an opportunity for Demo-crats to solidify their position. He and his administration saw a trend in Democratic success. "The Democratic Party held 12 of the 21 county court houses, eleven of the 15 congressional seats, both houses of the legislature, and most large municipalities. They read and agreed with newspaper sto-ries asserting that the balance in New Jersey politics was tipped for many years to come in favor of the Democratic Party."[79]

Governor Hughes also felt the election results represented a mandate.[80] He had promised school leaders more school aid if he won, and Democrats took the legislature.[81] He felt he had run on a platform "to meet the needs of the state," and he felt he had a mandate to enact innovative policy.[82] "[E]ven allowing for a high degree of public ignorance in the campaign, most people surely knew that they were voting for a strong activist state."[83] He saw this as an opportunity to break from the state's past.[84]

Table 3.1. Changes in Democratic Legislative Seats by County Characteristics, 1963 to 1965

County Type	Assembly					Senate					Dem. % change	
	N	1963 Democrats		1965 Democrats		N	1963 Democrats		1965 Democrats		Ass.	Sen.
		N	%	N	%		N	%	N	%		
Rural	18	4	22	5	28	13/9	2	15	1	11	6	−4
Suburban	22	13	59	19	86	5/11	3	60	10	91	33	31
Urban	20	11	55	18	90	3/9	1	33	8	89	45	56

Counties are classified on the basis of the percentage of urban density and the percent minority.* The counties are classified as following using 1960 census data: urban: Essex, Hudson, and Union; suburban: Bergen, Camden, Mercer, Middlesex, and Passaic; rural or transitional to suburban: Atlantic, Burlington, Cape May, Cumberland, Gloucester, Hunterdon, Monmouth, Morris, Ocean, Salem, Somerset, Sussex, and Warren.

The number of districts changed from 1963 to 1965 because the legislature had to comply with court orders mandating equality of population among districts. The solution of the legislature was to increase the number of seats in urban areas in the senate and to retain the practice of at least one representative per county.

* The information to classify counties came from the following sources. County demographic data came from *The City and County Data Book*, published by the Bureau of the Census, various years. The party of the legislators holding seats in specific counties was taken from various editions of the *New Jersey Legislative Manual*.

The Republican Party was weak,[85] and perhaps most important was Hughes's sense of what the party had to do with this opportunity. He "believed that a major threat to continued party success would be failure to implement campaign promises and to fulfill the responsibilities of 'full' power." [86] He saw this as an opportunity to exert leadership and as an opportunity to affect the historical perception of his administration.

The difficulty was that many party members disagreed with Hughes's interpretation of their situation.[87] The primary focus during the gubernatorial campaign had been whether a professor at Rutgers University who opposed the Vietnam War should be protected with "academic freedom" or should be disciplined in some way.[88] Many legislators did not think the focus of the campaign had been on broad state responsibilities, and they were not eager to take the initiative on taxes. They had to run again in two years, and were uneasy about being responsible for tax increases. It was still widely perceived among legislators that "taxes is losers."[89] Most of the state legislators were not issue-oriented, and did not share Hughes's enthusiasm for a series of bold policy enactments.[90] Freshmen legislators in particular were worried that supporting any sort of tax would hurt their reelection prospects.[91]

THE PURSUIT OF TAXES

The reluctance of the party to play the role of policy innovator and enact taxes became evident during the 1966 session. Hughes decided that he would pursue an income tax because it would be a fairer way to raise revenues.[92] He made it his number one priority, built his budget around it, and applied enormous pressure on Democrats to pass it, while Republicans completely opposed the income tax. After very difficult negotiations with the senate Democrats, he was able to get an income tax through the senate, and had assurances that the assembly would pass it. The night before the assembly vote, however, the thirteen-member delegation from Essex County announced they would not vote for the income tax. Several other county delegations soon indicated they were wavering and did not want to pursue the issue. The pursuit of the income tax collapsed because Democrats in the legislature saw more negatives than positives in enacting a state income tax in a state with a long history of low taxes and decentralized government.[93]

After the frustration of failing to obtain an income tax had subsided, Hughes regrouped and returned with a proposal for a 3 percent sales tax, which some had expressed a preference for earlier. The more conservative

Democrats were uneasy about directly taking people's income, but were willing to accept a sales tax, which was based on what people spent. Legislative Democrats, however, were still very uneasy about being the "tax party." They wanted bipartisan support to avoid a charge in the next election that the tax was a Democratic tax.[94]

In considering whether to join with Democrats, Republicans were affected by their desire for programs Hughes had included in his proposed budget. Hughes had proposed a budget with increased state aid, with most of it going to schools, but the aid was contingent on increased revenues.[95] This put pressure on the legislature to approve the new revenues. If more revenues were not found, existing programs would be cut, and the announced increase in school aid would not materialize. Republicans wanted to prevent cuts and they wanted the school aid. There was also a faction of progressive Republicans who felt that the party had too conservative an image and should show some concern for social problems. These more liberal Republicans were grudgingly willing to provide some votes.[96] They did not want the party to be seen as simply opposing everything. There was a price for Republican cooperation. They bargained for less school aid for lower-income Democratic areas and for college construction, and more for road construction.[97]

The sales tax eventually passed in April with several Republicans in each house voting for the tax. Table 3.2 indicates how legislators voted by party and by area. Of the 40 yes votes in the assembly, 29 came from Democrats. Of the 18 yes votes in the senate, 23 came from Democrats. Democrats had demanded and gotten some Republican support, but Democrats still provided the bulk of the votes.

The issue of equity of burden played a significant role in voting. Many urban legislators were opposed to the sales tax because they saw it as regressive. Since the tax was on expenditures, and lower-income individuals spend a higher proportion of their income on goods and services, they would pay a higher proportion of their income in taxes. This debate led to items such as clothing and food being exempt from the tax, and several urban Democrats voted against the tax.[98] Urban legislators were also opposed to the sales tax because many thought that there was more sales activity in the urban counties, so sales tax revenues would be greater in these counties. A state sales tax would take more money out of urban areas than out of other areas, which meant urban areas might pay more than their fair share.[99] Suburban legislators, on the other hand, were opposed to taxing income, which was higher in the suburbs, so the sales tax was an acceptable compromise.

Table 3.2. Partisan Support for the 1966 Sales Tax,
by Party, House, and Area

Party and Area	Assembly		Senate	
	No	Yes	No	Yes
Democrats				
Rural	1	4	0	1
Suburban	3	16	0	9
Urban	7	9	5	3
Totals	11	29	5	13
Republicans				
Rural	3	10	1	5
Suburban	2	1	1	0
Urban	2	0	1	0
Totals	7	11	3	5

Source: Votes were taken from the *Journal of the Senate* and *Minutes of the General Assembly.* The classification of counties is the same as for table 3.1.

CREATING A HIGHER EDUCATION SYSTEM

Hughes also used his reelection success and a Democratic majority in the legislature to return to the goal of creating a department of higher education. Hughes felt strongly that the existing administrative control of colleges was inhibiting growth of a system that could educate more of the children of New Jersey residents, and he chose to make this a major issue of his administration.[100] He devoted speeches to the importance of developing a separate higher education system. His staff plotted a strategy of how to overcome the lobbying of the elementary and secondary education community. He again convened a conference to study the issue. The conference recommended that a separate cabinet position be created. This proposal was resisted by the education department, which did not want to see any loss of control over the education agenda and the resources directed to education.[101] Hughes was able to get the commissioner of education to resign and to get the New Jersey Education Association to stay out of the

fight over the issue.[102] Hughes mounted a sustained effort to push his proposal through the legislature, and with a substantial crop of new legislators
after the 1965 elections, he was able, with some support from Republicans,
to secure a vote of 22 to 6 in the senate and 37 to 20 in the assembly.[103]
Hughes made a significant impact on higher education over four years. He
secured the existence of a community college system, and he secured the
independent existence of a system of higher education, which could expand on its own.

Interpreting Party Control

Democrats gained control of New Jersey state government for the first
time in fifty years in 1966, and it resulted in enactment of the first statewide general tax. An analysis of the relationship between party control and
taxes and spending might conclude that parties in New Jersey were "programmatic."[104] Democrats acquired control over government for the first
time in decades and the first statewide tax was enacted. But the behavior of
Democrats in 1966 does not accord with any such simple image of parties.
Neither the Democratic governor nor the Democratic state legislative candidates campaigned on a party platform that they would provide new programs and use an income or sales tax to pay for them.

Legislative Democrats did not embrace either an income or sales tax
with any enthusiasm. They voted for a regressive tax, the sales tax, though
they were able to win some exemptions that reduced the extent of
regressivity. They voted for a sales tax, but were eager to pass up claiming
credit for it as a Democratic tax. They sought bipartisan support to avoid
that possibility, and were able to pass it in the assembly only with the support of 11 rural Republicans. The urban contingent within the Democratic
party, which might be presumed to be the prime supporters of more state
taxation to provide more state aid, voted against it. It is difficult to see the
1966 sales tax enactment as the product of a cohesive party mobilizing
itself to enact a policy principle.

What, then, does party mean in this situation? The behavior of the New
Jersey Democrats illustrates several fundamental principles about parties.
First, the interpretation of partisan trends and election outcomes is highly
subjective. There was a struggle over the meaning of the 1964 and 1965
elections, and the interpretation of the governor won out. There is no certainty that winning a majority of seats will result in agreement that the
victory reflects a mandate. Second, whether events lead to change is very
conditional. Whether change occurs depends on the presence of a strong
leader who is willing to fight for an interpretation of events and present an

argument as to why change will help the party, and who also has a legislative party with the disposition to listen and eventually respond positively.[105]

The significance of parties is that they represent collections of politicians who differ, on average, in their dispositions about how to respond to situations. In 1966 Hughes reacted to events with the perception that the state should take on a greater role. Though the judgment must be speculative, a Republican governor elected in 1965 might have felt less of an inclination to respond to these problems and propose an income tax. Democratic legislators, with much reluctance, ultimately accepted Hughes's argument because they were more inclined than Republicans to want the programs and aid he proposed and because they were less hostile to a greater state role. Their acceptance was clearly not enthusiastic, but Democrats, given the optimism about the possible benefits of government action in 1966, reflected a disposition to respond.

Party, then, did ultimately mean something. Parties represent collections of politicians with differing dispositions to respond to issues. Elections or other events create the question of whether a response is appropriate, and parties vary in their disposition about how to respond. That disposition may be relatively passive, but it is still relevant. Democrats were willing to gamble and enact a change that Republicans had not enacted when they had control. The embrace of action by Democrats might not have been as enthusiastic as we often presume, but they did embrace change.

Tax and Aid Changes

The sales tax generated significant amounts of revenue for the state. State tax effort, defined as the percentage of personal income taken by the state through taxes, increased from 2.5 in 1966 to 3.3 in 1967, the largest recorded increase in the state's history. Over the same time period local tax effort declined from 5.9 in 1966 to 5.4 percent in 1967. Local governments still raised much more than the state, but the difference in tax effort between the two levels declined from 3.4 to 2.1 percent. The proportion of state and local tax revenue raised by the state increased from 29 percent in 1966 to 39 percent by 1968. The state was able to provide significant increases in aid to local schools. In 1965, before the state enacted the sales tax, real state aid per capita to schools was $8.66. By 1967 real education aid per capita was $16.64.[106]

From 1950 to 1967 Democrats played a major role in expanding the role of the state. Governor Meyner had taken the initiative to increase the gas tax to provide more school aid. The increases were not great, but they were increases. Major changes were brought about by Hughes and the

Democratic legislature. State legislators did so without enthusiasm, and only after much pressure from the governor. They had settled on a less progressive tax, but the state was now more involved in local affairs and provided more aid.

THE 1967 ELECTIONS: THE RETURN OF REPUBLICANS

The 1967 legislative elections provided a test of Hughes's argument that bold, innovative enactments would solidify the future of the Democratic Party. While the situation in 1965 was favorable to Democrats, in 1967 it was not. At the beginning of the year Hughes issued warnings that new taxes would be needed, which probably did not help the party's image right after enacting the sales tax.[107] The 1964 elections, while seen by some as the beginning of Democratic success, really contained the beginning of Democratic problems. The party came to be seen as liberal, very supportive of issues like welfare and minority rights, and tolerant of crime, which some argue drove away many traditional supporters.[108] Newark experienced riots in 1967, and many people blamed these on lenient, liberal Democrats. Republicans sought to exploit the issue in the 1967 New Jersey elections by blaming Democrats for problems.[109] Hughes's commissioner of education, appointed in April 1967, also caused problems for Democrats. In a speech he suggested that traditional school boundaries might have to be ignored to solve the integration problem. Republicans ran ads suggesting a Democratic victory in November would mean busing.[110] Finally, dissatisfaction with President Lyndon Johnson was growing, and state Republicans encouraged people to vote for Republicans to express their opposition to him.[111] How much these factors affected New Jersey in 1967 as compared to the enactment of the sales tax is impossible to tell.

Regardless, Democrats lost badly in the 1967 state legislative elections. While caution must be exercised in interpreting the 1967 results, it does appear that the sales tax votes had a significant impact. In the assembly, 8 of the Democrats voting against the sales tax decided to run for reelection. Six of the 8 won, and 5 of the 6 winners were in urban areas. Eighteen of the 29 Democrats voting for the sales tax chose to run. Their fate was very different. Only 6 of the 18 survived. Table 3.3 indicates success rates by area. The major losses came in the suburban areas in Essex and Bergen Counties, where Democrats had done so well in 1965.[112]

In the senate 5 of the Democrats voting against the sales tax ran, and 3 of them won. Twelve of the Democratic senators who voted for the sales tax ran, and only 3 won. The major loss of seats was again in suburban areas. In each house, those Democrats who voted for the sales tax lost

Table 3.3. Electoral Fate of Democrats Voting for
1966 Sales Tax, by Party, House, and Area

Party and Area	Assembly		Senate	
	Ran	Won	Ran	Won
Democrats				
Rural	2	0	1	0
Suburban	10	2	8	3
Urban	6	4	3	0
Total	18	6	12	3

badly. Democrats who did not vote for it fared well. The electorate apparently distinguished between Democrats based on how they voted for the sales tax.

Republicans, on the other hand, did not suffer for voting for the sales tax. Five assembly Republicans who voted for the sales tax ran and won. They were all from rural areas.[113] Three senate Republicans who voted for the sales tax ran and won. They were all from rural areas. All eight incumbent Republicans who ran in the assembly won. The only incumbent Republican senators who ran were those who voted for the sales tax. Democrats fared badly in 1967 and Republicans did not.

The ability of Republicans to vote for the sales tax and survive suggests that the 1967 vote may have been primarily a swing back to Republicans following the evaporation of the negative effect of the 1964 Goldwater candidacy. All across the Northeast the Democratic proportion of seats increased in the 1964 elections and declined again in the 1966 elections. In the Northeast the average proportion of seats won by Democrats in senates was 48.6 in 1962, 58.9 in 1964, 50.4 in 1966, and 48.5 in 1968.[114] The same pattern prevailed in state assemblies across the Northeast. General national trends surely affected the fortunes of Democrats in New Jersey. While these national patterns are very relevant, it is still important to note that Democrats differed in their fate depending on how they voted for the sales tax. Those opposing it survived at a much higher rate than those supporting it. The tax was initiated and primarily supported by Democrats, and that party image surely played a significant role.

This 1966–67 situation illustrates the enormous difficulties parties face in trying to predict how their policy choices will affect their subsequent electoral fortunes. Hughes thought he saw a trend and argued that certain policy enactments would cement that trend. Legislative Democrats evaluated the argument of their governor and a majority of them decided he was correct. Hughes and his supporters guessed wrong, and their error indicates the dilemmas parties have to face when they decide to enact change. It is never clear if the electorate will reward or punish politicians for tax increases, even if accompanied by significant increases in state aid. The Democrats brought about a change in the role of the state. Their actions were reluctant and nervous, and they subsequently lost power. But they did enact change.

The 1965 and 1967 elections also illustrate the crucial role of suburban swing districts. Democrats came to power in 1967 because they did well in those areas. They lost power in 1967 primarily because the lost in the suburbs. Table 3.4 indicates how areas of the state divided in their support for the parties for the 1965 elections and after the 1967 elections. The far right column in the table indicates the percent of seats lost in each area from 1965 to 1967 for Democrats. Republicans remained in control of the rural areas, and made significant gains in suburban areas to regain control. Democrats retained control of urban areas in both houses, but they experienced their biggest percentage losses in the suburban areas, which cost them control. Democrats had presumed that suburban areas would accept the sales tax as least harmful to them and that the increases in state aid would win votes. Democrats guessed wrong, as they would in subsequent years.

PARTIES AND THE HAVE-NOTS

The state took on a greater role in New Jersey from 1950 to 1967. Change in and of itself may be interesting, but the important political questions are who benefits from change and whether parties played a role in the change. The primary change over this time was an increase in state aid to schools, with greater funds distributed to communities with less property wealth. Every community received some increase in aid, but the greatest benefit was surely to lower-income individuals and communities. These benefits came about in several ways.

The initial increase in aid was financed by an increase in the gasoline tax. Since more-affluent individuals own more cars, and probably commute more, they paid a higher percent of these taxes. The sales tax is more complicated. On one hand, it is generally regarded as regressive, that is, as having a greater impact on low-income individuals. On the other hand, more affluent communities generate more sales tax revenue, which is then available for redistribution by state politicians. The most direct benefit for the less affluent comes from redistributive state aid made possible with these revenues. The property tax is generally seen as regressive in its effects on individuals, so greater reliance on this tax meant lower-income

Table 3.4. Changes in Democratic Legislative Seats by County Characteristics, 1965 to 1967

County Type	Assembly					Senate					Dem. % change	
	N in 65–67	1965 Democrats		1967 Democrats		N in 65–67	1965 Democrats		1967 Democrats		Ass.	Sen.
		N	%	N	%		N	%	N	%		
Rural	18–22	5	28	0	0	9–11	1	11	0	0	–28	–11
Suburban	22–31	19	86	7	23	11–16	10	91	5	31	–53	–60
Urban	20–27	18	90	15	56	9–13	8	89	4	31	–34	–58

Counties are classified on the basis of the percentage of urban density and the percent minority.* The counties are classifed as following using 1960 census data: urban: Essex, Hudson, and Union; suburban: Bergen, Camden, Mercer, Middlesex, and Passaic; rural or transitional to suburban: Atlantic, Burlington, Cape May, Cumberland, Gloucester, Hunterdon, Monmouth, Morris, Ocean, Salem, Somerset, Sussex, and Warren.

The number of districts changed from 1963 to 1965 because the legislature had to comply with court orders mandating equality of population among districts. The solution of the legislature was to increase the number of seats in urban areas in the senate and to retain the practice of at least one representative per county.

* The information to classify counties came from the following sources. County demographic data came from *The City and County Data Book*, published by the Bureau of the Census, various years. The party of the legislators holding seats in specific counties was taken from various editions of the *New Jersey Legislative Manual*.

individuals paid a higher percentage of their income in taxes. Reliance on this tax to raise money for schools also hurts lower-income communities, since they have smaller local property tax bases. To the extent the state moved to provide more aid, with more going to communities with less property wealth, this change created some redistribution that helped less-affluent groups. The replacement of further property tax increases with state aid helped all communities, but its effects were surely greater for lower-income communities.[115]

Democrats were the source of change, but not in any simple fashion. Meyner was the leader of the changes in the 1950s, but he did have to rely on Republican votes to be successful. Hughes was the leader of the sales tax enactment, but his party followed him reluctantly. The reluctance of the legislative Democratic Party to strongly support the sales tax illustrates the consequences of a Democratic Party without a clear lower-income electoral base. Many of the Democrats who won in 1965 came from suburban districts, where taxes were not popular, but state aid probably was. They hesitated to support the sales tax, because there was considerable ambiguity in how their constituency would react to the tax change. The lack of a cohesive class-based legislative party restrained the party. Hughes, on the other hand, won with a significant margin in 1965, he felt he had a mandate, and he was a liberal. He served as the forceful advocate for a greater state role and was able to persuade others to follow. If he had not done so well in 1965 he would probably not have been able to carry along an ambivalent legislative party. Democrats played the role of helping the have-nots, along with providing more aid to others, but, again, it was a reluctant move and probably only because a set of unique conditions pushed them along.

4

The Return of Republicans

DEMOCRATS INCREASED TAXES AND THE ROLE OF STATE GOVERNMENT IN 1966. IN the next election, held in 1967, Republicans gained control of the legislature with enough votes to control the state agenda. They held the legislature by a 3 to 1 margin, which was more than enough to override any gubernatorial veto of legislative proposals. Hughes, elected in 1965, still had two more years as governor, but the Republican margin was sufficient to dominate. The intriguing political question was what the Republicans would try to do with this power.

The 1969 elections increased Republican power and created a second opportunity for challenging the prior Democratic initiatives. In the 1969 gubernatorial election Democrats ran ex-governor Meyner as their gubernatorial candidate, while William Cahill ran as a relatively liberal Republican. Cahill won, with Republicans retaining their margins in the legislature. Republicans had complete control in 1970 for the first time since the 1953 session. Figure 4.1 indicates the percent of seats held by Democrats after each of these elections. Would Republicans repeal Democratic initiatives, or accept and ratify them?

In neither case did Republicans repeal Democratic policies. In 1968 the legislature approved a series of increases in minor taxes and some additional local aid programs. In 1970 Republican governor Cahill persuaded the Republican legislature to increase the sales tax from 3 to 5 percent. Rather than repeal the measures for the increased role of the state enacted by Democrats, Republicans ratified the prior changes and further increased that role.

It would appear that party meant little in New Jersey over these years. While the parties again did not fit any simple notions of how parties affect policy, this period of Republican control does tell us a great deal about how parties behave. Specifically, their behavior indicates how the political climate can affect party calculations, how Democratic pressures about social policy matter, and what happens when the political logic of a governor differs from that of his legislative party. Parties behaved as we might expect, if we consider the situation and political coalitions of the politicians involved and their interaction with the political context.

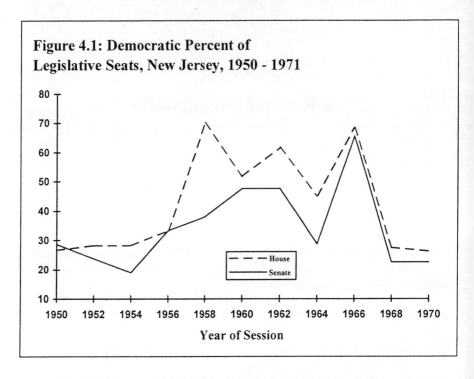

Figure 4.1: Democratic Percent of Legislative Seats, New Jersey, 1950 - 1971

THE HUGHES-REPUBLICAN LEGISLATURE BATTLE

Though the electorate rejected many Democrats in 1967, the Democratic governor Hughes was not inclined to scale back his program ambitions. He began the 1968 session with a record-breaking proposed budget of $1 billion. He put pressure on the legislature by noting that his budget included no funds for a Medicaid program, which the state needed to adopt by 1970. He indicated that the state would have to find funds to match federal funds for the Medicaid program, or the state would lose $12 million in federal funds.[1]

The pressure to pursue liberal social programs escalated in the next several months. The Select Commission on Civil Disorder reported in February and concluded that "a crisis existed in Newark and other cities" and that the state needed a "massive program to rehabilitate Negro neighborhoods."[2] Shortly after that Martin Luther King was assassinated, creating a sense of crisis and that something needed to be done in response. Hughes responded with a request for an additional $125 million for an urban aid program.

Much of the funding would be used to increase the proportion of local welfare costs paid by the state. The state system for delivering welfare had developed as an essentially localistic system.[3] As caseloads and costs increased, significant and uneven burdens were placed on local governments. The development of this system deserves some explanation. The initial efforts within the state to provide aid to the poor originated, as in many Northeast states, with municipal programs. The state first became involved when it adopted a program for relief of dependent children in 1899. When the Social Security Act of 1935 was passed to provide aid to the blind, old-age assistance, and aid to dependent children, the state elected to participate in the program, but assigned administration and sharing of costs to municipalities.[4] The state also continued to support a fourth program of public assistance, called the General Assistance Program. It provided funding to individuals who did not fit the criteria of federal programs, and whom local municipalities wanted to support. Differences in administration across municipalities led to a state commission study in 1953, which recommended shifting all federal programs to counties. Over the next several years federal programs were shifted to counties, while General Assistance remained a municipal program.[5]

The arrangement for paying for administrative costs and for direct public assistance benefits to individuals in the state in the late 1960s is shown in table 4.1. The federal government paid 50 percent, and 25 percent was paid by each the state and the counties. For federal assistance programs, the bulk of costs were being paid for by the federal government and counties. Other costs were distributed as shown.

As welfare rolls expanded during the 1960s, new pressures emerged to have the state intervene again in how public assistance was delivered and who paid for it. The decentralized delivery system had created several issues.[6] The essential difficulty was that there were differences across counties in the frequency of welfare cases, which created varying expenditure demands and tax obligations. A county with greater burdens would have to raise $19.20 per resident through local taxes, while another county might have to raise only $2.60 per resident. The counties required to raise the most had the lowest per capita income and the lowest property tax bases.[7] It was also the case that clients in different counties were being treated differently, even though state law prohibited that.[8]

The differences in tax burdens had led to criticisms that the burden of paying for public welfare was unevenly and unfairly distributed. Differential treatment of clients was criticized by some as illegal and unfair. Increases

Table 4.1. Distribution of Public Assistance Costs
in New Jersey State and Local Governments

Program Type	Purpose of Expenditure	Percent of Costs Paid By			
		Federal	State	County	Munici-palities
Federal benefit (categorical)	direct benefits	50	25	25	0
	county administrative costs	50	0	50	0
	social service costs	75	0	25	0
General assistance	benefit payments	0	75	0	25
	administration and services	0	0	0	100

Source: Governor's Task Force on Welfare Management, *A State Welfare System for the Poor* (Trenton: State of New Jersey, 1971), 4.

in welfare rolls led to complaints from local officials about the unfairness of having to generate local taxes for a state-mandated program. Hughes proposed that the state increase its share of costs from 50 to 75 percent.[9] Since welfare costs were greater in urban areas, this would free up greater funds in urban areas for other purposes.

Hughes also proposed that part of the funds from his package would go to renovate urban slums. Hughes proposed an income tax or an increase in the sales tax to fund these programs. He spoke of a need for "moral recommitment" and the need to meet a "crisis of massive proportions."[10] Another state commission, the Governor's Commission to Evaluate the Capital Needs of New Jersey, reported shortly after this. It concluded the state had massive unmet capital needs because of its years of low taxation and limited revenues, and recommended the state pursue $2 billion of capital construction on projects involving roads, colleges, water systems, and environmental pollution control. The commission recommended that the state adopt the income tax.[11] Hughes reiterated his support for the income tax, and suggested that the state use the funds to spend $1.75 billion over the next several years. The year of Republican control began with a litany of serious unmet needs in the state, with Hughes serving as the major proponent of the need to respond to the needs being expressed.

The Republicans were restrained but firm in their response to Hughes's proposals. They did not comment on the importance of the needs Hughes was speaking about, but they proposed to do much less for urban needs. They rejected increases in the sales tax or adoption of the income tax.[12] They proposed their own program of urban aid, totaling $90 million. The funds would come from increases in the gasoline, cigarette, and corporate income taxes, and from increased driver license and car registration fees. Perhaps most important were how they wanted to direct urban aid and their willingness to support the capital needs program. Their urban aid program consisted of a package directing more aid to suburbs than to urban areas. They eliminated aid for renovating slum housing. They also were willing to borrow only $890 million for capital construction.[13]

Given the margin of Republican control in the legislature, Hughes had little chance to defeat Republicans. He kept up his relentless claims of crisis[14] and attacks on Republicans, asking "will the legislature plunge into a dark of shame and neglect?,"[15] and apparently had an impact. A march on Trenton was arranged by the liberal wing of the Republican Party, and the legislators from Bergen and Essex Counties rejected their party's proposals in favor of more spending.[16]

The Republican legislative leaders then relented and added more to the urban aid program. Their proposal was still not very sympathetic to urban areas. Their "urban aid" program consisted of $25 million in school aid, with the same amount per pupil to every district in the state, and a rebate of the sales tax, with the rebate distributed on a per capita basis to each government. With both programs, affluent districts would get as much as low-income districts. Republicans were clearly trying to make sure that the suburban districts that brought them to power did not receive less money than other areas. They also agreed to increase the bond issue by $100 million, and included some money for urban housing in this amount.[17] Hughes continued to speak of the "shame" of the legislature,[18] and vetoed their urban aid legislation.[19] Republicans then overrode his veto and enacted their urban aid program.[20] Democrats chose to vote with Republicans, even though they did not like the distribution of aid. They knew they could not change the outcome, and as the senate minority leader explained, "How can you turn down money even though it does not go where the Governor wants it to go?"[21]

In 1969 Hughes and the Republicans experienced a similar battle, but on a much smaller scale. Hughes acknowledged that in an election year not much was possible,[22] and only late in the session did he propose another urban aid package and some small tax increases on banks and savings and loans.[23] The legislature ignored his requests and awaited the outcome of the 1969 elections.[24]

Hughes lost his battle with Republicans, at least on the surface. But this dynamic illustrates the importance of partisan political positioning and dialogues for outcomes. The political climate—riots the prior year and commissions indicating the state should do more—put pressure on Republicans to not ignore articulated needs. Hughes served as the advocate of minorities and cities and put pressure on Republicans to respond. The combination, plus anxieties in the liberal wing of the Republican Party, surely pushed Republicans to provide more help to cities than they had wished. His pressure also prompted Republicans to increase the bond and include urban housing. Without Hughes serving as an advocate for the have-nots, there may have been no aid package.

Cities and low-income communities did not get as much as Hughes wanted, but they did get increases in aid. State tax effort increased from 3.4 to 3.9, and the proportion of revenue raised by the state increased from 38.6 to 40.6. By 1970 real state aid to schools increased to $20.02 per capita from the $16.82 level of 1968. Hughes's pressure amidst the urban crisis, even with a veto-proof Republican legislature, resulted in an increased state tax effort and more state aid. Finally, Hughes was able to get the legislature to agree to increase the proportion of local welfare paid for by the state. Since welfare problems were more prevalent in urban areas, that freed up more funds in urban areas for other purposes than in affluent areas. The bond issue was approved in the November elections, so there were funds for more public college construction and urban housing. A focused argument by Hughes on the need to address problems resulted in an increase of aid for low-income needs. Hughes was clearly helped by the political climate, but it was his articulation of these concerns which was crucial.

The 1969 Elections and Complete Republican Control

The 1969 elections put the Republican Cahill in the governor's office, and Republicans retained their prior margin of control in the legislature. Republicans now had complete control and could impose whatever policies they wished. Their range of policy choices, however, was again constrained by events.

As Cahill took office, the state was faced with a $300 million deficit for the current fiscal year. Since it was late in the fiscal year, cutting spending would be difficult.[25] The state needed funds to match federal Medicaid funds, and local officials were putting pressure on the state to help them with local welfare costs. The state had adopted a modest Medicaid program, to be administered by the state, to begin January 1, 1970, that would create demands for state revenues.[26] Welfare costs were growing and creating more complaints, and further increases were expected.[27] Cahill's response represents a puzzle in understanding political parties. While he was a Republican, he proposed an increase in the sales tax from 3 to 5 percent.[28] The Republican legislature agreed to the proposal, though without enthusiasm. As the senate majority leader put it, "Some guys will vote yes and then go out and throw up."[29] The legislature passed it on the day he was inaugurated so he could sign it right away and begin collecting revenues by March 1, 1970. The tax again increased state tax effort, which rose from 3.9 in 1969 to 4.3 in 1971.

Cahill's behavior is puzzling, if we assume that Republicans are invariably conservative. Cahill was not. He had an activist view of government,[30] and said during the campaign that the solution to the state's fiscal problem was new revenues.[31] Cahill was more liberal than his legislative party and was willing to lead the effort for a tax increase.[32] The Republican legislature was not eager to raise taxes, but they were also not willing to cut large amounts from the state budget. The budget deficit had been widely and repeatedly discussed, so there was some public acceptance of the existence of a problem, which makes enacting taxes easier. State legislators also realized that local governments were experiencing rising costs because they had to pay part of the escalating costs of welfare and Medicaid. Legislators wanted to reduce some of that pressure and were willing to raise taxes to do so. The combination of a liberal Republican governor and severe fiscal problems resulted in a willingness to raise taxes.

REPUBLICAN CONTROL AND THE NEW STATUS QUO

Republicans, when they acquired power, ratified the greater state role that had come with the enactment of the sales tax in 1966. They did so for several reasons. First, despite the controversy of the 1966 sales tax enactment, it did not persist as a campaign issue in 1967. Republicans did not make repealing it a major issue in the 1967 legislative elections. It was not an issue in the 1969 gubernatorial campaign. The party had made no promises that it would repeal the tax. They were probably inclined to accept it because the need for it had been discussed for years, and it was regularly pointed out that New Jersey had lower taxes than surrounding states. The tax had also brought a significant increase in state aid, which no one wanted to reverse. Second, there was a persisting focus on social problems, which

Hughes used to create pressure on state legislators. Third, the state was experiencing fiscal problems, because of growing costs for federal programs. The combination of events made Republicans willing to accept this greater state role.

The 1969 and 1971 elections reassured Republicans that they were not going to be punished for accepting the sales tax, or for raising it. They experienced no significant losses in seats, and were not punished for adopting taxes in 1968 and 1970.

The Republican Party had not transformed itself into a liberal party, however. There were limits to their willingness to increase taxes. After passing the sales tax increase in 1970, Cahill established a Tax Policy Committee to study the entire tax system of the state. The committee recommended reducing local property taxes by shifting the burden to a state income tax. During the 1972 session Cahill sought to get such a change enacted. He failed to secure passage and was able to get only a few Republicans to vote for the proposal. When Cahill ran for reelection in 1973, several conservative Republicans entered the race, and Cahill lost.[33] The party had been willing to consider his requests when significant fiscal pressures existed, but they were not willing to consider enacting an income tax. That issue would be left for the Democrats.

Part III:

Schools, Inequality, and State Taxes, I

5

Schools, Democrats, and
the Income Tax

INTRODUCTION

THE ENACTMENT OF THE SALES TAX AND INCREASE IN ITS RATE IN THE EARLY 1970s did not end the issue of whether state government should do more. The issue of inequalities of tax bases among school districts became a central focus of state politics during the mid 1970s. A confrontation developed between the state supreme court and the legislature over whether the state should respond to these inequities and provide more state aid to reduce inequities. State politicians, and Democrats in particular, were presented with the issue of whether they would impose a new statewide tax to provide funds to equalize school finance. The result, after a protracted struggle, was the first income tax in New Jersey's history.

The income tax enactment again tells us much about just how parties become agents of change. Many state politicians had long believed that an income tax was the best way to end New Jersey's dependence on the regressive property and sales taxes. There were enormous demands on the state and reasons to enact a statewide tax that was sensitive to ability to pay. The Republican governor, in office from 1969 to 1973, had tried, unsuccessfully, to secure passage of an income tax. But it was a Democratic governor and a Democratic legislature that finally enacted the income tax legislation. Only when faced with the extraordinary situation in which the courts could be blamed for the necessity of imposing an unpopular tax did Democrats in the legislature take the political risk of voting for the tax that Republican and Democratic executives alike had supported as necessary

---

This chapter was written by Mary P. McGuire

for years. Democrats imposed the tax with little support from Republicans, despite the fact that the state supreme court forced the closing of New Jersey's entire public school system.

This enactment points to a fundamental difference in the dispositions of the two parties. Republicans were unwilling to support a tax even when there appeared to be no reasonable alternative. Democrats were willing (though by no means eager) to impose a progressive tax, even as they recognized the likely political risk. This chapter tells the story of the passage of the income tax and its aftermath. It is the story of a long political battle that locked New Jersey's judicial, legislative, and executive branches in a multiyear struggle. It was a struggle that set suburban interests against urban and rural interests, the needs of the poor against the preferences of the middle, and ultimately resulted in Democratic policies winning over Republican policies. In the end, it demonstrated that parties matter, but sometimes prefer not to.

The tale also indicates how parties can survive the enactment of an unpopular change. The Democratic Party was not repudiated in the 1977 elections. This presents an enormous contrast to the party's experience in the 1960s, when introducing the state sales tax led to political defeat for many Democrats. Why Democrats lost power in one case but not in another is important for understanding when parties get blamed and when they do not. As is often the case, context and circumstances proved to be important in saving the Democrats from electoral repudiation.

THE CONTINUATION OF SUBURBANIZATION AND ITS EFFECTS

The census reports from 1970 revealed that the income gap between blacks and whites and between urban and suburban dwellers in New Jersey had increased significantly since 1960.[1] This growing inequality took a toll on the state's cities during the 1970s. Welfare expenditures were increasing, and in 1970 Governor Cahill warned that expansion of the program would require more expenditure at the local and state level.[2] As the suburbs prospered, there was continual pressure to fund state programs that would allow the decaying urban areas to share in that prosperity. Governor Cahill proposed a $50,000,000 aid package designed to support the fiscally troubled city of Newark, but Democrats opposed it because they believed that it was not enough money for Newark and that such funds had failed to assist similarly situated cities.[3]

The only realistic actor to initiate and fund more urban programs was state government, but the state's practice of relying heavily on localities to fund and manage many services limited the ability of the state to respond to urban needs. By February 1971 Republican governor Cahill, who in January had called upon President Nixon to increase federal aid to crumbling cities like Newark,[4] presented a $1.78 billion budget that included twice the amount of municipal aid that had been available in 1970. He also chose to widely distribute the aid, making a large number of cities eligible for the aid. This diluted the effect the increase might have had.[5]

The ability of the state to respond to problems, however, was significantly limited by the tax system. Although New Jersey was a relatively high income state in the 1970s, the tax system exacted little from its citizens at the state level. Hence, compared to states with comparable wealth available, New Jersey had little revenue to spend on higher education, public education, institutions, and transportation.[6] Further, the state's low statewide taxes placed an enormous pressure on the revenue-raising capacity of local government, particularly local government in relatively poor cities. Urban cities were experiencing continuing decline during the 1970s as industry moved to suburbs. While the suburbanization of industry was a national trend that had been going on for two decades, New Jersey was particularly hard hit. "[I]n 39 major metropolitan areas of the country, 85 percent of all industrial and commercial growth, measured by jobs, ha[d] taken place in the suburbs. In New Jersey the rate ha[d] been 95 percent."[7] In 1974, the appellate division of the state's superior court ruled that a suit challenging the practice of county support for welfare should be heard. During that same year the legislative action committee of the New Jersey Conference of Mayors warned that without tax reform, the cities faced financial disaster. Hence, despite New Jersey's earlier efforts to increase state revenues, by the 1970s the state still had low statewide taxes. As a result, local governments were under enormous pressure to raise revenues and provide services, an all but impossible task for the poorest areas of the state.

ROBINSON V. CAHILL

For the state to play a greater role, it had to have more resources. The political difficulty was that passing an income tax to provide the revenues to allow the state to assist local governments and citizens in the poorest areas was politically unpopular. The beginnings of an end to this impasse emerged with a very significant court interpretation of the state's constitution. The crucial language involved the constitutional guarantee of a "thorough and efficient" education for all of New Jersey's children.

In 1871 the New Jersey State Legislature warned that local taxation could not be relied upon to provide equal educational opportunity.[8] In 1875 the legislature passed an amendment committing the state to provide a "thorough and efficient" education to all its children. It was this amendment that would support a 1973 challenge to New Jersey's system of financing schools through local property taxes. This phrase had had no impact since its adoption, but now it took on considerable significance and became a widely repeated and understood phrase in the state.

The challenge to the existing system of school finance came in the form of *Robinson v. Cahill*. The idea for the case originated when a young Jersey City lawyer, Harold Ruvoldt Jr., wrote an article for the *New Jersey Bar Journal* in 1969 arguing that the right to an education was implied by both the national and the state constitutions.[9] Since the right was constitutionally based, it was incumbent upon the state's financing system to secure that right. The article was brought to the attention of Jersey City mayor Thomas J. Whelan. He was struggling under budgetary pressures. Criticized for high taxes and poor services, he had been informed that the city's teachers were on the verge of striking for higher wages. He decided to use Rudvolt's reasoning to challenge the state's system of school financing in an effort to provide financial relief for his city or at least a reduction of public relations pressure for himself.[10]

Rudvolt was hired to make the city's case before the superior court. Rudvolt presented a case before the court in which he

contended that education was a fundamental interest and that delegation of responsibility for education by the state to localities whose property wealth varied widely constituted a classification of students on the basis of wealth, a constitutionally suspect distinction among citizens. The court, he argued, must strictly scrutinize the state's education finance system to determine if it denied some students equal protection of the laws as guaranteed by the Fourteenth Amendment of the United States Constitution and by the New Jersey Constitution. The quality of a child's education may not be a function of the wealth of the community in which he lives, the complaint alleged Rudvolt reinforced this position by contending that the youngsters harmed by the state's education finance scheme were predominantly minority group members. New Jersey['s] . . . school finance system . . . provided disproportionately fewer educational opportunities to black children such as Kenneth Robinson than to white children. The New Jersey Constitution assigned the responsibility for public education to the state government, and any failure to meet that obligation must be remedied by the state itself.[11]

As part of the case, he filed information on selected school districts that indicated the equalized tax base per student, the expense per student, the tax rate for the district, and the state aid per student for 1971–72. That information is presented in table 5.1. The evidence before the court painted

Table 5.1. School District Variances

	Equalized Value per Pupil, 1971 A	Expense per Pupil 1971–72 B	Equalized School Tax Rate, 1971 C	State Aid per Pupil 1971–72
Bergen County				
Ridgefield	85,602	1,338	.57	104.61
Englewood	79,643	1,743	2.07	105.36
Hackensack	79,665	1,471	2.11	104.62
Tenafly	72,347	1,339	1.90	104.74
Paramus	51,063	1,403	2.81	104.69
Dumont	39,289	1,020	2.55	104.29
Essex County				
Montclair	51,231	1,390	2.52	105.00
Bloomfield	49,816	1,060	2.01	104.63
Orange	35,403	1,199	2.72	118.72
Newark	19,815	1,121	3.69	317.80
Hudson County				
Secaucus	119,172	1,184	1.10	104.16
Bayonne	46,949	1,031	1,56	106.01
Jersey City	26,786	897	2.82	221.52
Hoboken	19,079	811	2.77	293.68
Mercer County				
Ewing Twp.	45,853	1,145	2.05	104.96
Trenton	20,724	1,013	2.80	305.00
Middesex County				
New Brunswick	55,974	1,488	2.23	105.65
Perth Amboy	31,339	1,293	3.20	167.48
Madison	25,505	1,069	3.20	221.51
Monmouth County				
Red Bank	55,974	1,488	2.23	105.65
Asbury Park	31,339	1,293	3.20	167.48
Morris County				
Madison	49,351	1,234	2.21	104.60
Parsippany-Troy Hills	43,189	986	2.19	103.74
Dover	36.988	901	2.00	106.13
Passaic County				
Clifton	75,527	961	1.24	104.84
Wayne Twp.	53,323	1,037	1.93	104.12
Passaic City	33,999	928	2.14	135.12
Paterson	23,232	857	2.57	259.88
Somerset County				
Bernardsville	73,786	1,234	1.75	104.93
Somerville	45.157	1,181	2.65	105.48
Union County				
Summit	68,498	1,230	1.82	104.61
Elizabeth	43,920	1,038	1.88	128.93
Plainfield	31,220	1,093	3.21	145.46

Note: The data are excerpted from an opinion by Superior Court Judge Theodore I. Botter, 1972. Source for table: *Robinson v. Cahill,* appendix A.

a bleak picture of inequality in education in New Jersey. In 1972, 68 percent of the cost of operating schools came from local property tax. School districts differed dramatically in the equalized assessed value per pupil. This resulted in very different per pupil spending levels, with some districts spending almost twice as much as others (Column B). It also produced a situation where those districts with the smallest tax bases imposed the highest tax rates (Column C), but still had far less to spend on schools. State aid (Column D) was limited in amount and was not distributed to counter local wealth differentials, so state aid did little to offset inequalities in local wealth.

Children in urban and rural areas had far fewer resources than their peers in the suburbs, where there were higher property values. The relatively wealthy parents in the suburbs were taxed at lower *rates* (not amounts, though) than those of the city and rural children. Within Bergen County, for example, Dumont imposed a property tax of 2.55 percent, while Ridgefield had a tax rate of only 0.57 percent. Despite that, Ridgefield spent 30 percent more per student than Dumont. Urban areas had lower property values, so even with higher taxes they had less to spend on students. As Harold Ruvoldt Jr., the lawyer who initiated the case, said, "Because the system is wealth-based, we're telling certain pupils that you're getting less [education] because you live in a poorer district."[12]

The existing situation of taxes and spending was problematic for two reasons. First, the scheme was unfair to taxpayers. Taxpayers throughout the state were being taxed at different rates in order to achieve the same public purpose, the education of children. Because the state constitution stipulated that the state was to provide a "thorough and efficient" education to all children, this meant that citizens were taxed at different rates in order to fulfill a public purpose for which the constitution made the state, not the school district, responsible.[13] Second, the scheme assured that some districts were able to provide their children with a thorough and efficient education while others were not.

The districts with lower per pupil spending also paid lower teacher salaries and found it more difficult to recruit the state's highest quality teachers. Low-spending districts also had low staff-to-student ratios, assuring that the children from New Jersey's poorest districts had the least support and attention.[14]

Not only were there inequalities in the system, but the problem had worsened over the past two decades as industry left the decaying city centers and moved to suburbs at an even faster rate in New Jersey than the rest of the nation, thus contributing to a steady decline of the tax base in the cities. To examine how change was occurring, we can return to the random sample of New Jersey school districts' 1952 tax rates discussed in chapter

2. The 1952 and 1969 tax rates for the sample districts are shown in figure 5.1. School districts are arrayed from those with the lowest tax base to those with the highest tax base. In 1952 there were not significant differences in tax rates across the groups of districts. By 1969 the average tax rates among the most affluent districts had declined, but tax rates were still high in the poorer school districts.

As middle- and upper-income families relocated to the suburbs, an increasingly higher percentage of the children living in city districts were from poor families in which the parents had a low level of educational attainment. Further, they were increasingly likely to be from non-English speaking and/or minority group families. They were thus a population difficult to educate, needing such expensive resources as English as a second language instructors and materials. Small, poor urban and rural districts faced difficulty raising school funds. The legislature had tried to direct more money to districts with high percentages of children whose families received AFDC, but these efforts had not focused on school finance issues.[15]

The state attorney general did not dispute the fact that there were children in New Jersey schools who were being taught in substandard facili-

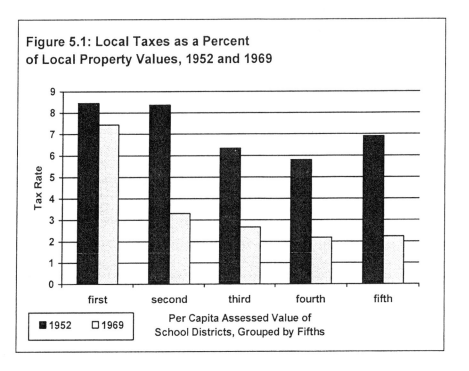

Figure 5.1: Local Taxes as a Percent of Local Property Values, 1952 and 1969

ties.[16] Dispute was over the relationship between expenditures and quality of education; the argument was made that more money would not solve the problems of low-income districts. The judge handling the case, Botter, was aware that there was disagreement over whether simply spending more money would improve the education of children in poorer districts. He spent six days questioning expert witnesses to attempt to understand the relationship. He was ultimately persuaded that less-qualified teachers, out-dated textbooks, inadequate physical plants, poor ratios of professional staff (psychologists, reading specialists, counselors) to students, and large class size contributed to poor performance.[17] Botter summed up his resolution of the conflicting evidence on educational quality:

> Clearly a large number of New Jersey children are not getting an adequate education. This is caused in part by insufficient funds in many districts despite high taxes. On the other hand, many districts provide superior education with less tax effort. More money should make a significant difference in many poor districts. However, the problems in older cities with large minority populations are more complicated. It is too much to expect that our school system alone can solve all these problems. But much can be done, and doing more will cost more. Education is no exception to this fact of life.[18]

His decision to reject the current system of school financing was not widely accepted, however. The City of Clifton Springs filed a friend of the court brief seeking to encourage the state supreme court to overturn Botter's decision. The city's lawyers argued that the case could cause an unleashing of equal protection rights that would destroy local government in New Jersey, allowing the court or legislature to order localities to provide more police or fire protection.[19] The position of Clifton Springs reflected the opposition of those who live in well-off communities capable of considerable self-sufficiency to helping those who live in communities with fewer resources and more vexing problems. This conflict would dominate New Jersey politics for at least two decades. It would ultimately prompt the court to seek to enforce its orders because the legislature and the governor were unable to reach agreement on how to respond to the court ruling.

New Jersey superior court judge Botter handed down his decision in *Robinson v. Cahill* on January 19, 1972. He found that the state's system of funding public schools was indeed unconstitutional. His decision was upheld by the New Jersey Supreme Court on April 3, 1973. The state supreme court's decision, written by Chief Justice Joseph Weintraub, said,

> It must be evident that our present scheme is a patchy product reflecting provincial contests rather than a plan sensitive only to the Constitutional

mandate. . . . Upon the record before us, it may be doubted that the thorough and efficient system of schools required by the 1875 amendment can realistically be met by reliance on local taxation. . . . There is no more evidence today than there was 100 years ago that this approach will succeed.[20]

ROBINSON V. CAHILL AND POLITICAL CONTEXT

Robinson v. Cahill was initiated by Jersey City for the purpose of altering a public finance policy that harmed the state's cities and benefited its suburbs. The case was to influence education policy, but its more profound effects were to be on fiscal policy. Once the city had won its case, the obvious policy change that would meet the state's newfound financial responsibility was the introduction of a statewide income tax. As a justice who endorsed the *Robinson v. Cahill* decision explained:

> The Court did not say that you had to have an income tax, but anyone with an ounce of sense would know that the only possible solution to the problem was the adoption of an income tax or something much worse [such as an increased sales tax or statewide property tax].[21]

Imposing a statewide income tax was bound to be politically risky. Voters are generally reluctant to turn over more money to the government. Middle- and higher-income earners, whose children already attended well-appointed suburban schools, were particularly likely to resent such a tax. Hence, the legislative branch was reluctant to enact the justice's "only possible solution." From the perspective of the executive branch, an income tax, which most states had already imposed by 1973, was the most reasonable solution to both the school funding problem and the state's wider budget pressures. Hence the court's decision created a political context in which there was both a need to effect politically undesirable legislation and a built-in tension between the state's executive and legislative branches. Evidence of response to that new context can be found in a brief analysis of efforts to effect a judicial review of the decision.

Although the New Jersey Supreme Court's decision would never be overturned, it would be challenged in at least three ways. Those opposed to the decision would challenge its validity by appealing it to the federal court system (see table 5.2), while its proponents tried to force the court to accept greater responsibility for enforcing it (see table 5.3). The legislature would further challenge it by refusing to pass the legislation required to comply. It would take until July 1976, and drastic action by the state supreme court, before the legislature would find a constitutional method of refinancing educational funding.

THE EMERGENCE OF STATE GOVERNMENT

Table 5.2. Challenges to the New Jersey State
Supreme Court's Authority on School Finance

Complainant	Grounds	Year	Outcome
New Jersey Attorney General	The New Jersey Suprem Court lacks power to redistribute funds, which is a legislative function	1973	Federal court refused to hear the challenge
Legislative leaders[a]	Asks U.S. Supreme Court to strike down state supreme court decision on the grounds it was a violation of separation of powers	1973	U.S. Supreme Court refused to hear
State Senate	Asks for a rehearing	1975	Court refused
Town of Elizabeth	Asks U.S. Supreme Court to stop closing of schools, as ordered by N.J. Supreme Court	1976	U.S. Supreme Court refused to hear

[a]Senate President Alfred N. Beadleston (Rep.) and Assembly Speaker Thomas H. Kean (Rep.)

The decision in *Robinson v. Cahill* created a political context in which legislators were forced to respond to an equality issue that threatened the status quo and challenged them to find a solution to problems faced by the state's poorer urban and rural districts, without offending constituents in relatively well-off suburbs. The efforts to escape the pressure that was created for lawmakers is evident in their challenges to the court's decision. Legislative members argued that the court had overstepped its bounds and violated the doctrine of the separation of powers in 1973. The legislative leaders claimed that the appeal had bipartisan support. The appeal may have been largely intended to show that the legislature had done every thing possible to retain the current system, as Kean suggested when he called it a "final step" and an "obligation" of legislators.[22] It nonetheless demonstrated a willingness to oppose the court's decision. By 1975, the senate was reduced to arguing that because the legislative branch could not make policy, the case should be reheard:

> We believe that [a rehearing] is the most effective way to expedite a revision of the educational and financial laws to the extent that such a revision

Table 5.3. Efforts to Encourage the Court
to Step Up Enforcement

Source	Action Requested	Date	Outcome
Plaintiffs from *Robinson v. Cahill*	Court-ordered income tax	Dec. 1973	Court refuses
Plaintiffs from *Robinson v. Cahill*	Asks court to impound school aid until legislature decides how to make school funding more equitable	Jan. 1975	Court refuses
Governor Byrne	Asks court to redistribute $640 million in state school aid from 426 wealthier districts to 138 poorer districts[a]	Jan. 1975	Court refuses
Governor Byrne	Asks court to move up deadline for new school financing plan from October to July	Feb. 1975	Court honors Gov. Byrne's request
Governor Byrne	Asks court to impose a state financing program	Mar. 1975	Court refuses
Governor Byrne	Asks court to move up deadline	Feb. 1976	Court honors Gov. Byrne's request

[a] Redistribution would have meant the 426 communities losing aid would have to raise property taxes between 20 and 30 percent to make up the school budget difference.

is mandated by the Constitution of this state. . . . As a result of more than six months' efforts to enact legislation that would comply with the mandate of *Robinson v. Cahill* the one point on which there appears to be near total agreement is that no one can agree what must be done to comply with the decision. [23]

Governor Byrne also tried to use the courts to his advantage in the political struggle over school funding (see table 5.3). His first strategy was to attempt to pressure the court to redistribute school aid [24] or impose an accepted state school financing program itself. His second strategy was to ask the court to compel the legislature to act quickly by establishing shorter deadlines.[25] Byrne's second strategy was ultimately successful.

The New Jersey Supreme Court faced a classic problem for American courts. While it clearly had the power to declare the financing system unconstitutional—several attempts to appeal the decision to the federal courts failed—its power to enforce the ruling was much less clear. As tables 5.2 and 5.3 illustrate, the Court was caught between the efforts of both opponents and proponents of the decision. Those who sought to maintain the status quo in school financing challenged the court's authority to enforce its decision by appealing to the federal court system and by asking the state supreme court itself to rehear *Robinson v. Cahill*. On the other hand, Governor Byrne, and others who sought to impose a more equitable school financing system, attempted to encourage the court to enforce the decision more energetically (see table 5.3).

The court's subsequent behavior indicated it was not inclined to be aggressive in enforcing its ruling. It originally failed to set a deadline by which it expected the legislature to have found a new way to finance education, it refused to honor Governor Byrne's request that it redistribute funds or design a new system (see table 5.3), and it accepted Public School Act of 1975 (S 1516), which called for the state to assume greater responsibility for public school funding but failed to provide the necessary funds. (A fuller discussion of the law is provided in the next section.) Further demonstrating the difficulty U.S. courts have in enforcing their rulings, each time the legislature failed to meet a court-ordered deadline an extension was granted and, until 1976, each time a new deadline was set the court failed to say what it would do in the absence of legislative cooperation. The court's hesitation to take an active enforcement role was probably based on a desire to keep the itself out of the political struggle that ensued and to avoid setting the court against the legislature in a potentially embarrassing power struggle. However, through its inaction the court contributed to the political deadlock that persisted for three years after its decision. It was not until the court took decisive action in July 1976, over three years after its original decision, that the New Jersey State Legislature was able to agree upon an income tax to raise money for school financing and tax reform.

As politicians avoided the situation and the court chose not to enforce its ruling, the disparity between schools in wealthy and poor communities remained a reality for the schoolchildren of New Jersey. By February 1975 Newark's schools were in such disarray that Governor Byrne announced that the state would supervise a reform program in the city. Two hundred fifty thousand dollars were to be withheld from state education aid to Newark public schools in order to hire administrative personnel to direct the reforms. In March, Mayor Gibson's budget proposed a school staff cut of 12 percent for Newark schools. By December 1975, a state-appointed auditor had begun work in an effort to improve the school district's fiscal practices.

While some thought an income tax was the only way to provide the revenues to rectify the inequalities in New Jersey's school financing system, there was little political inclination to impose such a tax within either party. Democrats, however, once again became important. Just as the need to increase the state's share of financial burden in the 1960s had left the Democrats with the unenviable task of initiating a sales tax, the same party was left to respond to yet another need to shift the fiscal responsibility up to the state level from the lower levels of government.

The Legislative/Executive Struggle to Change School Finance

The legislature in New Jersey typically waits for the governor to take the initiative on issues. The school finance issue emerged at a time when Republican governor Cahill was in office. In 1972 Cahill attempted to reform the state taxing system, but suffered a serious political defeat when his proposals were ignored. By the time the state supreme court issued its decision to uphold the superior court decision in *Robinson v. Cahill*, Cahill had been defeated in the Republican gubernatorial primary, due partly to charges of corruption in his administration and partly to his liberal reputation. That reputation increased his popularity among Democrats and Independents, but decreased it among Republicans. Cahill supported the court's decision and believed the income tax was the best way to reform the tax system, as well as the school financing system, but he was in no position to lead an effort to enact one. His defeat in the Republican primary rendered him an ineffective advocate for any new legislation in the Republican-dominated legislature. Further, as the court did not initially set a deadline by which the legislature was compelled to find a constitutional method of financing education, there was no way or need to pressure the members to act in what was bound to be a difficult election year.

When the supreme court refused to hear the legislative leaders' 1973 separation of powers argument (see table 5.2), Assembly Speaker Kean said "the new Governor and new Legislature which will assume power in January have a clear and definite responsibility—namely the development of an alternative method of financing public education in New Jersey."[26]

Despite this language about a "clear and definite responsibility," the legislative leaders did not offer proposals for a solution to the issue.

Democratic governor Byrne began his term in January 1974. He had won his office with a solid lead over his Republican opponent, Sandman. In addition he enjoyed the advantage of a legislature that was overwhelmingly Democratic. As often occurs in politics, parties are the beneficiaries of political shifts over which they have no control. That occurred all across the country in 1973 and 1974 as the public recoiled against Watergate and the Republican party, electing Democrats in record numbers. Democrats picked up support in such traditionally Republican areas as Bergen County, as indicated in table 5.4, and appeared to have wide enough popular support to carry out their agenda. This would seem to indicate that Governor Byrne should have been able to get the political support he needed for his programs.

However, the gains that gave Democrats control of the legislature suggested he would have problems. The major gains made in each house by the party came in suburban and rural areas, the very areas that would probably be least receptive to an income tax. In the assembly, Democrats had a majority, but 44 of their 65 seats were in suburban and rural areas. In the senate, 19 of 36 Democratic seats were in suburban and rural areas. Those tensions made it very difficult to enact changes to comply with the state supreme court's order concerning public school financing.

In addition, the campaign for governor in 1973 focused largely on the promise of integrity in government and involved little debate about school finance issues. Byrne even declared that New Jersey would not need a state income tax for the "foreseeable future." That statement was discarded soon after the election, however, and Byrne declared his support for a state income tax, in his view the most equitable way to reform the tax system and to comply with the New Jersey State Supreme Court's decision in *Robinson v. Cahill*. Like his Republican predecessor, the new Democratic governor supported the supreme court ruling. Further, he expected to be able to sign a bill that would bring the school financing into compliance by the court's deadline of December 31, 1974—in time to go into effect by July 1, 1975, the start of the fiscal year.

In May 1974 Byrne took a step that had caused painful defeats for his two predecessors and proposed a $800 million income tax designed to increased state aid to public schools, allow the state to assume some school expenses previously covered by local property taxes, and close the $300 million gap in the New Jersey budget. The story of what had to transpire before that proposal was accepted is involved, but it is a good example of the difficulty associated with enacting change in the role of state government, particularly when it involves an issue with as much symbolism as the income tax.

Reactions to the income tax proposal generally split along city-suburb

Table 5.4. Party Success by District Type, 1971 and 1973

Assembly

| County Type | 1971 Assembly | | | 1973 Assembly | | |
| | Total Seats | Party | | Total Seats | Democrats | |
		D	R		#	gain
Urban	22	14	8	23	21	7
Suburban	28	17	11	28	26	9
Rural	25	7	18	24	18	11
Totals	75[a]	38	37	75[a]	65	27

[a] The assembly had eighty members. Independents and members of third parties have been excluded from this table.

Senate

| County Type | 1971 Senate | | | 1973 Senate | | |
| | Total Seats | Party | | Total Seats | Democrats | |
		D	R		#	gain
Urban	11	6	5	10	9	3
Suburban	14	7	7	14	12	5
Rural	13	2	11	12	7	5
Totals	38[a]	15	23	36[a]	28	13

[a] The senate had forty members. Districts that were not easily classified and third-party senators were excluded from this table.

lines, with representatives from wealthy suburban areas indicating their opposition to changing the status quo. Like Hughes and Cahill, Byrne could not muster enough support for the tax. Byrne withdrew the tax package in July in order to avoid certain defeat in a senate controlled by members of his own party. After the withdrawal he announced that he would not reintroduce the tax package.[27]

Resistance to a change in the school finance and tax reform that included an income tax was so strong that it seemed unbendable, even though by 1974 the legislature was facing what was perhaps the worst fiscal crisis in New Jersey's history. The projected budget deficit was between $400 and $500 million, most New Jersey cities were on the brink of fiscal crisis (prompting the New Jersey Conference of Mayors to call for tax reform), twelve commuter bus companies faced shutdown unless subsidies could be raised, and state revenue yields from the sales tax and the state's lottery were shrinking.[28] The fiscal crisis and school finance issues converged to place enormous pressure on the Democrats, who controlled the legislature and the executive branch, to find new sources of revenue. While the party leadership agreed that an income tax was the fairest way to raise the needed revenues, there was no consensus among other elected Democrats. By November 1974, the inability to reach consensus prompted the release of an unusual statement from the assembly leadership:

> There is no consensus to date as to what constitutes a "thorough and efficient" education, as required by the New Jersey State Constitution, or as to the method by which a "thorough and efficient" education is to be financed. There is also no agreed course of action as to how to meet the problem posed by the anticipated shortage in the state budget for the fiscal year 1976.[29]

The electoral bases of the Democratic Party, following the 1973 elections, played a crucial role in determining Byrne's inability get his income tax proposal passed. Seventy-four percent of the seats Democrats picked up in 1973 came from traditionally Republican suburban and rural areas where opposition to an income tax was intense. In the senate, 77 percent of the Democrats' new seats came from suburban and rural areas. While Democrats controlled the legislature in 1974, their traditional urban and lower-class constituents were not a majority of the party, and could not provide enough votes to pass an income tax.

Republicans were not inclined to help Byrne. Following Byrne's announcement of his income tax plan at a joint legislative session in June, Assembly Minority Leader Kean criticized Byrne for submitting the "first wholly partisan tax-reform program in New Jersey's history" and for his "cavalier treatment" of the Republican minority.

But Democrats were not rushing to form cohesive party support for Byrne. Democrats held control of both houses by a better than three to one majority, but Mr. Byrne received only "a smattering of polite applause" at the joint session. Further, Assembly Majority Leader Joseph Le Fant, of Hudson County, refused to immediately commit his support. The senate minority leader indicated that the governor's plan did not stand "a snowball's chances in hell."[30] The legislature then refused to adopt the income tax.

Following the defeat of his income tax proposal, Byrne made a speech at a Conference of the New Jersey State League of Municipalities that was the beginning of a pattern of trying to build support outside the legislature for the income tax, as a means of pressuring the legislature. Byrne told his audience of municipal officials that it was their responsibility to convince the public of a need to increase revenues in order to overcome the budget deficit. Despite the last minute (December 23, 1974) efforts of Governor Byrne and twenty-four senators to come up with a school tax plan, 1974 ended without the court-ordered change in school finance.[31]

When 1975 began, New Jersey's leaders were still faced with a budget deficit and a court order to develop a new public school financing system. Byrne's 1975 request for a state supreme court redistribution of state aid to schools (see table 5.3) was apparently an effort to encourage public support for an income tax. Had the court complied, the 426 communities that would have lost state aid would have had to raise property taxes from between 20 and 30 percent in order to replace the state aid.[32]

The court denied Byrne's request for redistribution of school funds. Instead the court ruled that the old system should stay in effect for the 1975–76 school year in order to avoid chaos. The new deadline for the legislature was moved up to October 1, 1975. Governor Byrne went to court again in February 1975 to ask that the deadline be moved back to 1 July. Byrne argued that the legislature had shown a tendency to procrastinate and that the court should use its power to encourage more rapid compliance.[33]

Risking another political humiliation, Byrne in January 1975 again announced his plan to propose a statewide income tax. He attempted to increase support for his income tax proposal by a combining it with a sales tax reduction and a plan to use some of the income tax proceeds to supply property tax relief.[34] Prior to the introduction of his tax proposal Byrne had announced his plan to impound $66 million to head off the deficit. He would reduce all services and force all agencies to make cuts.[35] Newark mayor Gibson announced that this would lead to job loss for 370 city employees. The various announcements brought the reality of budget deficit into plain view for voters. When the tax proposal was made public in February it called for a sales tax reduction from 5 percent to 3 percent and a graduated income tax. Byrne also sought to drive home the need for an income tax by proposing a balanced budget, assuming no increase in revenues without an income tax, which provided for no increase in school aid. If the legislature did not act on his income tax proposal, state aid for schools would not change. The Jersey City lawyer who had originated the *Robinson v. Cahill* case filed an unsuccessful petition with the New Jersey Supreme Court requesting a court order to force Governor Byrne to increase state aid to education by $120 million.

Two separate income tax proposals failed in January, 1975. The first was a 5.5 percent surcharge on federal income tax. It was opposed by the Jersey City mayor, who believed that his city would benefit more from a court-ordered redistribution of school aid than from the income tax. The second was a $1 billion tax reform package, passed by the assembly but defeated in the senate, that included an income tax.

With his income tax proposal still unapproved and the July 1 deadline for a new system of financing schools fast approaching, Governor Byrne again tried to apply outside pressure on the legislature to impose new taxes. This time Byrne went directly to the people in an emotional address that was designed to personalize the budget cuts that would occur without passage of a tax package. Byrne argued that the biggest losers would be the state's six hundred school districts, which would lose $180 million in state aid. The aid cuts would lead to either drastic cutbacks in school programs or substantial increases in property taxes "which could drive some families from their homes." Byrne argued that other cuts "would virtually wipe out commuter buses and force railroads to cut service in half and increase fares on remaining trains by 55%." Further, he argued that "our state supported colleges would be forced to increase tuition for New Jersey residents by 50 per cent [and] similar crisis cutbacks in other programs would severely affect all the people in the state." He also warned the legislature that he would refuse to sign a bill that increased the sales tax, unless it were part of a package of taxes, in which case he would try to find a way to eliminate the sales tax increase.[36]

Despite the fiscal disaster looming before them and the agreement between the governor and the legislative leaders on the need for an income tax, the senate remained unwilling to pass any tax package or new school financing system. However, both houses were able to pass a toothless measure providing apparent additional funding for schools. The senate acted first, passing a "thorough and efficient" education funding bill that would increase state aid to local school districts from 32 percent to 38 percent of their budgets. The bill would commit the state to raising $300 million in additional school aid for the 1976–77 school year and $420 million for the following school year. However, the bill was not accompanied by a new tax effort to assure the funding. The bill also placed a cap on school budgets, limiting them to a 1 percent annual increase. This measure was needed to guarantee passage. Many senators feared that rapidly increasing costs would mean that the bill would cause an uncontrollable commitment for the state. The caps were also designed to equalize educational spending.

The bill would redistribute funds from the wealthy districts to poor ones, and the caps would prevent the districts that lost state aid from replacing it.[37] The assembly passed a similar bill in September. The assembly version raised spending on school aid by $314 million. The thorough and efficient legislation, in addition to increasing state aid to education, increased the state's authority to monitor both business and educational practices of the local school districts. However, neither version raised state revenues to fund the additional school spending. This meant that the politically difficult question of how to raise more money for schools was not addressed.

Following the June 28 rejection of a *fourth* income tax proposal by the senate, Byrne announced budget cuts of $378 million that threatened the jobs of state employees and reduced school aid and transportation subsidies. The lack of an income tax, he said, would probably lead to an increase in local property taxes. That prompted the legislature to focus on finding ways to replace the money that Byrne had cut. On July 15, Byrne and the assembly leadership agreed on a plan to restore $60 million of the $148 million cut from minimum school aid. The replaced money could be spent during the first half of the school year (July–December). This provision was meant to force the state legislature to consider the school financing problem again before the end of the year. In a compromise, the governor agreed to sign a version that would allow school funds to be replaced for the entire year with a provision that the governor would have to certify that there was sufficient money in the treasury to cover the spending by February 1, 1976. This would give the governor a way to assure that the legislature was making progress on school financing. Other cuts in higher education and transportation were also restored. Money was raised through an increase in the realty transfer tax, higher motor vehicle fees, increased taxes on gross receipts of unincorporated businesses, placing banks under the incorporated business tax, and a revision of anticipated revenue estimates reflecting an increase of $17 million.[38] It was clear that the legislature would go to great lengths to avoid enacting the income tax.

AMIDST IMPASSE, DEFINING THE STATE'S ROLE IN SCHOOL FINANCE

While the impasse about finding resources to address the school finance issue persisted, the legislature was willing to consider and define the obligation of the state regarding local school finance. The senate had passed legislation asserting the obligation of the state to provide a "thorough and efficient" education for all students in May of 1975. When it passed a bill identical to Senate Bill 1516 in September, the assembly accepted the senate's "thorough and efficient education" for all students. The law guaranteed the children of New Jersey a thorough and efficient education and mandated a $334 million increase in school aid for the 1976–77 school year.[39] Byrne signed the bill, which gave the state education department broader authority over all of the business and educational procedures in the local school districts.

The bill involved a significant change in the role of state government. The legislature, even while it fought imposing a state income tax, had accepted a greater role for state government in the area of education. In accepting that role, however, they did not want the state commitment to be open-ended. The law sought to contain that commitment to help local schools. The law placed a cap on local spending increases, because legislators did not want additional funds to just be absorbed as higher teacher salaries without any impact on education. They were trying to make sure that the greater aid did not just expand the public sector, but that the greater aid coupled with expenditure caps would reduce local property taxes, while providing more state aid for schools.[40] State government also had the right to review local performance and decide if it matched state expectations. State government would now be more involved in local education, but there was still reluctance to enact a new revenue source.

Byrne at this point joined with the legislature and asked the state supreme court to accept the new law, despite its lack of funding, and to advise him and the legislature as to when they must appropriate the necessary funds.[41] One month later, the court announced plans to hold public hearings on the new law.

ANOTHER ELECTION AND A CONTINUING IMPASSE

The November 1975 election worsened Governor Byrne's fiscal troubles. Voters rejected a bond issue that would have provided funds for mass transit, emergency institutional repairs, improving state hospitals in order to reinstate accreditation, pollution abatement, and new housing.[42] The election brought him further woes by reducing the Democratic control of the assembly from a 4 to 1 majority to a 5 to 3 majority, thus making it likely that he would receive less support for his programs than he had previously. Most of the Democratic Party's assembly losses were in rural and urban areas. The Democrats retained almost all of the seats they had picked up in suburban areas in 1973 (see table 5.5 below), but that created problems. After the 1975 elections, 51 percent of the assembly Democrats now represented suburban districts (senate elections were not held in 1975, as senate terms were lengthened to four years). These constituents were likely

Table 5.5. 1973 and 1975 Assembly Election Results

1973 Assembly

County Type	Total Seats	Democrats	Republicans
Urban	22	21	1
Suburban	28	26	2
Rural	24	18	6
Totals	74[a]	65	9

1975 Assembly

County Type	Total Seats	Democrats		Republicans seats gained	Democratic seats lost
		#	% change		
Urban	24	16	-23.8	8	-5
Suburban	30	25	-3.8	5	-1
Rural	24	8	-55.6	16	-10
Totals	78[a]	49	-24.6	29	-16

Note: Senate elections were not held in 1975, because New Jersey had switched to four-year senate terms.

[a] The assembly had eighty members. Independents and members of third parties have been excluded from this table.

to be adversely effected by any plan to use an income tax to equalize school financing. While the last three governors had concluded an income tax was necessary, and the Court's decision in *Robinson v. Cahill* seemed to make it unavoidable, it was difficult to for the Democratic majority to impose the tax.

Following the elections, Byrne tried different approaches to pressuring the legislature. First he announced that he would no longer lead the drive for an income tax and left the resolution of the fiscal crisis to the legislature. He planned to cope with the immediate shortfall by cutting funding for medical and commuter services unless the legislature was able to find an additional $60 million in revenues.[43] By the end of November, however, Byrne had resumed his tactic of trying to encourage outside pressure on the legislature to assure that the income tax and school financing remained priority items on the legislative agenda. In a November 15 speech to the New Jersey Education Association, he called upon teachers to use their political clout to encourage the passage of a statewide income tax to make education funding in the state more equitable. His speech followed a call by the association's delegate assembly for the passage of a graduated income tax.[44] Less than two weeks later, the governor announced his plans to ask the state supreme court to mandate a new system of funding for schools. He suggested three alternative solutions that the court might consider:

- A court order diverting local property taxes
- A $114 million diversion of minimum state aid from wealthy districts to poorer ones
- A redistribution of the entire $640 million in state school aid[45]

At the beginning of 1976 the school financing reform remained an unsettled issue. Byrne came under criticism from the AFL-CIO for his failure to consider alternative solutions to the state's fiscal problems. Labor leaders believed that Mr. Byrne's insistence on an income tax in the face of formidable opposition was leading to the loss of jobs for state employees.[46]

As the impasse dragged on, there were numerous theories of why change could not be enacted, aside from the obvious one that suburban interests did not want the tax. Some argued that the problem was simply that the court had failed to make explicit its planned method of enforcement of its order if the legislature failed to comply. As one Democratic legislator explained, "I'd be a damn fool to vote for anything until the Court actually tells me in no uncertain terms what it's going to do if I don't."[47] Others blamed a lack of leadership from Governor Byrne. One Republican legislator explained, "Anyone who expects us to approve a major new tax for school refinancing just because the court told us to doesn't understand the legislative process in New Jersey. That kind of response takes strong legislative leadership and a strong Governor to orchestrate it. And that was missing here all the time." For many years, new legislative leaders had been elected every two years, and only recently had the legislature switched to four-year terms. The frequent turnover had led to a history of weak leadership and a pattern of strong governors who filled the leadership gap in directing the legislature. There were many who felt that Byrne had been ineffective in filling that role.[48] The weak leadership, accompanied by redistricting that had freed representatives from local political machines and thus significant party influence, left the New Jersey legislature a body whose members were free to act independent of their parties. The result was what Thomas Kean called "mob rule."[49]

Legislators were not receiving pressure from constituents to deal with the school finance problem. The "crisis" was still primarily a problem for political elites. The mass public was not following the issue closely and was not yet convinced of the need for additional funding. Despite all the court decisions and missed deadlines, opinion polls showed that most of the public, even three years after the initial court decision, had not followed the case.[50] Finally, there was evidence of declining support among the public and legislators for the idea that the solution to education problems was more money. There was skepticism that more money would just mean higher salaries and little change otherwise.[51]

At the end of January 1976, the court upheld the thorough and efficient education law of 1975 despite the lack of funding for the additional $314 million in school funding required by the law. The court gave the legislature until April 6 to find a constitutional method of funding the additional aid.[52] However, three days later the senate majority leader, Joseph P. Merlino, predicted that the law would remain unfunded, as the senate was "paralyzed by right wing politicians."[53]

In his continuous attempt to keep the legislature focused on the issue, Byrne asked the court to move the deadline up to February 29. He argued that the legislature was unlikely to agree on the funding and that waiting until April 6 would cause irreparable damage to local school planning. The court responded by moving the deadline to March 15. In the same ruling the court ordered Governor Byrne to show any reason why the court could not choose one of several options for funding in the event that the legislature failed to raise the necessary funds. The court's alternatives included devising a new aid formula and distributing the money, balancing the school budget by sequestering funds from other programs, or closing the schools on July 1 by prohibiting the distribution of school funds under the old unconstitutional system.

The assembly passed an income tax to fund the law on March 15, in time to meet the court's deadline. The bill received support from the governor, the legislative leaders, labor, and schoolteachers. This was the first income tax passed by the assembly that included a homestead exemption (which precluded imposing the property tax on the first $10,000 of home value and was designed to cushion the blow of the income tax by limiting property taxes). It also included a minimum standards test of students to assure that education goals were being met. These two provisions allowed passage.[54] However, the bill was killed in the senate.

Several weeks after the court's March 15 deadline passed without legislative approval of a new system of school financing, Governor Byrne, in a weekly press conference announced that he doubted that the legislature would resolve the issue before the court announced what it would do if the

Public Education Law remained unfunded. Byrne theorized that uncertainty allowed the senators to believe that the court might choose an option that would not adversely affect their constituents.

Amidst the uncertainty concerning school funding, local school districts found themselves in a state of confusion. The city of Trenton ultimately refused to balance its budget or to lay off teachers. City leaders stated that they would rely on the legislature to fund the additional $375 million in school aid.

On May 13, 1976, after three years of extending deadlines, the court announced that, unless the legislature found a constitutional method of funding public schools before July 1, 1976, the court would order the schools closed on that day.[55] The court had apparently finally realized that the legislature would not take action unless there was a deadline that would have some impact on the public. Ten days later Governor Byrne announced that he would abide by the court's ruling and allow the schools to close on July 1.[56]

With the refusal of the United States Supreme Court to hear a challenge from the city of Elizabeth to the state supreme court's authority to order the closing of the New Jersey schools, the senate was under additional pressure to pass some form of income tax in order to change the school financing system.[57] On June 17, after refusing to pass an income tax five times, the senate approved the imposition of a flat 1.5 percent income tax on the citizens of New Jersey.[58] Four days later the flat income tax was defeated in the assembly.[59]

On July 1, 1976 the New Jersey public school system was closed down as the result of a state supreme court injunction that prohibited the distribution of funds raised under the unconstitutional school financing system. If members of the legislature had been waiting to see what the court would do if they ignored its demand that they find a way to constitutionally fund the public schools, the answer was now clear.

Following the closing of the schools, U.S. Attorney General Jonathan Goldstein asked the U.S. Court of Appeals to order the schools reopened. The court allowed Goldstein to file papers but refused to hear arguments. Seven hundred state board of education employees and four thousand summer school teachers became unemployed when the schools were closed. Handicapped children in year-round programs, children who needed summer school to avoid failing a grade or failing to graduate, and students who tried to use summer school to accelerate their education were hurt by the closing.[60]

Six days after the schools were closed, the assembly passed an income tax of 2 percent on the first $20,000 of income and 2.5 percent on income over $20,000. The legislative leaders, in meetings with members of the legislature, had realized that members wanted to make sure that they could bring home some tangible tax relief as a part of the change.[61] To respond to

that need, the bill included $25 million of money to be returned to locali-
ties for property tax relief, and a homestead exemption that amounted to
about $210 for each homeowner in New Jersey.[62] The senate passed the
same tax bill the next day. Governor Byrne signed it an hour later and
asked the court to lift the injunction that had closed the schools. New Jersey became the forty-third state to impose an income tax on its citizens.

The assembly roll call vote shows how the income and party of legislative districts were intertwined. Party was dominant, as table 5.6 indicates.
Only 8, or 17 percent, of the 47 Democrats in the assembly, opposed the
income tax. Conversely, only 2, or 7 percent, of the 28 Republicans supported the income tax, despite the property tax rebate that was designed to
soften the blow of the income tax for middle-class suburbanites. But parties clearly differed in their income bases, so the income of districts played
a significant role. In the lower-income districts, 20 of 26 seats were held by
Democrats. In these districts there were 18 votes for the tax (all Democrats), and 8 against (2 Democrats[63] and 6 Republicans). Sixty-nine percent of members from these districts (both parties) voted for the tax. In the
upper-income districts Republicans held 17 of the 24 sears. From these
districts there were 6 votes for the tax (6 Democrats and 1 Republican).
Only 22 percent of those from upper-income districts (both parties) voted
for the tax. The crucial areas were the middle-income districts. Democrats
held 20 of these 25 districts, and they were able to get yes votes from 15 of
these 20 members. The suburban Democrats voted for the bill, but there
were also some significant defections from that area.

Table 5.6. Assembly Income Tax Vote, July 1976

District Income	Total Dem. Seats	Democratic Votes				Total Rep. Seats	Republican Votes			
		Yes		No			Yes		No	
		#	%	#	%		#	%	#	%
Low	20	18	90	2	10	6	0	0	6	100
Middle	20	15	75	5	25	5	1	20	4	80
High	7	6	86	1	14	17	1	6	16	94
Totals	47	39		8		28	2		26	

Source: Votes were taken from the *Journal of the Senate* and *Minutes of the General
Assembly.* To classify districts by income, information was taken from the *Legislative
Districts in New Jersey* (New Brunswick, N.J.: Eagleton Institute, 1971. Districts were
arrayed from highest to lowest family income, and then grouped by thirds. There were
eighty seats in 1976, but there were some vacancies.

The vote in the senate (table 5.7) was similarly divided. In the lower income districts Democrats held 9 of 13 seats, and 8 of the 9 Democrats voted for the tax. In the upper-income districts, Democrats held 8 of the 13 districts, and 6 Democrats voted for the tax. Again, in the middle-income districts Democrats were able to get a majority of their members to vote for the tax, with 7 of the 12 Democrats voting yes. Only 28 percent of Democrats opposed the income tax, while nearly 90 percent of Republicans did so.

Table 5.7. Senate Income Tax Vote, July 1976

District Income	Total Dem. Seats	Democratic Votes				Total Rep. Seats	Republican Votes			
		Yes		No			Yes		No	
		#	%	#	%		#	%	#	%
Low	9	8	89	1	11	4	0	0	3	100
Middle	12	7	58	5	42	2	1	50	1	50
High	8	6	75	2	25	5	0	0	5	100
Totals	29	21		8		10	2		9	

Source: Votes were taken from the *Journal of the Senate* and *Minutes of the General Assembly.* To classify districts by income, information was taken from the *Legislative Districts in New Jersey* (New Brunswick, N.J.: Eagleton Institute, 1971. Districts were arrayed from highest to lowest family income, and then grouped by thirds. There were eighty seats in 1976, but there were some vacancies.

Republicans, despite the pressure from the court, had chosen to vote against the tax. They were the minority party, and the burden of governing was not on them. The Republicans arguably had an incentive to allow the crisis to continue. They could blame the Democrats for the crisis and also for the income tax that would inevitably pass. The public's reaction to the income tax was hard to gauge, and the Republicans might be able to use tax votes in the next elections.

Democrats could only hope that they could blame the court for making them enact the tax, and hope that they could structure the benefits such that they would get at least as much credit as blame for the change.

THE AFTERMATH: THE INCOME TAX AS A CAMPAIGN ISSUE

The beginning of 1977, an election year, looked bleak for the Democrats. Governor Byrne's popularity had plummeted, and he seemed easily beatable. As the primaries approached, the most prominent issue in the gubernatorial campaign was the income tax. A new law providing public funding for gubernatorial candidates encouraged multiple challengers, and Byrne faced ten opponents in the Democratic primary. He was criticized not only for the passage of the income tax itself but also for his statement during the 1973 campaign that New Jersey would not need an income tax for the foreseeable future. This left room for the argument that he had deceived the voters.

Byrne faced a significant challenge based on a statewide issue: the income tax. He responded with a significant first in New Jersey history. He ran the first extensive statewide television campaign, stressing his leadership in dealing with a significant problem.[64] Two weeks before the primary, Byrne admitted that he was mistaken in his failure to see the need for an income tax when he was running for governor.

His campaign succeeded. While fewer than half of New Jersey Democrats supported the income tax, the anti-income tax vote was divided among his opponents, and Byrne won easily. Several factors helped Byrne. His numerous opponents had difficulty getting name recognition in a state with no commercial television stations and no statewide newspaper. Candidates were forced to buy time in the expensive New York and Philadelphia markets to reach New Jersey voters. While the *Newark Star-Ledger* covered state issues and attempted to be a state newspaper, it had very low circulation outside of Newark.[65]

Byrne's win in the Democratic primary was statewide. He lost to the second place contender, Roe, in only three counties: Morris, Passaic, and Sussex. The governor won 30 percent of the Democratic vote in a field of 11 candidates compared to 24 percent for his nearest opponent. The five lowest-scoring candidates split 5 percent of the vote.

The only three Democratic assembly members who supported the income tax and lost their primary bids were from Jersey City. While all three lost to opponents who ran on an anti-income tax platform, their losses were due to their close ties to former Jersey City mayor Paul Jordan, who had problems. In the senate, all five who lost their primary elections were Democrats. Four of the five had voted in favor of the income tax. However, all five of the senators were also plagued by divisive local issues.[66]

Overall, Democrats experienced little damage from the income tax in their party primaries. The same would prove to be true in November when they faced Republican opponents. Although Byrne was unpopular throughout the campaign and Democrats sought to distance themselves from him and their party's pro-income tax platform, Byrne won a solid victory in November. The Democratic Party maintained control of both houses of the legislature, picking up five seats in the assembly for an impressive majority of 54 to 26 and losing only two seats in the senate and retaining a strong majority of 27 to 13. Voter preferences in the gubernatorial race were closely linked to opinion on the income tax. The only significant difference in the party platforms was their stands on the income tax issue, and it was the most prominent issue in the campaign. Seventy-five percent of voters knew that Byrne favored the income tax, but only 45 percent knew that Republican gubernatorial candidate Bateman opposed it.[67] Bateman's failure to make his position known to the majority of voters weakened his ability to attract support from those who opposed the tax.

Byrne won more of the blue-collar vote than expected, despite the opposition to the income tax and the decision of the usually Democratic AFL-CIO not to endorse a candidate in the gubernatorial election. The fact that most voters were unaware of Bateman's anti-income tax stance probably helped the Democrats retain that support. Democrats lost less of the blue-collar, anti-income tax vote than expected while gaining some of the usually Republican suburban commuter vote. Byrne carried traditionally Republican Bergen County, where Democrats also picked up assembly seats.[68]

During the campaign each of the candidates for the executive office faced problems in key counties. Byrne had problems in traditionally Democratic Hudson County. Blue-collar workers were opposed to the income tax, and Jersey City Democratic mayor Thomas F. X. Smith withheld support for Byrne until late September, stating that he would support whichever candidate would do the most for his city.[69]

Republican candidate Bateman also faced difficulties. In Bergen County, the Republican Party failed to unite after a divisive primary election. There was also significant support for the income tax in areas like Bergen County. Suburban commuters benefited from the income tax. Commuters to New York and Pennsylvania were already paying income taxes to those other states. The New Jersey income tax did not raise their tax bills, because they were now allowed to deduct their tax obligation paid elsewhere from their New Jersey state income tax. This change meant their net tax increase was significantly reduced. Meanwhile, they received property tax rebates. These changes rendered Republican criticisms less significant to many in the suburbs.

The election suggested that hostility to the income tax was not that great. The legislature had originally passed the income tax with a requirement that it would be repealed June 30, 1978. Given these election results, the income tax was likely to become a permanent fixture in the New Jersey. The 1976 legislature and governor had with much difficulty established an income tax, a tax that could would have a significant effect on the distribution of tax effort between local and state government in New Jersey and that had the potential to become a mechanism for the redistribution of wealth in the state.

The torturous path to passage of the income tax tells us much about how significant changes in the role of state government occur. Democrats enacted change, but they did so with a thorough reluctance. Unified Democratic control did not simply result in enactment of higher taxes. The composition of the legislative party created internal party conflicts that were almost impossible to bridge. The primary reason the party was finally willing to enact change was that the state supreme court created a public crisis by closing the schools. This created the pressure that gave legislators the excuse they needed to enact change. While government by crisis never pleases the critics of state government, in this case it gave legislators a reason to change the status quo and avoid political defeat at the next election.

THE INCOME TAX AND THE PUBLIC SCHOOL EDUCATION ACT OF 1975: WINNERS AND LOSERS

The income tax and the Public School Law were introduced as answers to the state supreme court's ruling that the state school financing system violated the state constitution. The court agreed with the argument that it was a violation of the constitution to provide a lesser education to children who lived in poor neighborhoods compared to their counterparts in wealthier districts. The 1973–76 battle was protracted, but the enactment of the income tax was major transition in tax policy for the state. What did that tax do to the role of state government, and did it change the distribution of educational opportunities in New Jersey?

The tax produced an immediate and significant increase in state tax effort, as shown in figures 5.2 and 5.3.[70] Tax effort is the percent of all personal income of state residents taken in taxes by either state or local taxes. Figure 5.2 presents the change in tax effort for each year from the prior year. That is, the tax effort for any year is subtracted from the next year to indicate how much it changed in one year. As figure 5.3 indicates, there was a major increase in tax effort after 1976. The last major increase had been in 1967 when the sales tax took effect. The effect of a significant increase in state taxes, with a local property tax rebate, was that local tax effort dropped, and, by the late 1980s, for the first time in the state's history, state tax effort was equivalent to local tax effort. Figure 5.4 tracks state and local tax effort, beginning in the 1950s. As might be expected, and as figure 5.5 documents, the result was that the state was raising an increasing proportion of all state and local taxes.

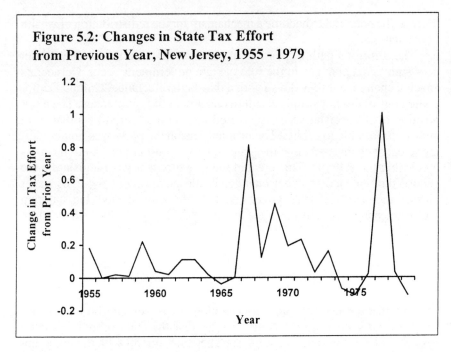

Figure 5.2: Changes in State Tax Effort
from Previous Year, New Jersey, 1955 - 1979

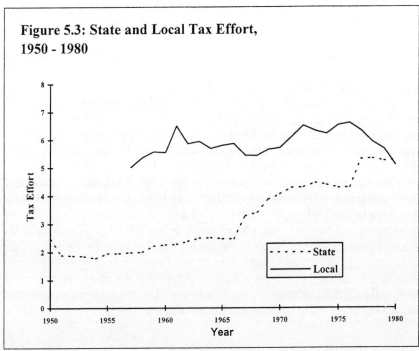

Figure 5.3: State and Local Tax Effort,
1950 - 1980

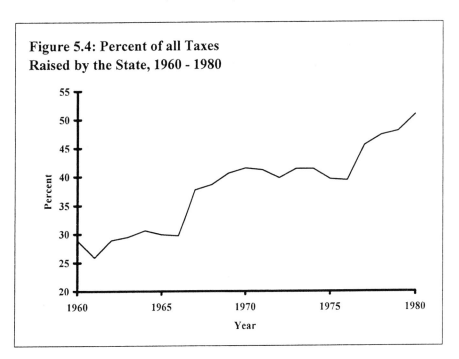

Figure 5.4: Percent of all Taxes
Raised by the State, 1960 - 1980

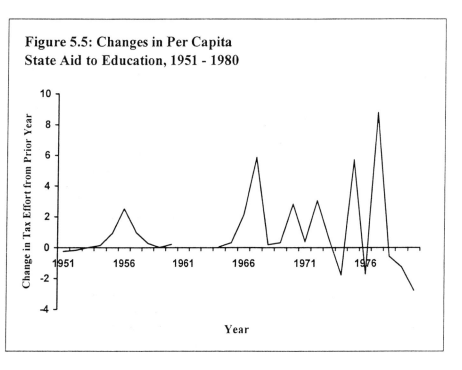

Figure 5.5: Changes in Per Capita
State Aid to Education, 1951 - 1980

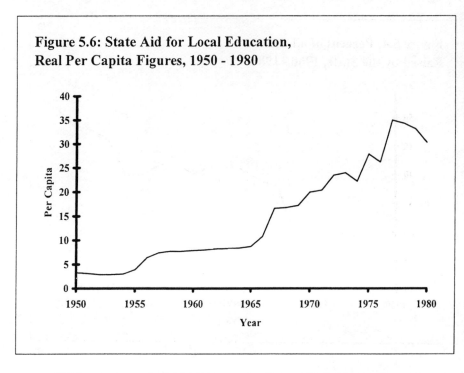

Figure 5.6: State Aid for Local Education, Real Per Capita Figures, 1950 - 1980

The battle over the income tax was about whether state government would do more for schools and for local governments in general. It was also about whether the state would involve itself in reducing local taxes. In New Jersey the consequence of this enactment was a greater role for the state and a greater reliance upon state government to raise revenues.

The battle focused on equity in the funding of education. Did the changes enacted reduce the extent of inequality? Figure 5.4 presents the changes in real per capita state aid to local education. There was a significant change in state aid to education immediately after enactment of the income tax. The result, as shown in figure 5.5, was a significant increase in total real per capita state aid to education right after the enactment of the income tax. In 1975 the state provided 32 percent of all local education spending, and by 1979 it provided 40 percent. The state was now more involved.[71]

THE REDISTRIBUTION ISSUE

The impetus for change was the issue of the state's obligation to address inequality issues. Did the 1976 income tax enactment change that situation significantly? Despite all the controversy about this issue, the evidence does not suggest a significant change in inequality occurred. Assessments of change, to be sure, depend on how data are viewed. Poor districts received the greatest amount of school aid funds, on a per pupil basis, but in terms of total dollars the bulk of the money from the income tax was being returned to the suburbs in the form of property tax rebates. A symposium at the Woodrow Wilson School in 1977 showed that after a year the income tax had done little to reduce the inequalities experienced by the poorer city school districts.[72] Inequalities in local tax rates had declined somewhat, but were still enormous. In 1976 the tax rate for the twenty-three poorest school districts was 149 percent of the state average, while in the wealthiest suburbs it was 40 percent of the average. In 1977, the income tax rate in the cities had fallen to 139 percent of the state average, while in the wealthy suburbs it had risen to 47 percent.[73] Margaret Goertz, a longtime critic of the school finance situation, argued that the narrowing gap in property tax rates and the property tax rate decreases were a symptom that "heavy tax burdens in the poor districts and budget caps on all [districts] led them to substitute state aid for locally-raised education revenues. The result was a significant drop in school tax rates rather than a lessening of expenditure disparities."[74]

In 1978 the problems of unequal educational spending were still enormous, and those differentials in spending were still associated with educational success.[75] It remained the case that the best predictor of per pupil spending in a district was the wealth of the community.[76] As early as 1978 the Newark Urban Coalition was planning to go to court to try to have the law reshaped.[77] To critics there was little evidence that the momentous battle over taxes had produced any real change in the inequality between school districts.

How could a conflict so focused on raising revenues to address issues of inequality have such limited impact? It is clear that the change resulted in a greater state role, but that change did not significantly alter the existing inequalities. Democrats very reluctantly enacted an income tax, and Republicans were not willing to vote for the tax. But Democrats were unwilling to tackle the redistributive role.

This outcome, again, tells us much about parties. The party's willingness to redistribute was shaped by the composition of the party. The New Jersey Democratic Party was not a collection of liberal legislators. It was a party dominated by suburban and rural legislators. In attempting to negotiate an income tax deal, the party had to give the legislators from the suburban areas something to secure their vote. The compromise entailed adding the property tax rebate program and creating a school aid formula that did not give all the additional funding to urban and local income districts. Suburban areas fared well in the distribution, which meant that the cities received little benefit. The specifics of that formula will be explored in the next chapter, when another lawsuit about school finance will be discussed. The party had enacted a change that made a major difference in the role of state government within New Jersey. But parties work with the members they have in negotiating legislation, and in this case the party had to have suburban votes. That lead to a distribution package that was limited in its degree of redistribution. Change occurred, but it was constrained by the internal composition of the party.

CONTEXT AND POLITICAL ACTORS

The story of the imposition of New Jersey's income tax supports our assertion that major change requires an appropriate political context as well as party inclination. Once again political actors in New Jersey decided to increase the state government's responsibilities. This time, it was in the form of an income tax intended to equalize school spending. Once again, the purpose of a shift in power from the local to the state level was to reduce inequality within the state. The effort to equalize school spending reflected values typically associated with the Democrats, not inconsequentially the party in control of New Jersey state government in 1976. Despite the apparent simple correlation between Democratic control and the imposition of the statewide income tax to equalize school spending, the New Jersey income tax case is instructive precisely because it demonstrates the role that political context plays in effecting change in the balance of responsibility between local and state governments. Without the *Robinson v. Cahill* decision, the income tax would have been unlikely to have been enacted in 1976. Even with the decision, a Republican majority would have been less likely to choose an income tax solution. Without the increase in suburban support for the Democrats, a Democratic tax proposal would probably not have included property tax relief. Hence, the political context that made school funding an issue for the legislature interacted with the values of the party in control and the preferences of that party's least secure supporters to create the specific tax policy that was adopted in 1976.

The case is also interesting because it is an example of the trend toward greater state responsibility for social spending that occurred without federal pressure. It clearly demonstrates that increasing state budgets for and decreasing local control of social policy cannot be wholly explained as a state response to conditions attached to federal aid opportunities.

6

The Return of
Republican Influence

THE ENACTMENT OF THE INCOME TAX IN 1976 AND THE INCREASED STATE AID TO
local education significantly increased the state's fiscal role. The survival
of Democrats in the 1977 and 1979 elections indicated there would be no
revolt over the income tax, and that it was now part of a new status quo.
Brendan Byrne, facing the two-term limit imposed on governors, had to
leave office, setting the stage for a new governor. In 1981 Republican Tom
Kean won the gubernatorial election with the narrowest margin in state
history. He followed that in 1985 with the widest margin of victory in history. In 1985 Republicans also gained control over the assembly. The crucial issue, in a state where the governor has enormous power, was what the
new Republican governor would do with his power. In what direction would
he take state government?

The 1976 decision to enact the income tax and increase state aid would
seem to have resolved for at least the short run the issue of the role of state
government. It was now doing much more for local governments than it
had ten years prior. The issue, however, persisted. The 1980s presented
state politicians with several situations involving the issue of state responses
and responsibilities. First, a serious recession prompted the issue of whether
services and aid would be cut, or whether taxes would be raised to maintain state revenues. Second, a lawsuit filed in the 1970s about open housing
became an issue the state could not avoid, so some state response had to be
formulated. Third, another lawsuit was filed challenging the school finance
system. Fourth, members of the legislature sought to establish a state planning commission. A decade that might have been one of just presiding over
a new status quo became one filled with contention revolving around the
role of state government.

137

THE GUBERNATORIAL CAMPAIGN

The 1981 gubernatorial campaign presented voters with a relatively clear choice. Thomas Kean, who was in the assembly from 1967 to 1977, had unsuccessfully sought the Republican nomination for governor in 1977. He had a reputation as a moderate Republican from his years as a member of the assembly. While in the legislature he had sponsored legislation creating the State Department of Environmental Protection. He also sponsored legislation to help parents with college costs, and he proposed the state's first rent-control law.[1] Yet he had voted against the "T & E" law, or the law that specified that the state should "provide to all children, regardless of socioeconomic status or geographic location, the educational opportunity . . . to function. . . ."[2]

Despite his relatively moderate background, during the 1981 campaign he emphasized an agenda compatible with that of President Ronald Reagan and focused on trying to make the business climate more attractive.[3] He proposed eliminating the corporation net worth tax over four years, cutting the 9 percent corporate income tax in half in two years, and reducing the state sales tax by 1 percent by his third year in office. His proposals would not increase the role of state government. Kean, using the "supply-side" logic popular at the time, argued that his tax cuts would get the economy moving.

His stance on education also expressed a more conservative position. When Kean was questioned about education, he expressed concern that increased funding was going to create more administration and bureaucracy.[4] During the campaign he made his position very clear about whether more money for education was necessary. He stated:

> Quality public education in New Jersey remains as far out of reach today as it was six years ago, despite the expenditure of billions of dollars. What this money has purchased is a rapidly expanding bureaucracy which has placed self-interest ahead of the interests of the state's schoolchildren.[5]

His Democratic opponent, Jim Florio, was also a former member of the state assembly, and was currently a member of Congress. He announced his candidacy in Washington to call attention to his criticisms of Reagan's budget cuts, which he called "radical."[6] Florio, noting that the state would be losing federal funds, said it was not the time for corporate tax cuts. He emphasized that such cuts "would result in either sharp cuts in state programs or sharp increases in local property taxes."[7] Florio had a strong environmental record, having sponsored the legislation to establish the Superfund cleanup program. He had voted against a reduction in income tax rates

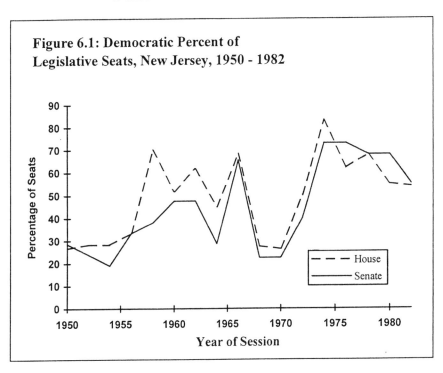

Figure 6.1: Democratic Percent of Legislative Seats, New Jersey, 1950 - 1982

proposed by Reagan, charging that it favored the rich. During the campaign Florio called Kean's tax-cut proposals "voodoo economics," and he resisted Kean's challenge to pledge he would not raise the state income tax as a way to resolve the state's fiscal problems.[8] During the campaign, Kean said he "did not want to raise taxes under any circumstances," while Florio said, "I am not prepared to unequivocally say that in the Florio administration there will never, ever be a tax increase—that would be irresponsible."[9] On education, he agreed with Kean that administrative costs in education needed to be reduced, but never articulated a specific set of proposals that would differentiate him from Kean.[10]

The election, won by Kean with the smallest margin ever recorded, 1,677 votes, split the electorate along fairly traditional lines. Florio received greater support among Democrats, women, liberals, blacks, families with a union member, and those with low family incomes. Kean received greater support among Protestants, conservatives, and those with higher incomes. Despite divisions along these lines, the poll results did not suggest that current issues played a significant role in affecting how the candidates were seen. When asked who could be trusted to keep taxes and spending down, 37 percent chose Florio and 45 percent chose Kean. When asked who could be trusted to help the elderly and poor, 55 percent chose Florio and 48 percent chose Kean. Voters did not see significant differences between the candidates on immediate policy issues. It also did not appear that the campaign was followed closely by the electorate.[11] Late in the campaign, a majority of voters could not indicate if they had a favorable or unfavorable image of either candidate. There was little in the election results that suggested that Kean had strong support for the tax cuts he proposed during the campaign. It also appeared that Kean's effort to link himself to Reagan had not produced any great gains.[12] The Republicans also did not experience any significant gains in the legislature. Democrats held both houses before the elections, and the elections did not change that. The percentage of seats held by Democrats remained the same in the assembly, while they dropped from 68 to 55 percent of the seats in the senate. Democrats had smaller margins of control in the two houses, but they still controlled the legislature, as shown in figure 6.1.

As governor, Kean faced a majority Democratic Party with an electoral base very different from that of Republicans. Democrats won 70 percent or

Table 6.1. Electoral Bases of Democrats, Assembly,
and Senate, 1982 (Percentage of Seats Won by
Each Party, by District Type)

| | Assembly | | Senate | |
	% Rep	% Dem	% Rep	% Dem
Per Capita Income				
Low	21	79	21	79
Middle	33	67	25	75
High	79	21	79	21
Percent Nonwhite				
Low	73	27	80	20
Middle	50	50	33	67
High	8	92	8	92

Note: The groupings for income are: low: 0–$7,299, middle: $7,300–$9,099, high: $9,100 and above. The groupings for nonwhite are: low: 0–8%, middle: 9–17 percent, high: 18 percent and above. The groupins were done so as to divide the districts into three groups with roughly the same number of districts in each group. The groupings for income and percent nonwhite were done separately. This ensures that each grouping has a reasonable number of districts.
Source: Bureau of Government Research, *1984 New Jersey Legislative District Data Book* (New Brunswick, N.J.: Rutgers University, 1984).

more of the seats in middle- to lower-income districts and 90 percent in districts with a high percentage of nonwhites. Table 6.1 presents the success of Democrats by type of legislative district in the 1981 elections. Given its electoral base, the Democratic Party was likely to have some differences with a Republican governor.

1982: THE ECONOMY AND POLITICAL CHOICES

Governor-elect Kean indicated he did not intend to raise taxes during his term, and that he would pursue business tax cuts to stimulate the economy.[13] The reality of the economy, however, quickly altered his agenda. The national economy declined in the early 1980s, and the recession produced a decline in state tax revenues in New Jersey. By March 1982 Kean was announcing that he expected a deficit of $729 million for the upcoming fiscal year. In his first budget proposal, Kean sought to fulfill his campaign promises and to cope with the revenue shortfall. He proposed that the corporate income and business net worth taxes be cut. To raise revenues to replace business taxes, he proposed to extend the sales tax to gasoline and cigarettes, to raise mass transit fares, and to increase tuition at the state university by 10 percent. His proposal would have cut state aid to local governments.[14]

Democrats immediately expressed their opposition to his plans, and made it clear that distribution effects were paramount in their concerns. The Democratic Speaker of the assembly, Alan Karcher, said "As a condition precedent to any real discussion, he's got to recant on a tax break for the rich."[15] Later he said, "It's Robin Hood in reverse. It taxes the poor to give to the rich." The poor and the middle class would be forced to bear the burden of his proposals.[16]

Negotiations produced compromises. Kean got the legislature to agree to elimination of the business net worth tax. The tax on cigarettes was raised five cents, with most of the votes coming from Republicans, since Democrats did not want the tax to be defined as a Democratic tax.[17] Kean could not muster enough votes to extend the sales tax to gasoline.[18] Kean and the legislature eventually agreed to cut the budget by $186 million, largely through small cuts in state aid to local education and by reducing new transportation funding. Additional revenues were raised by reducing the ability of business to claim depreciations against their tax obligations.[19]

The June budget passage did not end battles over state aid and taxes, however. The state's economy continued to deteriorate, and by December the governor and legislature were once again meeting to discuss what to do about declining revenues. Kean pushed the need to confront the issue by signing an executive order in early December that would begin cuts in state programs on January 1, 1983, if no solution was reached by that date. Kean put the legislature in the situation that, if they did not act, local governments, and particularly urban school districts, would receive less state money.

The issue of cutting state programs and aid, which was an option politicians might have embraced, was quickly resolved. Both sides approached negotiations as if the former state role should be maintained. To prevent cuts, Kean proposed an increase in liquor taxes, and the previously proposed 5 percent tax on gasoline. Many legislators wanted an increase in the income tax as a solution,[20] but Kean said he would veto an increase in the income tax.[21] Kean then indicated that he would support an increase in the state sales tax from 5 to 6 percent.[22]

The battle became an important example of how party constituencies and philosophies affect public policy decisions. Now that an income tax had been enacted, there was a clear vehicle for Democrats to propose revenue solutions that were progressive. Democrats proposed an income tax increase. The existing income tax was 2 percent on earnings up to $20,000 and 2.5 percent on earnings above that. Democrats proposed making the tax much more progressive, with the rate rising to 3.5 at $50,000, 4.5 at $60,000, 5.5 at $80,000, and 6.5 at $100,000 and above.[23] The Democratic Speaker of the assembly, Alan Karcher, made it clear that many of the constituents of Democrats made so little that they would not pay any of this tax increase, and that ability to pay should be an important principle. He commented:

> This [increase in income tax rates on the affluent] won't affect most people in Democratic districts. The median income in Newark is $13,000. In Camden, it's $11,000, and in Perth Amboy it's $16,000. Where the tax will have an impact is in Alpine, where the median family income is $78,000, and in Bedminster, where it's $60,000. And there are no Democrats representing those districts.[24]

Republicans were much more worried about having all income groups bear a burden, and less supportive of the "ability to pay" principle.[25] Democrats pursued their plan and passed an income tax. Kean promptly vetoed it.[26] After further negotiations, the two sides eventually agreed on an increase in the sales tax from 5 to 6 percent (wanted by Republicans), and an increase in the income tax (wanted by Democrats).[27] Democrats accepted a smaller increase in the income tax, with the change involving just a 1 percent increase for those making more than $50,000.[28]

The party positions on taxes were reflected in legislative votes on the issue. Kean ended up being the advocate for the sales tax, with Republicans in the legislature carrying the battle for that tax. In the assembly and senate, as shown in table 6.2, two-thirds of Republicans voted for the sales tax, while most Democrats voted against it. Democrats, on the other hand, were much more supportive of the income tax.

Table 6.2. Percent of Each Party Voting for 1982
Sales and Income Tax Increases, Assembly and Senate

	Assembly		Senate	
	No	Yes	No	Yes
Sales Tax				
Republicans	14	72	26	68
Democrats	66	34	48	38
Income Tax				
Republicans	33	53	72	28
Democrats	26	67	9	68

The 1982 confrontation was the most prominent tax battle Kean faced during his eight years in office, but it was not the only one. Later tax issues became less of a confrontation with the legislature, but they also indicated the differences between the parties, and how tax issues often became entangled with issues of state obligations. In 1985, with the economy growing, a surplus emerged in the state budget. Kean proposed a 10 percent cut in the income tax, with a maximum cut of $75 for any person.[29] This would reduce state revenues and give taxes back to the public. The Democrats chose the route of using the additional revenue to propose allowing residents, for the first time, to deduct their local property taxes from their gross income before calculating their state tax obligation.[30] This would preserve state revenues and put the state in the position of picking up part of the costs of local taxes. Kean would have reduced the state's role, while Democrats pursued the route of maintaining and enhancing the state's role. Indeed, the Democrats proposal would increase the connection of citizens to the state, because they would annually see a deduction connected with the state. Kean eventually agreed to the Democrat's proposal.[31]

In summary, the 1982 tax confrontation illustrates how issues of the state role get dealt with and how this issue is so often intertwined with tax issues. As a gubernatorial candidate, Tom Kean argued that cuts in state business taxes would help the economy. His agenda was altered by something he could not control (though he probably could have anticipated it):

the decline in the economy. He was immediately faced with the issue of whether he would reduce state support to local governments or raise taxes. Campaign agendas are not irrelevant, but politicians must continually adjust as events change.

The political disposition of politicians play a crucial role in the responses to these situations. Kean, with a prior reputation as a moderate Republican, did not immediately choose to cut programs. He was willing to maintain state programs, but he proposed regressive taxes to raise additional revenues, and he publicly tried to make the Democratic legislature responsible for failing to resolve the problem.

The conflict quickly became not whether state programs should be maintained, but who should bear the burden of raising additional funds. Issues of equity of burdens are never far from the surface when the issue of the role of state government emerges. In this case, Democrats explicitly played the role of making this an issue. Kean resisted, and only gradually moved from selective, regressive taxes to a more broad-based regressive tax, the sales tax. Democrats, with a lower- to middle-income constituency, proposed a progressive tax increase and remained cohesive throughout the negotiations. The issue of maintaining state aid was resolved, with the state having a higher tax effort and a more progressive tax system. Events dictated the emergence of the issue, but parties and their constituencies shaped the way the issue was resolved.

The Democratic actions changed the tax structure. In the midst of a battle over how to preserve state revenues and programs, Democrats focused on making the progressivity of any tax increases the central issue. Democrats were able to make the income tax more progressive by increasing the percentage paid by those with higher incomes. Their position in favor of a more progressive tax system did not make it as progressive as they wanted, but their presence and negotiating increased the degree of progressivity. Democrats enacted the income tax in 1976, and in 1982 they led the effort to make it more progressive. Figure 6.2 indicates how the 1982 battle changed tax rates by income levels.

The 1982 tax decision also had a significant impact on state tax effort. Figure 6.3 shows the changes in state tax effort from year to year for the period 1955–89, which includes all the years Kean was governor. The 1982 tax increase was the major increase in tax effort during Kean's administration. The decision to increase taxes rather than respond by cutting programs became significant as the 1980s unfolded. There were no declines in tax effort until the late 1980s, which meant that state tax effort remained higher than in the 1970s.

Perhaps most important is how the tax structure put in place by the 1982 decisions, in combination with growth in the economy, shaped the

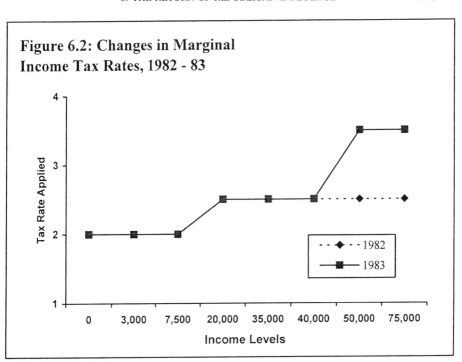

Figure 6.2: Changes in Marginal
Income Tax Rates, 1982 - 83

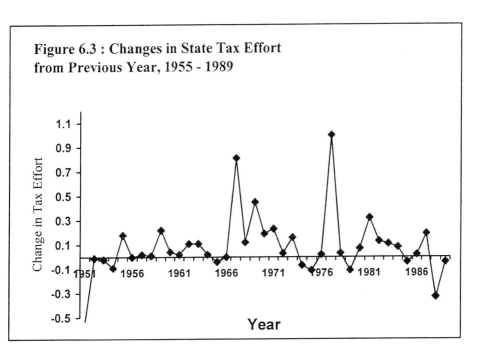

Figure 6.3 : Changes in State Tax Effort
from Previous Year, 1955 - 1989

subsequent role of state government. The national and state economy grew significantly, and with a higher tax structure in place, the state realized steady and large revenue increases as growth occurred in the 1980s. This made it possible to provide more state aid without having to impose additional taxes. Kean, who had won with a tiny margin in 1981 while emphasizing more conservative positions, chose to move towards the middle on this issue as the next election approached.[32] As the economy grew, Kean largely accepted the greater flow of revenue, and continually chose to propose increases in state aid for school districts.[33] The legislature generally accepted his proposed increases. The growth in the economy and the subsequent greater revenue allowed the legislature and the governor to avoid serious fights over distributing school aid throughout his eight-year term.

The result was steady increases in state aid, particularly for education. Figure 6.4 indicates changes in real per capita state aid for local education since the 1950s. During the 1980s there were real increases in aid in each year. Figure 6.5 indicates the total real per capita state aid to education. While the 1976 income tax resulted in a brief increase in education aid, it then declined through the early 1980s as the recession cut revenue flows to the state. The economic growth of the late 1980s made it possible for state government to provide steady increases after that.

While more revenue made it easier to provide more resources to schools

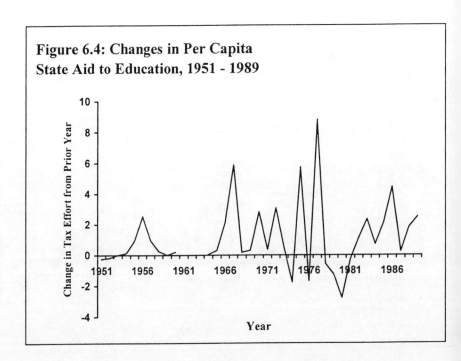

Figure 6.4: Changes in Per Capita State Aid to Education, 1951 - 1989

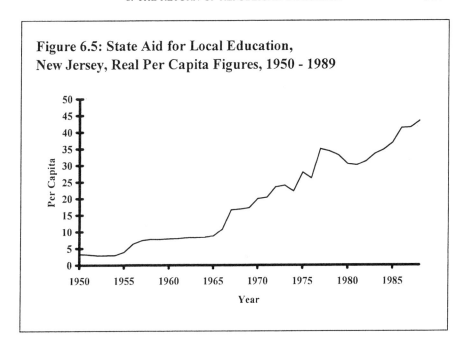

Figure 6.5: State Aid for Local Education,
New Jersey, Real Per Capita Figures, 1950 - 1989

and local governments, there were still differences about the fiscal obligations of state government. Kean, for example, was willing to provide more
state aid to schools, but he continually argued that the mandated state aid
formula was too generous. The school aid law enacted in the 1970s contained required year-to-year increases, but Kean resisted fully funding the
formula. He wanted the formula studied and the increases required from
year to year revised downward.[34] He vetoed an attempt by the Democratic
legislature to fully fund the school aid formula in 1984,[35] and he did not
propose an increase large enough to fully fund the state aid formula until
1985, when the state had a large surplus.[36] His actions in other areas also
indicated his reluctance to have the state play a greater role. While he increased municipal aid by $400 million over his eight years,[37] he often pro-
posed that aid be increased only if there was a repeal of the state law allowing
the deduction of local property taxes from gross state income.[38]

On the other hand, he was willing to propose that the state assume the
costs of welfare provided by municipalities and the costs of local court
systems.[39] Both of these changes would have increased the relative role of
state government. In both cases the legislature was unwilling to go along,
largely because these positions provided some local patronage jobs. On
balance, however, as a Republican, he did not serve as a significant advocate of the state generally assuming more responsibilities. The state budget

and state aid increased significantly during his tenure, but much of that was driven by growth in the economy.

Kean was not alone in taking this position. The legislature also did not aggressively push an agenda of having the state assume more responsibilities. Democrats lost the assembly in the 1985 elections, but the senate remained Democratic while Kean was governor. While Democrats had disagreements with Kean over taxes and their progressivity, they did not confront Kean with an agenda to significantly increase the fiscal responsibilities of state government. They generally sought somewhat larger increases in state aid. Like Kean, however, they were making decisions amidst a growing economy, and the additional revenues allowed legislators to make marginal increments in aid without major political confrontations.

THE STATE AND HOUSING OPPORTUNITY: *MT. LAUREL*

Suburbanization redistributes populations and wealth across municipalities. As people move to suburbs, the issue emerges of how much they, and particularly the affluent, should be allowed to use zoning laws to deny access to low-income individuals. Should there be equal opportunity to live in suburbs, and what does equal housing opportunity mean within a capitalistic *and* democratic society? Our individualistic economic culture emphasizes the right of individuals to enjoy the fruits of their labor, find a home that reflects their wealth, and protect that investment. But our democratic culture emphasizes the beliefs that government should act to pursue collective concerns and try to ensure some equality of opportunity, and that government should not be used to deny equality of opportunity. These values come into conflict when individuals seek to use local government zoning powers to shape housing opportunity. It is then that the issue emerges of whether state government has any obligation to intervene to affect local practices that structure opportunities.

The *Mt. Laurel* cases in New Jersey contained all these issues, but with a unique twist.[40] There was already a low-income, minority population in Mt. Laurel when this issue emerged. The dispute was over whether they would be allowed to remain there. This issue began to evolve at the local level in the late 1960s, but it became a state issue by the mid 1980s.

In the 1950s Mt. Laurel was a small municipality with a population of about 3000.[41] Mt. Laurel was far enough away from Philadelphia and Camden that few people chose to live there and commute to that metropolitan area. As suburbanization occurred in the 1960s, and bridges and roads were built, the affluent began to move to outlying areas like Mt. Laurel. The population increased significantly and by 1970 was over 11,000.

During the 1950s the town had a vague zoning plan that contained little detail. During the 1960s the town developed a comprehensive plan that defined the types of housing that could be built and designated where each type of housing could be built. That plan allowed only single-family residences.[42]

A minority population had been living in the town for some time, working in various low-income jobs. The issue was whether, as change occurred in the community, provisions would be made to allow them to stay. The housing that minorities had lived in was either eliminated as new roads were built or it was gradually deteriorating. Most minorities lived in an area called Springville, which was comprised of run-down, substandard housing. Housing for minorities became an issue because of how the local community reacted to the housing issue.

> According to state law, local officials had to ensure that the housing was made fit for people to live in or else make other arrangements for displaced residents. Because they were unwilling to do either, local officials usually waited until a family had moved out before conducting an inspection. Then, with no tenants whom they were legally obliged to relocate, they plastered the dwelling with yellow stickers that read "Unfit for Habitation" and razed the condemned homes.[43]

The decline in housing opportunities for the low-income individuals already living in the town prompted a response. The Springville Action Council, formed in 1967 to address problems of low-income groups, in 1968 proposed a set of thirty-six garden apartments—low-rise buildings with some surrounding green space—to be built in the Springville area. The state agreed to provide some matching funds. The proposal was presented to the local planning board, which had to approve a variance for multifamily units.

The plan was met with considerable resistance. The township council lodged numerous objections about the appropriateness of the land site, about the competence of the builders, and about where the site would get water and sewage.[44] The plan was reviewed at repeated meetings, with many residents from newer developments raising objections. Finally, in October 1970, the mayor, Bill Haines, was invited to a meeting of the all-black African Methodist Episcopalian Church to announce the town's response to the plan. The mayor announced that the town would never approve the group's request, and concluded with the statement, "If you people can't afford to live in our town, then you'll just have to leave."[45]

Frustration with the resistance of Mt. Laurel officials led to involvement by the Camden Regional Legal Services, one of the federally funded groups whose mission was to help represent the rights of low-income individuals. The lawyers involved in this case thought the case was particularly interesting because it involved the rights of those already in the town, and not "outsiders" trying to get in as growth occurred.[46] In May 1971, the group filed *Southern Burlington County NAACP et al. v. Township of Mt. Laurel.* The case was filed in state courts because the lawyers thought they might have a better chance of success with the activist state supreme court.

The prognosis for the plaintiffs was not good. The state supreme court, in the 1952 case *Lionshead Lake v. Wayne,* upheld local zoning ordinances setting minimum floor-space requirements, and concluded that the general welfare referred only to a town's current residents. In a 1962 case, *Vickers v. Gloucester,* the court allowed using local zoning ordinances to exclude trailer parks.[47]

The *Mt. Laurel* case embodied fundamental issues about notions of equality of opportunity and the obligations of state government. To the plaintiffs, the issue was whether individuals of different levels of income had the right to live in an area. Did all individuals have rights of access or only those with higher levels of income? To many of the residents opposing rights of access, the issue was very different. Did those who had earned a certain level of success have the right to do what they thought was necessary to protect it? To them low-income groups were seen as dangerous because they brought different values and sometimes crime, and it was thought their presence would threaten the home values of better-off residents. The clash was serious and involved the most basic issues of what equality of opportunity meant. Did opportunity involve the right to live anywhere, or did opportunity involve the right to compete in the economy and live in an area only if sufficient economic success occurred? The contrast with education finance is important. Education involves developing people so they can compete in society, and discriminating against children involves denying them the very chance to develop. Purchasing a home is very different to many, however, because it reflects what people have achieved at some later point in life. Liberals argue that the two are heavily intertwined because the source of differentials in education resources is housing segregation by class and race, but to those resisting, education involves opportunity and housing involves achievement.

The issue also captures a fundamental clash over notions of community and the role of state government.[48] To the defendants, the lawsuit was an attack on the essence of community, because it challenged the right of residents to try to guide their own fate. Those in the town did not see exclusion operating, but the market.[49] Those with more money simply had the means to afford more expensive houses. They did not see zoning laws as manipulating the process, but as the means to preserve and protect a community. Those living there should be allowed to determine what would serve their best interests, and there should be no external intrusion. To critics the world could hardly have been seen more different. They saw a systematic pattern of using local ordinances to segregate people by race and class. Local zoning laws were granted by state government, and state powers were being used to create islands of segregation. Their notion of community was far broader, and they objected to the use of local powers to shape opportunities. They felt state government had an obligation to limit the ability of local towns to exclude people.

After a trial in the Burlington County courts, the local judge ruled that Mt. Laurel's zoning ordinance was unconstitutional and constituted economic discrimination.[50] The judge ordered local officials to work with the plaintiffs to identify local housing needs and develop a program to respond to those needs. Town officials, however, made it very clear that they were going to resist the order and would not work with local low-income residents. The case was appealed to the state supreme court.

In 1975 the state supreme court made the first of its rulings on the *Mt. Laurel* case. The ruling surprised many. The court, referring to the state constitution, ruled that zoning practices in Mt. Laurel constituted economic discrimination. The court did not make the basis of the case racial discrimination. The most surprising aspect of the ruling was that the court ordered *all* municipalities to rewrite their zoning ordinances to assure that a "fair share" of poor families in the region could live there.[51]

As is true with all major court decisions, the crucial matter is how local compliance with the ruling proceeds. The immediate future did not prove to be bright for those seeking more low-income housing. Most municipalities took little action to comply.[52] Mt. Laurel responded within the year by dedicating twenty-three acres of swampy, unusable land for low-income housing. In a related case, the state supreme court undermined its previous ruling, and ruled that a locality had only to make a "good faith" effort.[53] It appeared the court might back off its earlier ruling.

The lack of change at the local level led to more lawsuits about housing opportunities. While these cases were pending, the composition of the court changed, and those changes proved to be very significant. After some lengthy trials, the state supreme court in 1983 issued a ruling, known as *Mt. Laurel II,* which finally made the legal issue a major state political issue. In the 1983 ruling the court ruled that the behavior of the towns was illegal. The usual practice of the court is to issue a ruling and then wait for lawsuits about inaction in complying with the ruling. In this case, however, the court established two significant mechanisms designed to affect the extent to which there would be more housing activity. To encourage more building, the court sought to harness the economic interest of builders. The court decreed that

> Developers who agreed to set aside 20 percent of their units for [low-income housing], fixing a price at below-market levels, were entitled to jump the queue for project approval. If they didn't get a quick okay from local planners, they could sue the township in a Mt. Laurel trial court.[54]

To speed action on cases of local resistance, the court also set up three regional trial courts across the state to handle only Mt. Laurel–type cases. This would expedite the consideration of cases and make it more difficult to engage in protracted resistance to efforts to build low-income housing. The judges, working with various advocate groups in the state, developed guidelines for the number of housing units each municipality had to build. In some communities, the announced goal for new low- to moderate-income units was three thousand to four thousand.[55] The normal process of waiting on compliance was replaced with a system designed to encourage efforts to confront local resistance. That process achieved the goal the court desired. Within a year, builders from all over the state were filing the majority of suits, and cases were piling up to be heard by the new trial court system.[56]

The issue was now a statewide political issue, and politicians were drawn into it. The issue was what position the state should take on this question of equality of opportunity. For state level politicians—the governor and state legislators—this was an issue fundamentally different from school finance. Both school finance and housing involve questions of equality of opportunity. School finance requires redistributing money, never attractive to some politicians, but it can be done without disturbing a community's composition, and is for the sake of children. In addition, if taxes are imposed and more revenues result, part of the policy resolution can be some additional money for all districts. No visible intrusion into a community occurs, vulnerable children are served, and at least some benefits are seen in all districts. Housing is a much more difficult issue for politicians, because creating more opportunities means using state power to visibly intrude into communities to affect housing construction. Providing low-income housing also means helping those who are adults and have not achieved economically in society.[57] To critics, it means helping the less successful and perhaps jeopardizing the situation of those who have worked to get into certain communities. It involves much more risk to politicians.

Governor Tom Kean wasted no time staking out a position on this issue. When he first took office in 1982, he rescinded the order of the prior governor, Brendan Byrne, that gave state funding preference to communities that voluntarily complied with the Mt. Laurel ruling. He also dismantled the housing grants program, eliminating sixty of sixty-three state planners. When the *Mt. Laurel II* decision was announced in 1983, Kean denounced it as "communistic."[58] In his 1984 state of the state address he proposed a plan to resolve the issue. He proposed the creation of a state agency to focus on planning for statewide growth. This agency, the Council on Affordable Housing, would decide how many new units were needed and where housing was needed. Perhaps the most important proposal was that municipalities would be able to contract with other municipalities to fulfill their fair share of housing obligations. Kean sought to pose the issue as whether the obligation was to provide affordable housing *someplace* in the state, or whether it was to provide some affordable housing almost *everywhere*. He argued the state was only obligated to provide affordable housing somewhere, and the issue was not one of economic integration. The state would be involved in helping promote housing, but not in intruding on local autonomy.[59] He also sought to use urban renewal funds only to rehabilitate existing urban housing, which meant accepting the existing distribution of low-income housing.

Differences between some members of the Republican and Democratic Parties quickly became relevant. Conservative Republicans, angered by the court decision, introduced a bill to curtail the powers of the court. They proposed a moratorium on judicial implementation of *Mt. Laurel II*. Liberal Democrats differed significantly. They criticized the governor for condoning economic segregation and suggesting a policy approach that would leave it untouched even as population shifts were occurring. Democrats controlled both houses and proposed and passed the Fair Housing Act. It established a statewide planning agency, taking control from the courts, but it preserved the fair-share requirement and the right of builders to seek to build. Once again Democrats were more comfortable with state action. The bill accepted some of Kean's proposal and allowed up to one-third of a municipality's housing obligation to be transferred to another municipality. The bill passed with only Democratic support and was sent to Kean, who vetoed it.[60]

The hard bargaining between the governor and the legislature then began. Many suburban state legislators in both parties did not want to allow extensive building of low-income units in suburban municipalities. Kean proposed that a municipality be able to transfer 50 percent of its obligation. He also asked that the state agency be allowed to set ceilings on how much affordable housing any municipality had to accept. To pick up votes from suburban representatives, more local officials were placed on the state board, COAH, which would supervise the plan, and the time required to comply was extended to twenty years.[61] The bill finally passed, with a majority of votes coming from Republicans, but with enough Democrats to provide the margin. The original liberal, Democratic sponsors of the Fair Housing Act passed by Democrats voted against it.[62] The legislation discontinued the special housing trial courts set up to handle housing cases, and replaced them with a state agency with strong ties to local interests, and with limits on how much municipalities had to do to comply. Cases being considered by the regional trial courts were transferred to the state agency to be resolved. The bill eliminated judicial handling of these cases. The state supreme court was soon presented with another housing case, which gave it the opportunity to indicate whether the change would be accepted by the court. In a 1986 ruling, the court unanimously upheld the new law, and effectively allowed a political resolution of the situation.[63]

This administrative approach to the housing issue soon led to a diminished state effort in this policy area. The staff of the public advocate's office, which had traditionally served to represent housing discrimination cases, was reduced. The COAH allowed towns to include housing for senior citizens and rehabilitated housing in the number of affordable homes created. The state estimate of the number of new affordable homes necessary to build to respond to needs was reduced dramatically, from 245,000 to 145,000. The fair-share number of units each town had to create was decreased. A state report in 1993 indicated that only 14,000 units of Mt. Laurel–related housing had been built since 1985.[64]

The evolution of the housing issue suggests that advocates of a greater state role lost. The outcome is less than clear, however. The difficult question is the baseline for judging change. If the standard is the ruling in *Mt. Laurel II* and the housing quotas created shortly after that, the events subsequent to 1985 indicate a clear loss for advocates of having the state play a role in opening up the suburbs. On the other hand, the series of *Mt. Laurel* decisions and the 1985 legislation did make consideration of housing needs a state issue. It created a small state bureaucracy to assess housing needs. State government was now more involved, though clearly on a limited basis, than it had been before. The courts in the 1950s and 1960s ruled that zoning was a local issue, but now the court's interpretation was that a broader community at least needed to be considered. The change in the presumption of a state role is important. The ruling and the legally defined state role created the potential for a slow, incremental intrusion of the state into this area. Whether that potential is used is determined by politics, but there is a mechanism for state action that did not exist before. The significance of the role can be seen in the actions that followed resolution of *Mt. Laurel*. The state bureaucracy did not give up on *Mt. Laurel*, and obtained a court order requiring Mt. Laurel to comply with a plan to build 140 town houses for low- and moderate-income families. On April 11, 1997, the town planning board unanimously approved the plan, which allowed the town to obtain federal aid to complete the project. The battle took over twenty-five years, but it changed to some extent, at least, the expectation of the role of state government.[65]

Parties played less of a role in this issue than with school finance. Polls showed that 70 percent of the public was opposed to the state intruding into local zoning,[66] and both parties had substantial segments of their constituents who did not support state efforts to open up communities. There were strong reasons for both parties to not support a greater state role in this area. Republicans, with a base in suburbs and rural areas, were opposed to state action in this area. Democrats, and particularly liberal Democrats, sought to expand the state role, but they were in the minority in their party. Suburban Democrats were unwilling to encourage state intrusion into local zoning practices, and they would only support legislation that provided for a limited ability of the state to intrude. Because the parties lacked clearly different constituency bases, no major party battle developed on this issue.

A State Planning Commission

The Mt. Laurel issue triggered focus on another possible state role, and again revealed differences between Republicans and Democrats on this issue. In rendering the *Mt. Laurel* decision, the State Supreme Court referred to the State Development Guide Plan. This had been prepared by the Department of Community Affairs in the 1970s. The court ordered that the document be a part of the process of promoting affordable housing, and ordered that the document be periodically revised. Kean, who was hostile to state planning, responded by abolishing the State and Regional Planning Division in 1983. A Democratic senator, Gerald Stockman, responded with a bill requiring a state plan. After extensive negotiations, the legislature passed the bill and Kean signed it in 1986. The legislation specified that all groups (the poor and minorities) and interests (conservation and development) receive consideration in the plan. Kean then delayed eight months in appointing an executive director. The final plan, one of the most comprehensive state plans ever developed, was not approved until 1992.[67]

Planning documents often have little impact, and the effect of this change should not be overestimated. But another state responsibility had been redefined, at least in law. Planning and zoning had been local responsibilities, and now, at least in the statutes, it was also a state obligation. A Republican had resisted the change, while Democrats had been the advocate of a greater state role.

The Renewal of the School Aid Issue:
Abbott v. Burke

The Kean administration faced one last major controversy over the role of state government. The critics of school finance were not satisfied by the enactment of the income tax and the distribution of school aid that followed. Almost immediately after the enactment of a new school aid formula in 1975 and 1976, critics began tracking how the money was being spent.[68] Their criticisms of the distribution of school aid were relatively simple. First, much of the money raised by the 1976 income tax had *not* gone for education. Some of it went for property tax relief, and some of it went for revenue sharing for cities. Second, and most significant to the critics, not enough of the money had gone to equalizing revenues across school districts. The composition of the Democratic Party in the legislature in 1976 was primarily suburban and rural (see the prior chapter), and the dominance of the nonurban portion had resulted in a desire to lower property taxes and support for a distribution pattern favoring suburban and rural areas.

The agreement in 1976 had not specifically directed that state aid be distributed to suburban and rural areas, but that occurred indirectly. State aid was distributed through several categories: as equalization aid, special education aid, and transportation aid. Each of these was distributed according to its own formula. Equalization aid is distributed in a way that districts with poorer tax bases receive more. This aid is redistributive. Special education aid, however, is not explicitly redistributive because it is distributed on a per pupil basis, and special education problems, while more prevalent in lower-income districts, occur across all districts. Transportation aid is distributed on the basis of the number of students who must receive public transportation to get to school. Since this is most likely to occur in suburban and rural areas, these areas receive more transportation aid per pupil than urban areas. These three existing categories—equalization, special education, and transportation—for distributing aid were preserved in the 1975–76 laws. The additional aid distributed in 1976 ($400 million) was added to this existing system. Of this $400 million in additional state aid, only $244 million went to equalization aid, thus limiting the amount of redistribution.

The net effect of all sources of revenues—locally raised, equalization aid, and categorical aid programs (funds given for specific purposes)—is shown in table 6.3. The first column indicates categories of districts, grouped from lowest per pupil tax base to highest per pupil tax base. The average per pupil tax base for each group is shown in the second column. The average amount of equalization aid per pupil for each group is in column 3. The next two columns present the per pupil average for transportation and special education aid. The column labeled total categorical aid is the sum of transportation, special education, and all other types of aid, excluding the equalization aid. The total of locally raised, equalization, and all categorical aid is presented in the next column.

Table 6.3. Local Revenues and State Aid, 1984–85

Tax Base per Pupil Group	Equalized $ Value / Pupil	Tax Rate	Local Revenue	Equal Aid	Transp Aid	Spec Ed Aid	Total Categorical	Total Revenues[a]	% Rev from State Aid[b]
						Per Pupil Figures			
1	42,608	1.71	728	2,132	68	168	529	3,482	76.6
2	78,767	1.37	1,080	1,840	103	186	489	3,514	66.7
3	126,618	1.42	1,802	1,369	158	192	443	3,687	49.3
4	163,644	1.43	2,338	999	155	171	405	3,825	36.9
5	205,364	1.45	2,971	592	138	168	368	4,041	24.0
6	260,755	1.39	3,613	320	135	169	371	4,409	15.8
7	450,666	.86	3,867	289	145	169	377	4,695	14.3
State Avg	190,401	1.23	2,349	1,073	129	175	426	3,952	38.1

[a]Includes Federal Impact Aid.   [b]Percent of total revenue from state aid.

Source: Edward H. Salmon, "Public School Finance Reform in New Jersey" (dissertation, University of Delaware, 1991), 40–44.

The critics argued that by putting so much money into categorical aid, the state did not have enough money to really equalize school expenditures. Even though state equalization aid was larger per pupil than any other category of aid, and was very redistributive, the distribution of other state aid on a nonredistributive basis mean that less-affluent districts still had revenues below the statewide average, and they still had students with more problems. The critics also argued that suburbanization was continuing,[69] and the relocation of jobs and property values was making it more difficult for urban school districts to raise enough money.

This argument was made even though the state was now engaging in extensive redistribution across school districts. The last column of the table indicates the percentage of all revenue per pupil coming from state aid, including equalization and all other forms of categorical aid. The percentage of revenue from state aid for the poorest group of school districts was 76.6, which was considerably higher than in the 1960s. Despite that greater state assistance for the poorest districts, the critics remained focused on the continuing inequality in absolute revenues per group of districts. They argued that the education a student received, teachers' salaries, the quality of buildings, and the availability of programs received were still dependent on the property wealth of a district.[70]

These data became the basis for another lawsuit. The Education Law Center, based in Newark, filed a lawsuit on February 5, 1981, for Raymond Arthur Abbot, a student in Camden, versus Fred G. Burke, the commissioner of education. They drew on the following section of the New Jersey Statutes, N.J.S.A 18A:7A-4, which states, "The goal of a thorough and efficient system of free public schools shall be to provide to all children in New Jersey, regardless of socioeconomic status or geographic location." The argument of the lawsuit was that the socioeconomic status of individuals was still connected to geography, and students in the poorest districts got less of an education.

The executive branch, representing the state, responded to the lawsuit and took the conservative position. They argued that, in many cases, the problems with poor schools stemmed from their own practices. They responded with findings that there was corruption and mismanagement in poorer districts, resulting in the waste of resources that could be used to improve the quality of education in those districts. The state argued that money does not determine outcomes in education.[71] The state also responded by trying to delay responding to the issue by trying to avoid a trial. State officials argued that a trial should not proceed until all administrative remedies had been exhausted. They wanted the issue submitted to the Office of the Commissioner of Education to see what the commissioner could do to respond to any possible problems. The state supreme court eventually ruled in 1984 that the issue was constitutional and should be handled by the courts.[72] A lower court judge, after reviewing the evidence, ruled that the state supreme court was likely to find the existing state law unconstitutional.[73] The Office of Administrative Law in 1985 then began to gather more information and hear testimony. In 1986 a trial finally began,[74] and continued until 1988. The lower-court judge ruled that the existing system was unconstitutional.[75] He then delivered the case to the state commissioner of education, who was allowed to respond. He ruled that the system was fair, and an appeal by the plaintiffs then went to the state supreme court for a final decision.

The commissioner's response indicated the position of the Kean administration. The commissioner repeated the argument that poorer districts mismanaged and wasted money.[76] He did not contest many of the facts about disparities of resources and programs. He argued, however, that the law does not require that all students have the same programs, and that neither the state constitution nor the state supreme court had yet mandated that all children receive identical programs and services.[77] Inequality existed, but there was no requirement to have equal spending, and it did not matter anyway.

The Kean administration chose to contest the lawsuit by arguing that the existing system was not unconstitutional. The lengthy process by which the case was considered allowed his administration to avoid any final decision in the case during his two terms in office.[78] The case finally went to the state supreme court in 1989 for final decision, and by then the 1989 campaign for governor was underway. Faced with a two-term limit, Kean knew that his administration would not have to face the consequences of a decision favorable to the plaintiffs. The legislature was also able to avoid the case because there was no ruling. The case ruling and the decision about what to do about the ruling would not become an issue until the next administration.

PARTIES AND DEFINING THE STATE ROLE

As a Republican governor during the Reagan years, the Tom Kean administration did not seek to repeal the role of state government. Faced with a declining economy, Kean did not seek to cut state support. Indeed, he created a situation where the legislature would be responsible if programs were cut. When the economy grew, he was willing to put much of the increased revenues into more state aid. Yet his behavior illustrates the role Republicans often play when confronted with issues. He proposed regressive taxes to deal with a recession. He strongly opposed a strong state role in creating greater accessibility to housing outside central cities for low-income groups. He curtailed efforts by state agencies to be active in this area, and led the fight to limit the state role in distributing affordable housing across municipalities. He resisted making planning a state responsibility. Finally, when presented with a case about continuing inequality of school finance, he chose to resist any further state efforts in this area. His approach was to seek to contain change.

Democrats, while not always aggressively pursuing a liberal agenda, were more willing when faced with an issue to pursue a relatively liberal position. They were more willing to respond to a recession with a progressive tax increase. They were willing to fight for a state role in planning following the *Mt. Laurel* cases. They supported a state planning commission. Parties mattered, but primarily in how they reacted.

While the parties were arguing about what role the state should take, the state ultimately took on a greater role in the 1980s. The tax increases enacted in 1982 helped to generate greater revenues, and the pressures of Democrats played a significant role in pushing Kean to agree to increase state funding, as long as revenues were increasing. Again, while the parties often struggled to play their roles, and this was particularly true for the Democrats, they did pursue positions and policies we might have expected, and the role of state government increased.

Part IV:
Schools, Inequality, and State Taxes, II

7

Schools, Democrats, and Taxes
(and Electoral Retribution)

DEMOCRATS GAINED CONTROL OF STATE GOVERNMENT IN 1990, FOR THE THIRD time since 1950. Much as was the case with prior new administrations, they faced a series of pressing problems. There was a recession, creating a budget deficit. There were growing complaints about local property taxes, and, again, complaints about inequities in tax assessments across local governments. The second major school finance case was also about to be announced, which could create additional demands on state government. The issue for Democrats was what would they do with this power and how would they handle these problems.

When Jim Florio assumed power as governor, he responded to these situations with a major proposal to restructure the tax system and the level and distribution of school aid. His program was heavily redistributive, with much more aid going to less-affluent school districts. The legislature, with great reluctance, and some modifications, enacted his proposal. The electorate virtually erupted, with extensive demonstrations and statements of anger. Democrats were obliterated in the legislative elections that followed. In 1966 the party had presumed that enacting the sales tax would help the party be seen as responding to problems, but they had guessed wrong. In 1990 the party made the same mistake, and they paid for it dearly at the next election.

As with prior situations, the concern is why did Democrats did this. What led the party to enact this legislation and believe that the party would not harm its political situation? What was the impact of these policy proposals for the role of the state and the situation of the have-nots? Finally, what impact did these events have on state politics and on debates about state issues?

163

THE 1989 ELECTIONS

There were many issues that might have dominated the 1989 gubernatorial campaign. There were public concerns that a growing recession would reduce state revenues and create budget problems. The issue about local property assessments and inequities in taxes had surfaced again. Some cities had not reassessed in ten years, and assessment was required annually. Taxes varied tremendously across municipalities, and local property taxes were rising.[1] A state commission issued a major report in 1988 detailing increasing program burdens on local governments and arguing that state government should increase its taxes so the state could assume the responsibility for such locally funded and financed activities as the courts, welfare, and psychiatric hospitals.[2]

The school finance issue was also lurking. The *Abbott v. Burke* case was being considered by the supreme court and there was considerable suspicion that the court would be inclined to accept the argument that the existing system was unconstitutional. As noted in the prior chapter, the plaintiffs were pursuing an argument that the growing disparities in local tax bases were interacting with provisions of state law to increase the differences in per pupil revenues available to local schools. Since the state formula was alleged to accentuate local differences in wealth, it was expected that the court would invalidate the state law providing for the distribution of state aid.

None of these issues was central in the election, however. The campaign focused on other issues. Jim Florio, the Democratic gubernatorial candidate, had run against Republican Tom Kean in 1981, and lost by 2,000 votes, the closest election in the state's history. In 1989 he ran an aggressive campaign against the Republican candidate, Jim Courter. Florio attacked Courter early on with ads showing illegal toxic waste barrels on Courter's land, and kept up a variety of attacks during the campaign. Courter stumbled several times in his campaign presentations, taking contradictory positions on several issues, such as abortion, and Florio was able to portray him as a weak candidate. Florio won with 62 percent of the vote, a landslide.

Florio's discussion of important public policy issues was reasonably clear, but they did not prove to be directly relevant. While there were rumors during the campaign that state revenues were not coming in as expected and that the *Abbott v. Burke* decision was imminent, there was no specific situation candidates had to react to. Both issues involved the question of whether the state might need to raise taxes. Florio's response to questions about the school finance situation is particularly important. On one hand, during the campaign he said that he thought the state was wrong in opposing the court case. Florio argued that the state needed to change to a foundation plan.[3] Foundation programs first set a minimal amount of expenditure per pupil in districts. The state then requires that each local district tax itself at some minimal rate as its contribution to this minimum expenditure rate. The state makes differences in expenditure levels from the minimum, after local contributions are considered. Districts with wealthy tax bases generate more from the required tax than poor districts do, so the state ends up providing more compensatory aid to poorer districts.[4]

Florio said during the campaign that he saw no need to raise taxes. When asked what he might do if the courts threw out the existing school finance system, Florio said he "would stand by his no-new-taxes pledge even if that happens and would not seek to raise taxes."[5] Yet he refused to sign a "no new taxes" pledge. He did not want to tie his hands, but he did not expect that new revenues would be needed. Governor Kean had indicated that the state would end the 1990 fiscal year with a surplus of $300 - 400 million. Florio intended to cut spending for some programs, and the combination of a surplus and cuts would provide sufficient revenues to address the school finance issue.[6] Florio, therefore, had indicated his support for changing the state school aid formula, but he did not think a tax increase would be necessary. The difficulty that developed was that the state budget situation proved to be very different from that which Florio assumed when he indicated his policy preferences. Despite all this ambiguity, it is clear that Florio had not suggested during the campaign that he would raise taxes, and he could claim no mandate for such actions.

The legislative elections also presented limited clarity as to whether a policy mandate existed for Democrats. Democrats gained control over both houses of the legislature, but the election did not produce a significant shift in their situation. As shown in figure 7.1, Democrats had controlled the senate with 24 seats in 1987, and they retained 23 seats in 1989. In the assembly the number of seats held by the Democrats increased from 38 to 43. The changes were not significant.

There were also no signs of a shift in the Democratic constituency base. As shown in table 7.1, following the 1989 assembly elections there was little change from the situation that prevailed in 1987. In 1987 assembly Democrats won most of their seats in lower- and middle-income districts. In 1989 the only change of any consequence was that Democrats gained four seats in middle-income districts and two in upper-income districts. Senate Democrats derived most of their seats from a very similar set of districts. The limited change from 1987 to 1989 in the assembly and the similarity of party electoral bases in the two houses provided little evidence that the elections had produced a statement of support from the electorate for something new.

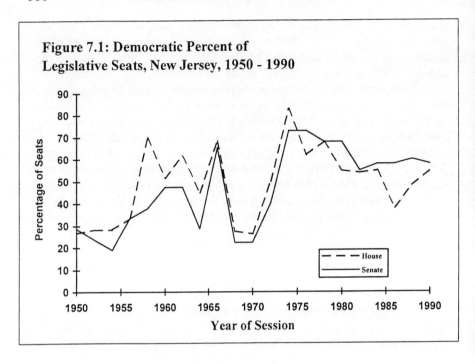

Figure 7.1: Democratic Percent of
Legislative Seats, New Jersey, 1950 - 1990

Table 7.1. Democratic Legislative Seats,
by District Income Level, 1987 and 1989

| | Assembly Districts | | | | | | Senate Districts | | |
| | 1987 Elections | | 1989 Elections | | | | 1989 Elections | | |
Income	N	N	% won	N	% won	Δ%	N	N	% won
Low	26	19	73	18	72	-1	13	11	85
Medium	28	13	50	17	65	15	13	9	69
High	28	6	21	8	29	8	14	3	21
	80	48	43	43	54	6	40	23	58

Note: Districts are classified on the basis of the per capita income of district residents in 1987. The relevant data were taken from the *1990 New Jersey Legislative District Data Book.* Districts were arrayed by income levels, and then divided into three equal groups.

DEMOCRATIC CONTROL AND RESPONDING TO
BUDGET AND SCHOOL FINANCE ISSUES

Jim Florio was not reluctant to have government take action to respond to state problems. Upon taking office, he immediately used state actions to address two problems. Car insurance rates in New Jersey were among the highest in the nation, and consumers were angry about them. Florio got legislation passed that rolled back insurance rates on cars. He was also concerned about the enforcement of environmental regulations in the state, and moved to reduce the discretion of those who did environmental inspections and issued warnings.[7] Florio was not reluctant to have state government play a significant role addressing problems.

But the crucial issues faced by Democrats as they assumed control were budget problems. While Kean had announced that there would be a surplus in 1990, by late 1989 and early 1990 it was known that the state was running a deficit for the fiscal year to end in June 1990, it was expected to reach $600 million. That is, it was forecast that the current budget would end up short of revenues. It would be necessary to quickly cut spending or impose new taxes.

The other issue, of course, was school finance. Florio had the choice of waiting for the court to issue its ruling or he could take decisive action before the ruling. The difference between a Kean, a Republican, and Florio, a Democrat, is important in this case. While Governor Kean argued against dealing with the distributive aspect of the school issue and sought to delay having to respond as long as possible, Florio did not hesitate in the school area and otherwise.

Florio offered several proposals to respond to all these problems. To resolve the budget problems, he proposed a 1 percent increase in the sales tax. It was his proposal to resolve the school funding issue, however, that was most significant. He could have chosen to propose legislation that provided aid to just the twenty-eight lowest-income districts that the court mentioned, but he decided to tackle the entire system of school finance. He proposed a package that would significantly increase aid for most school districts. The twenty-eight poorest districts would get large funding increases, but lower- to middle-income districts would also receive significant increases, and would get almost one-half of the funds. More-affluent districts would not receive increases, but would not have their aid be cut immediately. These districts would receive a gradual four-year transition of declines of aid to give them time to adjust.

His proposal went beyond what was required, and it would result in a significant increase in state taxes and in the role of the state in funding local schools. The question is why he made a proposal that went so far. His reasons were much like those of Governor Hughes, who had also proposed a significant increase in taxes. First, he thought providing more equality of education funding was the right thing to do. He saw the issue as "not about urban-suburban differences, but children." Second, he thought that the election had given him a mandate. During the campaign he had criticized the state for supporting the existing state school finance law, and for opposing the *Abbott v. Burke* case.[8] Third, he thought that the public desired someone who would take on tough issues and be decisive. "I sense there is now a desire out there to have somebody make some hard decisions."[9] He also thought his proposal would be more politically saleable because it provided greater state aid to middle-income districts. It would be easier to get suburban legislators to go along with the proposal, because he could point to specific increases in state aid that they would receive.[10]

Finally, the income tax increase was significant in how it targeted burdens. His proposal was to increase taxes on only the affluent, defined as all those with incomes above $55,000 per year, and families making over $100,000. Most of the tax increase would be paid by households making more than $100,000.[11]

The program would increase state involvement in school finance and it would do so with a clear redistributive focus. Lower- to middle-income districts would receive almost all the funds. Upper-income districts would face caps on how much they could spend on schools, and they would be weaned of school aid in subsequent years. Part of the funds from the income tax would be used for school finance, but part would be used to fund a property tax rebate program for families with incomes of less than $65,000.[12]

The set of proposals was, in some ways, remarkable. During the Reagan years there had been less emphasis on public policy designed to achieve more equality. Yet at the same time the newspapers had been filled with stories of growing disparities in the distribution of income between the top and bottom levels of society.[13] Even Republican analysts were arguing that inequality was likely to become an issue.[14] Florio's proposals were seen by some as a direct attempt at a Democratic response to that growing inequality.

> "What Jim Florio has done is set up a test case for the Democratic Party," said Representative Robert G. Torricelli, a New Jersey Democrat from suburban Bergen County. "For a decade, Democrats have been intimidated from offering substantive alternatives to the politics and rhetoric of Ronald Reagan. Now they are watching Jim Florio because he represents either the last defeat of a terrible decade, or our first success story in a new time when politics in America can be redefined."[15]

Florio gambled that his bold proposal would get him credit for dealing with a problem and would create a broad Democratic coalition. He had proposed a redistributive program with significant levels of aid going to middle-income districts and with most taxes paid by the affluent. This would allow him to create a coalition built around lower- to middle-income districts. It was presumed that the higher taxes would be paid by "more affluent areas, which the administration regarded as politically expendable since they generally voted for Republicans anyway."[16] The key was that he wanted to make sure middle-income districts benefited so they saw the Democratic party as helping them. As Florio put it:

> The difference between working people in the era of Roosevelt and working people in the era of Reagan is that, although they were suffering hardships in both, in the 1980s Reagan somehow convinced them that government was their enemy. Our policies cannot be aimed at just the poor.[17]

The key was whether middle-income districts would see themselves as part of this coalition. As a journalist and a state legislator, respectively, summarized the situation:

> [Journalist:] [I]f Florio can convince such voters [the modest middle class] that they are winners in his tax plan, the Governor can dramatically reshape politics in the state. But if those people often called "working class" and "middle class" feel they are Florio's victims, New Jersey's Governor is likely to be remembered as just one more failed liberal.

> [State legislator:] "He is either going to be a great success or a great failure. My district is a Reagan Democratic district. If you treat them like they are rich, if you leave them out of the coalition, we lose them."[18]

The court finally issued a ruling on June 5, 1990.[19] The court's ruling was clear. It focused on revenues and spending and on twenty-eight urban districts with severe problems.

> We find that under the present system the evidence compels but one conclusion: the poorer the district and the greater its need, the less the money available, and the worse the education. The system is neither thorough nor efficient.[20]
> . . . students in poorer districts have not been able to participate fully as citizens and workers in our society. They have not been able to achieve any level of equality in that society with their peers from affluent suburban districts. We find the constitutional failure clear, severe, extensive and of long duration.

> The Act must be amended, or new legislation passed, so as to assure the poorer urban districts' educational funding is substantially equal to that of property rich districts.[21]

The court, however, had not condemned the entire state funding system. They found that "the record did not show there was any constitutional violation in other districts."[22] The ruling left the state with the obligation to address funding problems in the twenty-eight districts, but the court issued no requirements about actions that needed to taken about the fiscal situation in other districts.

THE LEGISLATIVE REACTION:
FEAR AND ANGUISH AMONG DEMOCRATS

Democrats in the legislature received the proposals with considerable anxiety. Many of them thought it was the right thing to do and were receptive to his claim that they would look courageous. But Florio's proposals went beyond what the courts required. He was using the issue to try to address inequality across the entire system of school finance and at the same time build a broader political coalition for the party. Legislators did not like the way the issue was being handled. They worried about the ability to build the coalition Florio presumed was possible. A liberal Democrat who had supported Florio was worried that "Democrats would have to overcome years of racial distrust between blue-collar whites and poor minorities."[23]

Democrats were also being attacked by the teachers' union. As a part of his proposal, Florio wanted to change who paid teachers' pensions. The costs of pensions were at that time paid by the state pension system. Florio wanted to shift these costs to local school districts to produce more fairness. With the existing system, local school districts negotiated their own retirement programs, but costs were paid by the state. Wealthy school districts paid higher salaries and granted higher pension benefits than poor school districts. This meant that the state was subsidizing the already higher benefits in wealthier districts. Florio wanted to shift this to local districts for two reasons. If school districts knew they had to pay the costs of pensions, they would be less likely to negotiate generous benefits. Having wealthier districts pay for pensions would also be fairer, since they had the tax bases to support higher benefits. The emphasis was again on the redistributive effects of changes. The New Jersey Education Association supported the other parts of the school aid package, but was strongly opposed to this and promised to campaign against anyone voting for the proposal.[24]

Democrats also faced heavy criticism from Republicans, who argued the tax increases would make the state a high tax state and drive away business.[25] Republicans were also quick to charge that Florio was engaging in "Robin Hood" politics and was trying to introduce class politics into state politics by pitting district against district.[26] The fact that in some counties most school districts would lose aid after four years while districts in other counties would receive large increases gave credibility to that argument. Some legislators wondered whether they would survive when the change was presented as such obvious redistribution.[27]

Finally, there were anxieties about rushing Florio's school finance proposals through the legislature.[28] Legislators and advisors tried to persuade Florio that the way to handle the issue was to drag it out and create pressure from the court so the legislature would have to enact a change.[29] The legislature had enacted an income tax in 1976, but only after a long avoidance of the issue and being virtually forced to do so by the court. In that case there had been enormous publicity about that pressure, and no legislators had lost reelection because of the vote. Some legislators wanted to repeat that scenario. Florio was not inclined to wait and hope for a public drama that would compel him to act. He felt he was elected to resolve problems, and "professionalism did not allow me to be enthusiastic about the theatre component [of politics]."[30]

Legislators also wanted there to be some Republican votes so the vote would be seen as bipartisan. The 1982 tax increases had been bipartisan, and no legislators lost in the next election because of their vote for a tax. They felt that bipartisan support would help in this situation. The difficulty was that Republicans were not interested in supporting Florio's package, and Florio did not offer to negotiate with them.

Republicans were unsparing in their criticism and would not vote for the proposals. They did not believe that the election had given Florio a mandate to raise taxes. Florio had won by a large margin because their candidate, Jim Courter, had run a poor campaign, and did not demonstrate he understood state issues well.[31]

There were also numerous criticisms and protests by groups opposed to the tax increases. The sales tax on paper products was the object of particularly strong protests. It came to be known as the "toilet paper tax," and opponents used this as a symbol of a regressive and unfair tax on a commodity that everyone had to have.

After heavy pressures from Florio, Democrats in both houses finally passed his tax and state aid packages. The process of assembling a party willing to go along with a major change in taxing and spending policies was not easy and was built through appealing to diverse motives. Some legislators went along because they thought this was the right thing to do.[32]

Others were committed liberals from low-income districts that would benefit from these programs. Some thought the governor had won with a large margin of victory and that his popularity would carry him. Others, worried because they were from marginal districts, believed the governor's argument about how this would help the party. Some, who probably should have been worried, had won previous elections with comfortable margins, and they thought they would be safe. Others viewed the governor as powerful and thought he might be able to use those powers to harm them. The 1947 constitution made the New Jersey governor one of the most powerful in the nation. The governor was the only elected official in the state and had control over all state patronage. He had a line-item veto and could affect budget provisions. For all these reasons, Florio was able to persuade a sufficient number of Democrats to vote for the proposals.[33]

The proposals were bundled together as one large package of taxes and state aid as a means to get the pain of voting for taxes over in one concentrated event. The legislative leaders wanted this because they felt it would be easier to impose party discipline and keep all Democrats unified if legislative enactments did not drag out and give opponents more time to mobilize.[34]

The vote on taxes was a straight party vote, with a few legislators deciding not to vote. While a "party vote" is often expressed as "just" party politics, the vote ultimately reflected the class division that existed between the parties and that was implicit in the issue. The parties had different bases, and the vote reflected those differences. The vote in lower-income districts was almost exactly the opposite of that in upper-income districts for votes in both houses. The vote in middle-class districts was divided and embodied the essence of the Democratic gamble. All Republicans in these districts voted against the increases, while all Democrats voted for them. The bet was that Democrats would survive.

The party had again taken a gamble, and had done so with considerable reluctance. The initiative for a major change in taxes had again come from the executive branch because the governor thought it was the right thing to do, because he thought the package would create a broad political coalition that would sustain the party in the future, and because he thought he would get credit for resolving a problem. The legislative party, while enacting his proposals, once again did not fit the image of a collection of believers with strong support for the policy change. They were inclined to agree with a liberal Democrat that this was a good policy, but there was enormous ambivalence. They now had to wait and see if Florio was "an emerging national figure blazing a path for a timid national Democratic Party or a quirky ideologue leading his troops to political disaster."[35]

Table 7.2. Votes for the Sales and Income Tax, 1990, by District Income Level
(All Republicans Voted No)

District Income	Assembly						Senate					
		Sales		Income				Sales		Income		
	Num	No	Yes	No	Yes		Num	No	Yes	No	Yes	
Low	25	7	18	7	18		13	3	10	3	10	
Medium	21	7	14	9	17		13	5	8	5	8	
High	24	17	7	20	6		13	10	3	10	3	
Total	80	31	39	36	41		40	18	21	18	21	

Counties are classified on the basis of the per capita income of district residents in 1987. The relevant data were taken from the *1990 New Jersey Legislative District Data Book*. Districts were divided into three income categories. Districts were first ranked from lowest to highest income, and then divided into thirds.

PUBLIC REACTION

The Democrats knew there would be opposition to the increased taxes. There had been protests in the state capitol while Florio's tax proposals were being considered. The expectation, however, was that an enactment of significant change in mid 1990 would give the party time to make the case for the benefits of the change by the November 1991 elections.[36]

The party ran into more problems and hostility than they expected, however. There was considerable lack of information and confusion about specifics of the whole package. Many people only knew that taxes were going up, and were not sure of what benefits would follow. Legislators reported walking their districts and encountering the perception that everyone was going to experience higher taxes and only the lowest-income districts would get additional aid.[37] The timing of tax increases and increases in state aid were also creating problems. The sales tax increase went into effect first to cover the deficit in the budget. The increases in income taxes and in state aid would not take effect until 1991, but there was a perception that taxes were going up immediately.

There was also strong opposition to the taxes and to the redistributive aspects of the state aid. Legislators reported receiving hundreds of calls of complaint.[38] Those living in affluent areas resented the taxes and the allocation of more state aid to low-income districts. "He is trying to send all the money to the poor areas. Half of the folks there are not interested in going to school anyway."[39] Districts that were scheduled to receive more state aid for schools were skeptical, because they saw no immediate increases.[40] Perhaps most disturbing to Democrats was that even those in poor areas were unhappy with the taxes. They expressed concern that government would get more money and they were skeptical that they would really benefit.[41]

The depth and persistence of the antitax sentiment surprised the governor and the legislators.[42] Florio's ratings plunged in the polls.[43] Groups organized and continued their protests. Republicans played a major role in criticizing the tax increases. The Republican Party leadership in the legislature made it a point to give Democrats a "daily pounding" about the issue.[44] They promised to make the tax issue the cornerstone of the 1991 campaigns.[45]

The 1990 elections provided indications that Democrats were in trouble. Senator Bill Bradley, a popular figure, was surprised by a very close race against a largely unknown local politician, Christie Todd Whitman. He had not taken a position on the tax increase. It was presumed that Bradley's low vote was because voters were expressing their general hostility to higher taxes at him as a Democrat. Many local Democratic candidates lost. The results encouraged opponents of the taxes, and they promised to work even harder against Democrats in 1991.[46]

LEGISLATIVE DEMOCRATS TRY TO SALVAGE THEIR SITUATION

Democrats began the 1991 session with a realization that they were in trouble. The economy continued to falter, and even after the increase in taxes the state appeared to be headed toward a deficit of approximately $600 million. Politicians recognized that it would be difficult to explain how they had increased taxes but still faced a deficit.

> [M]ost politicians here [in Trenton] now agree that Mr. Florio grossly misread the public mood in 1990 and overestimated his ability to reach the hearts and minds of average people. "We all know now that he misjudged the public reaction," said Senator Gabriel Ambrosio, a Democrat from [suburban] Bergen County and a longtime supporter of Florio. "Communications were bad. The message was too complex."[47]

Legislative Democrats responded to the negative image of themselves by proposing and passing a program to divert some of the intended school aid to property tax relief. The benefits were targeted specifically at middle-class suburban areas. They proposed diverting $450 million of the revenues. The funds would come from reducing the amount of state aid that would go to the poorest urban areas, and would create an image of legislative Democrats as more conservative than Florio.[48] The property tax rebates would be given to families making less than $65,000 a year.

CHANGING THE ROLE OF THE STATE: TAXES AND AID

The Democrats had enacted major changes in taxes and state aid. The impact on levels of taxes and aid were significant. Figure 7.2 presents the year-to-year changes in tax effort for New Jersey. The 1991 change represents one of the three major changes enacted since 1950. Democrats enacted all three major tax increases. The increased revenue allowed for a significant increase in state aid to education. Figure 7.3 presents the per capita state aid to local schools, in real dollars, over time. In 1992 there was a major increase in state aid to education. The Democrats had shifted the level of state taxes and of state support for local education. Their problem, however, was that the change had not been well received among the middle class, the very constituency Democrats were seeking to win over.

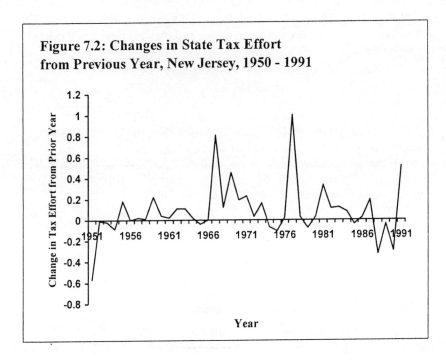

Figure 7.2: Changes in State Tax Effort
from Previous Year, New Jersey, 1950 - 1991

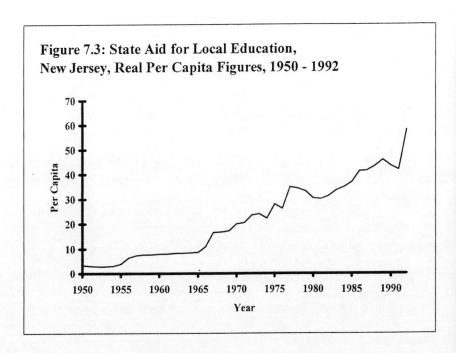

Figure 7.3: State Aid for Local Education,
New Jersey, Real Per Capita Figures, 1950 - 1992

THE 1991 ELECTIONS: THE WRATH OF THE ELECTORATE

The 1991 elections became a very partisan campaign. Republicans made Florio and the taxes he had proposed the major issue in the campaign.

> Our strategy is quite simply to focus voter attention on the disastrous record of the Democrats and of Jim Florio. What we are doing is educating voters for the first time that the incumbent Democrats are responsible, telling them that Jim Florio could not have done it alone. They did it together.[49]

The party blanketed the state with flyers that pictured Democratic candidates with Florio, and ran radio ads that continually linked incumbent Democratic legislators to him.[50]

Florio and Democrats in the legislature were not passive, but the lines of attack varied. Florio urged Democrats to fight back, and to defend what they had done.[51] He urged voters to make the election a referendum on President Bush.[52] Democratic legislators took other approaches to the election. Some Democrats decided, given the public reaction to their party, that it would be a good time to retire. In the senate, 7 of the 21 Democrats who voted for the income tax did not run for reelection. In the assembly, 11 of the 39 Democrats did not run for reelection. Others focused on portraying themselves as unassociated with Florio.[53]

The election decimated the Democrats.[54] The Republicans gained so many seats in both houses that they had a veto-proof majority. The strategy of Democrats had been to adopt a program that would appeal to the middle-class districts, and it was in those districts that Democrats experienced their biggest losses. Table 7.3 presents the changes in party success by the income of districts. In lower-income districts Democrats lost a few seats (from 18 to 14 in the assembly and from 11 to 9 in the senate). In middle-income districts their number fell from 17 to 5 in the assembly. In the senate it fell from 9 to 2. They also experienced some losses in upper-income districts, and particularly in the assembly. The significant drop, however, was in middle-income districts. The income tax vote did not hurt Democrats in low-income districts. In the assembly, 12 of the 14 Democrats in low-income districts who voted for the tax and ran won. In middle-income districts 11 Democrats ran who had voted for the income tax, and 7 of the 11 lost. In the senate 7 of the Democrats in low-income districts who voted for the tax ran and all won. In middle-income districts 5 Democrats ran after voting for the tax, and only 2 won.

Table 7.3. Changes in Democratic Legislative Seats by District Income Levels, 1989 to 1991

District Income	Assembly					Senate					Dem. % change	
	N	1989 Democrats		1991 Democrats		N	1989 Democrats		1991 Democrats		Ass.	Sen.
		N	%	N	%		N	%	N	%		
Low	26	18	72	14	54	13	11	85	9	69	−18	−17
Medium	26	17	65	5	19	13	9	77	2	15	−46	−62
High	28	8	29	2	7	14	3	21	2	14	−22	−7
Total	80	43	54	21	26	40	23	58	13	33		

Counties are classified on the basis of the per capita income of district residents in 1987. The relevant data were taken from the *1990 New Jersey Legislative District Data Book*. Districts were divided into three categories. Districts were first ranked from lowest to highest income, and then divided into thirds.

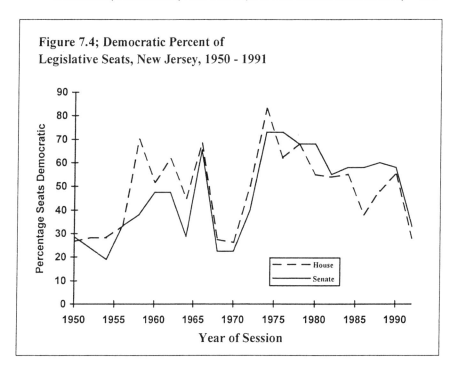

Figure 7.4; Democratic Percent of
Legislative Seats, New Jersey, 1950 - 1991

The election results also sharpened the role of race. After the 1989 elections Democrats had an electoral base built around districts with a high percentage of minorities and districts with moderate-income and minority percentages. The 1991 elections reduced Democrats to a base of heavily minority districts. Table 7.4 presents districts sorted by their income level, and the percentage of nonwhites.

In 1989 Democrats had some success in low- to moderate-income districts, though that success depended on the percent of nonwhites. In the assembly, in the set of districts with low to moderate income, and low to moderate percentages of nonwhites, Democrats won 11 of 26 districts in 1989. In the 10 districts with a low percent of nonwhites the party won 2 of 10. In the 16 districts with a moderate percent of nonwhites the party won 11 of 16. The 1991 elections left Democrats with none of these 26 seats. After 1991 the party did not have a single seat in low-income, largely white districts. Its success had not been great in 1989 in these districts, but it had no seats following the 1991 elections.

The same pattern prevailed in the senate. After the 1989 elections Democrats won 8 of the 13 districts with low to moderate income and minorities. In the 1991 elections the Democrats held 1 of 13. The party lost all of its base in low-income, primarily white districts in both houses.

Table 7.4. Democratic Success in 1989 and 1991
by Income and Racial Composition of Districts

	Assembly			Senate		
Percent Nonwhite	Income Low	Moderate	High	Income Low	Moderate	High
1989						
Low	0/1	2/8	2/16	0/1	3/4	0/8
Moderate	3/8	6/8	4/10	3/4	2/4	2/5
High	15/15	9/10	2/2	8/8	4/5	1/1
1991						
Low	0/2	0/8	0/16	0/1	0/4	1/8
Moderate	0/8	0/8	0/10	1/4	0/4	0/5
High	2/16	5/10	2/2	8/8	2/5	1/1

Election campaigns had not specifically focused on race. Republicans had focused all their attention on Florio's tax increases. Race did matter, however. The main focus in the school finance issue had been the twenty-eight urban districts that were heavily dominated by minorities. The underlying issue to many opponents of the taxes was that money was being wasted on "folks not interested in going to school anyway."[55] Florio has sensed considerable resentment to the direction of resources to minorities. In numerous meetings across the state, residents would angrily talk about "them" getting all the money, with a clear reference to minority groups.[56] The Democrats had fallen victim to the same problem troubling the national party. Many voters, whether accurately or not, perceived that the benefits were going to minorities and that white, working-class, and middle-income districts were not benefiting.[57] Democrats had sought to build a coalition around low- and middle-income groups to address problems of inequality of school finance. The goal was to benefit whites and nonwhites, but the coalition had not materialized.

For the third time Democrats had taken on a major change in taxes and for the second time they had lost badly in the next election. Republicans had gained a veto-proof majority, and faced a now unpopular governor. They again faced the issue of what they would do with power. Would they roll back the taxes and cut state aid, or would they redistribute existing state aid to help their constituents?

8

The Return of Republicans
and Tax Cuts

For the third time since 1950, republicans acquired power following a Democratic tax increase. When they acquired power in 1970 and 1982, they were faced with a soft economy and declining revenues, and Republicans had accepted past tax increases and even enacted new ones to maintain revenues. But 1991 was different in two ways. First, in 1992 the economy was recovering from a recession, rather than heading into one. Second, in 1991 Republicans had made opposition to taxes a primary theme of the campaign, and when they acquired power they felt an obligation to act on that theme.[1] The important question is why Republicans made cutting taxes a campaign issue, and why they acted on this theme.

Not only did Republicans act, but they acted swiftly. At a press conference the day after the election, the new Speaker of the assembly, "Chuck" Haytaian, pledged that the Republican-controlled legislature would cut taxes, and consider revising the Quality Education Act, which provided the formula for distributing state aid to schools.[2]

Republicans: From Promises to Specifics

Republicans were, however, cautious in the magnitude of the tax cuts proposed. While they had campaigned against the entire $2.8 billion Democratic tax increase, they promised only limited tax cuts and for future years instead of the current one. The Republicans were receiving reports that the existing budget might have a deficit (as could the next year's), because the economy was weak and revenue yields were lower than expected, and the Republicans were careful in how they presented the sequence of their proposals.[3] They began their legislative program with tax cuts rather than details of what programs might have to be cut. They realized that it

181

would difficult for Democrats to oppose tax cuts, and, as promised, by April of 1992 they enacted a cut of one cent in the sales tax. The cut would apply to the 1992–93 budget year.[4] They offered no specifics about what program cuts, if any, would be necessary because of the lost tax revenues.

Democrats had to decide what role they would play as the opposition. They had enacted the tax increases to respond to a shortfall in revenues and to try to resolve the issue of inequities in school finance. They had, however, suffered a resounding political defeat for their actions, so they had to decide what to fight for. Democratic legislators followed two paths of action. On one hand, legislators found it politically difficult to oppose the tax cut, and almost all voted with Republicans to cut the sales tax. On the other hand, they used the tax cut vote opportunity to continually raise the issue of who would bear the costs of cuts.

The Republicans suggested, early in the session, that they would alter the formula for distributing school aid. They indicated they wanted to lower and cap the amount going to the thirty "special needs" districts and distribute more to smaller, suburban districts.[5] They also suggested they might cut back on the property tax rebate program. Both programs—school aid and property tax rebates—had clear beneficiaries. The school aid program of 1991 had allocated large increases to low-income school districts (Camden would have received a 26 percent increase), and caps in increases would hurt largely Democratic constituents. The property tax rebate program had a sliding scale of benefits, with higher benefits going to those with lower incomes. Since retired senior citizens generally have lower incomes and their own homes, many of the benefits went to them. The program also provided benefits to renters, based on their income, even though they did not directly pay property taxes.

Republicans suggested the property tax program had become a "vote-buying scheme" and had gotten "out of control." Republicans saw this as a program "redistributing tax dollars to people who have never paid a dime in property taxes."[6] They also noted that Democrats had increased funding for the program in 1991, and that despite rebate checks being mailed out just before the election, the program had not done Democrats any good in the 1991 elections.[7]

The reduction in the sales tax rate was expected to cut $608 million from the state budget. Democrats, while reluctant to oppose a tax cut, approached the situation by calling attention to how reduced revenues might harm specific programs. Their focus was on programs generally beneficial to the nonaffluent. Both legislative leaders and Governor Florio continually expressed concern about the impact of a tax cut on property tax rebates, school aid, aid to mass transit, and tuition charges at the state university.[8] The Democrats devoted particular attention to the effects of cuts on the elderly.[9] The elderly vote, and they are a group it is difficult for Republicans to oppose, unlike low-income constituents. Democrats attended all legislative sessions with "Who Gets Cut?" buttons.[10] Democrats did not vote against the tax cut, but they did act as advocates of programs beneficial to their constituents, and they made an issue of the consequences of a tax cut.

Governor Florio chose to veto the repeal of the sales tax. He returned the bill to the legislature, and insisted that Republicans provide a balanced budget and indicate where the cuts would be. Perhaps most important, Florio staked out his concern for a clear set of interests. He insisted that cuts not hurt school aid, property tax rebates, aid to mass transit and municipalities, college tuition support, the Jersey Shore, or programs for children, the blind, and the physically disabled.[11] He said the question was whether state government would maintain its role supporting programs that help those with clear needs. He made it clear that his priority was maintaining programs beneficial to the less affluent.

Some Republicans were nervous about the override issue. Polls showed the public divided in support for the tax cut, and 60 percent did not want the cut if it meant cuts in services.[12] Nonetheless, the party overrode the veto in both houses.[13]

Republicans then announced their program cuts. They proposed cutting Florio's submitted budget for 1992–93 by $1 billion. The major cuts came from cutting the property tax rebate in half, reducing aid to transportation, and cutting Social Services. Republicans again characterized the property tax rebate program as "an income redistribution program." They drastically reduced the rebates renters could collect.[14] The poor were expected to bear a significant portion of the costs of the cuts. State aid to municipalities for general assistance, the state's public welfare program that was not assisted by federal money, was to be cut by $18 million. They reduced funding for affirmative action and equal opportunity programs in each department, and consolidated them into the State Personnel Department.[15] Perhaps most symbolic was the elimination of the cabinet-level Office of Public Advocate, an office devoted to filing public interest lawsuits, and particularly those helping the poor. The Republicans only bow to political reality was to preserve the property tax rebate for those over sixty-five, while cutting it back for everyone else.[16] The elderly vote more than others, and they are more likely to vote in elections in odd years, when no national offices are involved, when New Jersey state elections are held. It was difficult to portray the elderly as undeserving.

Florio again accused Republicans of trying to "punish the poor, the sick, the elderly, the state's public schools, and college students."[17] Democrats in the legislature echoed those accusations, and voted against the budget, arguing that the sales tax cut amounted to only $77 per person. Republicans responded that it was a "taxpayer's budget."[18] Florio vetoed the budget and Republicans accused Florio of trying to scare people with threats of chaos.[19] After some delay because one Republican senator (necessary for the override) held out for smaller cuts in the property tax rebate program, both houses overrode Florio's veto.[20]

The Republicans, who had swept into office with an antitax campaign, fulfilled part of their promise. They repealed part of Florio's tax package, and reduced his proposed budget by $1.1 billion. The choice of cuts was important. Florio had increased the sales tax and had increased the income tax on the affluent. Republicans decided not to repeal the income tax increase, probably because Democrats would have been able to criticize them for tax breaks for the affluent. When it came to program cuts, however, the Republicans made their biggest cuts in state programs that affected Democratic constituents. Florio had significantly increased property tax rebates and state aid to schools. Republicans cut back rebates and reduced the large increases to urban school districts. Democrats had attempted to label the Republicans as unfair, but it did not deter the Republicans.

The debate, while it may seem to have had no impact, was part of the process of parties seeking to represent their constituents, to create their image, and to attach a negative image to the opposing party. Democrats talked about who would get hurt by cuts, and accused Republicans of hurting those groups. Republicans continually emphasized their commitment to lower taxes and reducing the size of state government. They were less concerned with redistribution issues—who would be helped and who would be hurt. The parties were staking out positions about state obligations, which inevitably involved questions of who would benefit.

The Republicans did not stop with the budget in their approach to fiscal problems. Florio had increased taxes and state aid as a way to resolve the controversy about inequality in the financing of schools. The Republicans differed considerably in their approach. Not only did they cut back on funds for schools, but they initiated discussions about a constitutional amendment to resolve the school finance problem by removing the "thorough and efficient" phrase from the constitution.[21] Democrats attacked the proposal as one that would "create two separate New Jerseys divided along geographic and economic lines."[22] There were also criticisms from civil rights groups, churches, and civil liberties groups, and shortly thereafter Republicans announced they were dropping the constitutional issue from consideration.[23] They indicated they would begin studying plans to revise the formula for distributing school aid sometime in the future, and suggested that money spent on urban areas was "wasted" and that those areas should receive less.[24]

Republicans and Democrats made their sympathies clear. Republicans were concerned with lowering taxes and less concerned about inequality of school finance. They thought that the problem with urban schools was not a lack of money, but that much of the available money was mismanaged. Money was not the solution. Democrats were more concerned with the state resolving the problem of inequality of school fiscal resources, and they were willing to accept higher state taxes to give the state the resources to respond. The Republicans rejected those arguments and used their new power in 1992 to repeal some of the programs that increased the role of the state.

They did not, however, repeal the entire Florio package. That may be because the magnitude of cuts necessary would have been too great, and the criticisms of Democrats might have started to have some impact on the party's image. The Republicans chose to fulfill their promises, but to be somewhat cautious in doing so.

The 1992 battle over taxes and the state budget was apparently all the victory the Republicans wanted to claim for that election cycle. In January 1993, with the economy improving and state revenues up, Florio submitted a budget that proposed an increase of $.9 billion, from $14.7 billion to $15.6 billion.[25] The Republicans expressed no interest in further cuts, and passed the budget with minor changes. The Republicans had staked out their positions in 1992 with tax and program cuts. Florio had staked out his position with a veto of the tax cut. The Republicans now were willing to wait to see what voters thought of Jim Florio, the Republicans' repeal of the sales tax increase, and their cuts in state programs.

The only agreement between the two sides was that in the short term they would avoid the issue of school finance and equality of school spending. The issue was once again in the courts and neither side wanted to discuss the issue until necessary. Following the reallocation of state aid to property tax rebates in 1991, the state's poorest schools had filed suit that the state funding was insufficient to provide the resources necessary for an adequate education.[26] A lower court subsequently decided in 1993 that the 1990 state aid package had not done enough for the poorer schools, but that decision then went to the state supreme court for review.[27] Everyone knew that this decision would take a while, so the issue could be avoided for some time.

THE 1993 CAMPAIGN

Jim Florio had endured low job approval poll ratings through much of 1991 and 1992. His situation in 1993 proved to be volatile, and a remarkable example of the dynamics of public opinion during a campaign. A January poll had him losing to three possible Republican candidates, even though none were known by more than 38 percent of the public.[28] Then polls in February indicated that Florio's approval rating had risen, with 36 percent saying he was doing an excellent-to-good job, and 41 percent saying he was doing a fair job.[29] For the first time since 1990 more people thought the state was headed in the right direction than thought it was headed in the wrong direction.[30] Yet 51 percent said he should not run for reelection.[31]

Christie Todd Whitman won the Republican primary in June. She had sprung to prominence in 1990 when, as an unknown freeholder (an elected county official) she had challenged and almost beaten the popular U.S. senator Bill Bradley. Much of the vote for her was presumed to be a product of general hostility toward Democrats because of the 1990 tax increases. Nonetheless, she was articulate, and had a reputation as a moderate Republican, which carried her to a seven-point victory in the primary.[32]

Meanwhile Jim Florio was busy trying to reshape his image. He stressed his moderate side and emphasized his fight to ban semiautomatic weapons, his crime-fighting measures, and his efforts to reform welfare. He presented himself as a responsible person who tried to do the right thing. He also attacked Whitman as a rich woman out of touch with the average person. When the Whitmans released their tax returns, the returns indicated they had made more than one million dollars in income every year.[33] She and her husband owned a large farm, which received tax deductions as a working farm, and Florio continually referred to her "estate" and tried to portray her as a wealthy person getting undeserved tax breaks. She also had to admit that she had hired an illegal alien as a nanny during the 1980s, and owed some back social security taxes on the wages paid to the woman.[34]

She, in turn, accused him of waging class warfare, and brought reporters to her farm to convince them it was a working farm.[35] She also stressed during the campaign that she was pro-choice on abortion, and that she supported affirmative action. It was difficult to portray her as a simple conservative. She presented herself as a social moderate and a fiscal conservative.

Nonetheless, Florio's attacks had an impact, and by mid June Florio had a lead in some polls.[36] Polls in late September indicated that more people thought he had "the honesty and integrity for the job," "understood the needs and problems of people like you," and "had offered specific proposals about how to solve New Jersey's problems." The only issue he lost was "If the candidate is elected, what do you expect to happen to your taxes?" Forty-seven percent said taxes would go up if Florio won, and only 36 percent said they would go up if Whitman won.[37]

Florio was also making gains on the evaluation of his 1991 tax proposal. By late September, a poll indicated that 49 percent thought he had done the right thing in raising taxes, and 42 percent thought he had done the wrong thing. That same poll put the race at 50 percent for Florio and 31 percent for Whitman.[38] What was once thought to be a sure loss for Florio had turned around.

Whitman then uncorked a major surprise. She promised that, if elected, she would cut income taxes by 30 percent over three years. There had been hints for a month that she would propose a tax cut, but the magnitude of the cut surprised everyone, including many members of her own party.[39] The proposal was shrewdly packaged to ward off attacks that a Republican opponent was favoring the wealthy. As shown in table 8.1 and figure 8.1, New Jersey had a mildly progressive income tax structure when Florio began. His 1990 changes had eliminated all taxes on the lowest income bracket, kept the individual rates from $3,000 to $35,000 the same, and steeply increased rates on those at $35,000 and above. A mildly progressive tax structure was converted to a more progressive structure. Whitman accepted that fundamental shift to a more progressive tax structure, and went one step further by eliminating all taxes for the second-from-the-bottom income bracket. This would allow her to claim she was helping low-income individuals more than Florio had. She could also claim she supported higher taxes on higher-income individuals. The largest percentage cuts went to those at the bottom, even though the actual dollar amounts were small. The smallest percentage cuts went to those at the upper levels. Her proposal largely accepted the more progressive tax structure, but shifted all the rates down for every income bracket.

Whitman claimed that the tax cut would reduce taxes by $1.053 billion by the time it was implemented. The claim was that at the end of three years, by 1997, the annual flow of tax revenues to the state would be $1.053 billion less than it was currently. She claimed the revenue loss could be handled by eliminating inefficiencies and unnecessary overhead costs, establishing a hiring freeze, and limiting growth of the budget to 3 percent a year.[40]

The announcement certainly came as a surprise to the Florio campaign. His campaign advisors were ecstatic and sure no one would believe a proposal with cuts of this size.[41] Florio's own initial reaction was that no one would take it as a credible proposal.[42] He criticized it as "voodoo redo," drawing on George Bush's critique of proposed tax cuts by Ronald Reagan during the 1980 presidential campaign. He was also quick to point out the distributional consequences of her proposals. "Under her proposal 5.5 percent of the taxpayers get 40 percent of the benefit. For that 5.5 percent—the richest 5.5 percent—the average tax break is $4,534. For the [remaining] 94.5 percent the average tax break is $185."[43] Florio characterized her plan as "insulting the intelligence of New Jerseyans. Three years in the making.

Table 8.1. Tax Rates on Single Individuals in New Jersey
by Income Bracket, from 1989 through Whitman's Proposals

Income brackets	1989 rates	Florio plan rates	Whitman porposal	% cut in rates
$0–3,000	2.0	0.0	0.0	n.a.
3,000–7,500	2.0	2.0	0.0	100
7,500–20,000	2.0	2.0	1.4	30
20,000–35,000	2.5	2.5	1.75	30
35,000–40,000	2.5	5.0	3.5	30
40,000–50,000	2.5	6.5	4.875	25
50,000–75,000	3.5	6.5	4.875	25
75,000+	3.5	7.0	5.6	20

Source: All information for table 8.1 and figure 8.1 is from "How Whitman Sees the Bottom Line," *New York Times,* 22 September 1993, p. B6.

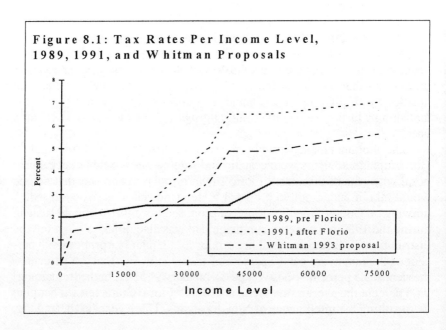

Figure 8.1: Tax Rates Per Income Level, 1989, 1991, and Whitman Proposals

One page of so-called spending cuts, with no specifics. And one page of very specific tax cuts, mostly for the rich. Two pages, that's it."[44] The press were skeptical that the numbers added up. They presented the proposal critically, presenting interviews with "experts" who questioned whether it was doable.[45]

The proposal presented a contrast between the candidates for the rest of the campaign. Florio and Democrats said that in 1990 they had acted responsibly and in the public interest and deserved voter support. They claimed the Whitman proposals lacked credibility among the public. The Whitman camp said "We've made the contrast now. People kept saying she isn't giving the voters a reason to vote for her. Now she has."[46] When questioned about whether the proposal was a gamble, one advisor responded: "When you're trying to win a close game, throw deep."[47] Legislative Republicans added to the contrast. They claimed credit for cutting the sales tax and lowering spending. In a familiar refrain heard across the country, the Speaker of the assembly, Chuck Haytaian, argued the choice was between "tax-and-spend" Democrats, and "the party which will cut your taxes."[48] Whitman's theme was to continue to remind voters of Florio's tax increases and contrast it with her tax-cut promise.[49]

THE 1993 ELECTION

The reactions to the contrasting campaign positions provided an important lesson in the dynamics of campaigns. Her proposal initially seemed to have no impact. A poll conducted at the same time Whitman released her proposal showed Florio ahead by 51 to 30 percent. The most discouraging result to Whitman was that only 10 percent thought she would cut their taxes, while 30 percent thought she would raise taxes.[50] Florio's ads used newspaper editorials critical of her plan to attack her proposals.[51] Polls in mid October showed Florio with a comfortable lead.[52] But polls in late October showed the race tighter.[53]

Ultimately, Whitman won by a narrow margin of thirty thousand votes. The legacy of the 1990 tax increases and the appeal of Whitman's cuts proved too much for Florio. Whitman managed over the last six weeks of the campaign to create a contrast and to convince enough voters that she had a credible proposal. The exit poll, parts of which are shown in table 8.2, reveals several important aspects of her electoral coalition, the decisions people made, and the limits of some campaign appeals. Florio had tried to make class an indirect issue by portraying her as wealthy and out of touch. He also tried to make class a direct issue by arguing that the bulk of her tax cut, in dollars, would go to the affluent. The appeal did not work.

Whitman was able to win 46 percent of those with only a high school education. She also got 49 percent or above in every other education category, preventing a class division of the electorate.

Table 8.2. Exit Poll Results, 1993 New Jersey
Gubernatorial Election

	% of electorate (read down)	1993 vote (read % across)	
		Florio	Whitman
Education			
high school or less	32	54	46
some college	25	45	55
college graduate	24	44	56
postgraduate	18	51	49
Percent agreeing raising taxes in 1990 was:			
right thing	41	93	7
wrong thing	55	17	83
Percent saying cutting taxes by over 30 percent over the next three years without cutting services is:			
possible	47	25	75
not possible	51	73	27
Decided for sure whom to vote for::			
in last two weeks	30	42	58
after Labor Day	10	53	47
before Labor Day	59	53	47

Source: "A Portrait of New Jersey Voters," *New York Times,* 4 November 1993, p. B9.

It is not possible to know why Florio was not able to convince the less affluent that they would lose with Whitman's proposals. Florio sought to portray Whitman as rich to convince less-affluent voters that they were unlikely to do well with her approach. Whitman's best move during the campaign may not have been the tax cut, but the way the proposed tax cuts would be distributed by income levels. Her proposal gave the largest percentage cuts to lower-income groups, which makes it much less clear that the affluent are the beneficiaries of the cuts. The affluent would get more in net dollars, but not in percentage terms. The newspapers regularly presented her proposals in terms of the percentage cut by income level, so they were probably seen in those terms.[54] For whatever reasons, Florio's attempts to make class-impacts an issue failed during the campaign.

The most important voter divisions were around the past tax increase and her tax proposal. Florio lost the retrospective judgment battle and that cost him votes. Fifty-five percent of those voting thought the 1990 tax increase was the wrong thing, and only 41 percent thought it was the right thing. Of those who thought it was the wrong thing, 83 percent voted for Whitman. Florio got a very strong vote (93%) out of those who supported the tax increase, but only 41 percent supported his decision. Florio also lost by a close margin the battle over whether her tax-cut proposal was feasible. Fifty-one percent thought it was possible to cut taxes by over 30 percent without cutting services, while 47 percent thought it was not possible. These opinions translated into clear differences in vote choices, with 75 percent of those saying such a cut was possible voting for Whitman. Finally, much of the last few weeks of the campaign was a battle to shape opinions about taxes, and of the 30 percent who decided in the last two weeks, 58 percent went for Whitman. Tax opinions were crucial to the 1993 elections, and Whitman won the battle.

The obligations of state government, while only sporadically a specific focus in the campaign, had been a part of the debate. Implicit in Florio's arguments was the claim that the state was not wasting money and needed the revenues raised in 1990. Whitman was able to win with an argument that there were savings that could be found, and with an argument that state monies were not the answer to all the problems faced by government. The next question was whether she would fulfill her promise.

The legislative elections also indicated support for Republicans. As shown in figure 8.2, the 1991 sweep by Republicans was largely preserved. The party in 1993 held on to almost all the seats they had won in the previous election. Democrats picked up a few seats in each house, with the gains coming in lower- and middle-income areas.

Table 8.3. Changes in Democratic Legislative Seats by District Income Levels, 1991 to 1993

District Income	Assembly					Senate					Dem. % change	
	N	1991 Democrats		1993 Democrats		N	1991 Democrats		1993 Democrats		Ass.	Sen.
		N	%	N	%		N	%	N	%		
Low	26	14	54	18	69	13	9	69	9	69	15	0
Medium	26	5	19	10	38	13	2	15	5	38	19	23
High	28	5	7	2	7	14	2	14	1	7	0	−7
Total	80	21	26	30	38	40	13	33	15	38		

Counties are classified on the basis of the per capita income of district residents in 1987. The relevant data were taken from the *1992 New Jersey Legislative District Data Book*, published by the Bureau of Government Research, Rutgers University. Districts were divided into three income categories with one-third in the lower category, one-third in the middle, and one-third in the upper category.

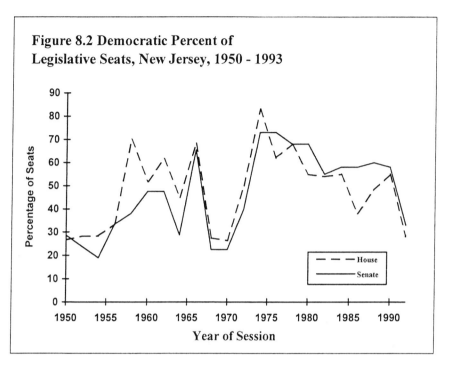

**Figure 8.2 Democratic Percent of
Legislative Seats, New Jersey, 1950 - 1993**

HITMAN'S AGENDA

Whitman wasted no time in indicating whether she would fulfill her campaign promise about taxes. At a press conference shortly after the election, she said:

> As I said over and over again, what I talked about in economic policy was not a campaign promise, it wasn't a political promise, it was a promise for governance. And that's how we're going to do the business of New Jersey.

She confirmed that position by publicly turning to the Speaker of the Assembly and asking him, "Are we going to do this?" He said yes.[55] She then surprised even her own supporters by announcing at her inauguration that she wanted to have the first phase of the tax cut take effect during the current fiscal year.[56] She proposed an immediate across-the-board cut of 5 percent in the state income tax rate, to be retroactive to January 1, 1993.[57]

Her plan was not received with enthusiasm by everyone. Some state fiscal experts pointed out that there was expected to be a deficit in the state budget beginning on July 1, 1994.[58] School boards, teachers' unions, mayors, and county executives expressed concern about state aid. They were worried that a declining state effort would eventually lead to higher local property taxes.[59] The New Jersey Education Association, representing teachers, said they would fight any attempts to cut costs by reducing aid to education.

Whitman responded with an argument rarely heard from state officials about state obligations. She said that increases in local taxes would not be her fault.

> I can't guarantee anything over areas over which I have no control. What I want to see stay the same is the current level of municipal aid, but if the municipalities are going to go into their own negotiations, and not institute discipline on themselves, or counties are going to do the same thing and continue to give contracts that are far above the rate of inflation or what they can anticipate in seeing new revenues from the state, then they are going to have a problem. There's going to have to be a level of discipline imposed at all levels of government.[60]

Whitman did not accept the premise that the state should continually provide more resources to local governments. More importantly, she was willing to explicitly place some of the blame for local property tax increases on local governments. She was trying to lower the expectations of what state government could do and shift the focus to the behavior of local government officials.

She was also willing to take on a group with enormous interest in not rolling back the state commitment: the teachers' union, or NJEA. This group had opposed Florio because he used some of the school aid for property tax rebates. They were well financed and politically active.[61] They knew her income tax cuts would mean less state aid for schools. She also announced a plan to require recertification of all teachers, which angered the NJEA and produced threats of retaliation.[62] She appointed a commission to study school finance, which ended up focusing on teachers' pay. There was growing public concern about the pay of teachers, and the commission gave direct expression to that concern.[63] The chair of the commission was quoted as saying:

> We are paying teachers $65,000 a year in the north part of the state. You get tenure, you get great benefits and great working conditions. Maybe $65,000 for 180 days work is adequate now.[64]

Whitman and members of her administration regularly pointed out that the New Jersey teachers were among the highest paid in the nation, and suggested that local school boards had to take a tougher approach in negotiating contracts. They also called attention to local superintendents making as much as the governor.[65] When almost one-half of all school budgets were rejected by local voters in April of that year, she and her aides said the results were proof that taxpayers were echoing Whitman's antitax message.[66] She was trying to alter the expectation that the answer to local budget problems was always more state aid. Her answer was to suggest that perhaps some public employees were paid too much, and that local officials were the culprit.

The legislative Republicans were uneasy about her plan to cut taxes right away. Some worried that significant cuts would produce higher property taxes and make the public angry with Republicans for going too far the other way. They were worried about repeating the lesson of 1990, when Democratic legislators blindly followed the governor too far, and were rejected at the polls.[67] The problem of deciphering elections and discerning mandates was still there, but now the Republicans were the party that had to decide the meaning of an election. The party now held all branches of the state government, but the victory for Whitman had been by a very slim margin, and much of the vote had been driven by a reaction to Florio. They had also lost a few legislative seats. The party did not know if the election was enough basis for repealing decades of laws promoting the growth of state government.

The legislative party expressed its unease by agreeing to her tax cut, but with an eye on minimizing immediate political damage. They accepted the idea of a 5 percent across-the-board cut in income tax rates, but they also wanted to eliminate all taxes on those making less than $7,500. This change would help ward off the claim that Republican tax cuts favored the wealthy. They also proposed eliminating a surcharge on the corporate income tax six months earlier than expected. They proposed to pay for the cut not by reducing state aid, but removing $300 million from various surplus accounts.[68] Whitman accepted the proposal as within the confines of her general idea, and this legislation became the package that passed both houses and was signed by Whitman.[69]

While Democrats criticized the proposal, they struggled to find an effective line of attack. The retiring state party chairman continually tried to focus attention on the argument that a state income tax cut would increase local property taxes. He argued that the tax break per person or family was small, but the lost revenue would have significant consequences for local property taxes. He argued that Florio had improved the situation. Under Governor Tom Kean, local property taxes had increased by an average rate of 12 percent a year, but under Florio, with increased state aid, the increases had averaged only 3 percent a year. But even he recognized that this was little known or appreciated.[70]

The Democrats faced two crucial problems. The proposal to remove all those making less than $7,500 from the rolls made it harder to exploit the fairness issue. While the argument could have been made that larger dollar reductions would go to upper income groups, Democrats did not press it. They either did not think of this counter or they did not think it would work. Their most serious problem was that the argument about the impact of state tax cuts on local property taxes was a hypothetical one. They had no evidence, and would not for quite a while.

Furthermore, Whitman argued that even if there were future increases, they would be a result of local decisions and not due to her actions. Her argument was that increases should not be seen as automatic and inevitable. They could be contained by local officials, but only if she could just get them to readjust their expectations of state bailouts. She also was arguing that many of the local public employees, particularly teachers, were already making enough. The difficulty that opponents faced was that it was impossible to marshal evidence about potential increases in local property taxes, and it was difficult to argue that local officials should not be accountable. In addition, while many argued that schools should be well funded, the stories about high administrative costs and teacher salaries made it more difficult to argue that the schools needed more money.

Whitman persevered in her tax-cut proposals. In her March 15, 1994, budget message she proposed moving immediately to the next phase of the tax cut. The 10 percent cut would be for families making less than $80,000 and individuals making less than $40,000. Those making more would get smaller percentage cuts.[71] She argued that the budget could be cut. She said that the state workers pension fund was overfunded and did not need as much money as was being put into it to meet future obligations. Her proposal was crucial, because it meant a significant reduction in state contributions to the pension system, which would free up revenues to fund state programs and state aid to local governments. She could maintain existing programs without cuts. She also argued that the state should stop a practice of subsidizing the social security payments of public employees. A provision of the federal social security law from the 1950s had reduced the benefit payments to state public employees, and the state had enacted a 2 percent subsidy in 1959. Federal law was changed in 1966, restoring the benefit, and New Jersey in 1994 was the last state still providing the subsidy.[72]

Public employee groups and the NJEA opposed it,[73] but their complaints had little impact. They were a group not popular with the general public to begin with, and the changes were not presented as cuts, but as appropriate adjustments that were justified. The change in the contribution to the pension fund was the most difficult to counter, because it involved a dispute over actuarial calculations, which most people did not understand at all.

Republican legislators still worried about endorsing the cut, because polls showed that voters did not want a cut if it meant property tax increases. Democrats criticized the cuts saying they did not amount to much per family and would lead to property tax increases. The media, however, focused on tax cuts, and there was little evidence of surging property taxes to present.[74] The legislature accepted her proposal and enacted the tax cut.[75]

In January 1995 she again returned with a proposed tax cut. She wanted to complete the final 15 percent in the 1995–96 fiscal year. Once again, she emphasized that the full tax cut would not go the affluent. The 15 percent cut would go only to those individuals making less than $40,000 and those families making less than $80,000.[76] She also repeated her argument that the state should not be held responsible for local taxing and spending decisions.

> Some argue that these tax cuts will force up property taxes. That simply isn't so. The state does not collect a penny of property tax. The state does not spend a penny of property tax. Those functions are the exclusive domain of the counties, the municipalities and the school districts. Property taxes reflect local spending decisions.[77]

Her budget again kept state aid at existing levels, which meant that increases in local expenditure would have to be paid for with local property tax increases. As before, her critics argued that her tax cuts were hurting them, but they seemed to accept that they had lost the battle to shape public opinion.[78] Even party leaders in the legislature conceded that public employees' salaries were rising too fast.[79] The legislature, after some tinkering, accepted her proposed 15 percent cut in the income tax. Whitman had fulfilled her promise to cut taxes by 30 percent.

Whitman had succeeded in enacting a significant reduction in tax levels. But what she accepted is also important to note. When Jim Florio proposed revising the state income tax rates, he turned an essentially flat tax structure into a progressive one. He imposed much higher taxes on the affluent, which generated much more state revenue. Whitman proposed a tax cut that essentially accepted his change. Her final revisions not only accepted a progressive tax structure, but made the system even more progressive. She gave smaller tax cuts to those with higher incomes, and removed those at the very bottom from the tax rolls. The changes are presented in table 8.4, and figure 8.3.

This acceptance of a progressive tax system got little attention, though the net changes by income levels did appear regularly in newspaper stories. The important matter is that Whitman did not cut taxes on the affluent as much as she proposed in 1993, which made it harder for Democrats to attack her for "favoring the rich." As mentioned, during the 1993 campaign she had been accused of being rich and out of touch. It was important that

Table 8.4. Tax Rates on Single Individuals in New Jersey
by Income Brackets, from 1989 through 1996

	Florio plan rates	rates	Whiteman proposal & cut in in rates	Final 1996 rates	% cut in rates
Income brackets					
$0–3,000	0.0	0.0	n.a.	0.0	n.a.
3,000–20,000	2.0	1.4	30	1.4	30
20,000–35,000	2.5	1.75	30	1.75	30
35,000–40,000	5.0	3.5	30	3.5	30
40,000–75,000	6.5	4.875	25	5.525	30
75,000+	7.0	5.6	20	6.37	9

Source: New Jersey Statutes Annotated, 54A:2-1, 1996 pocket

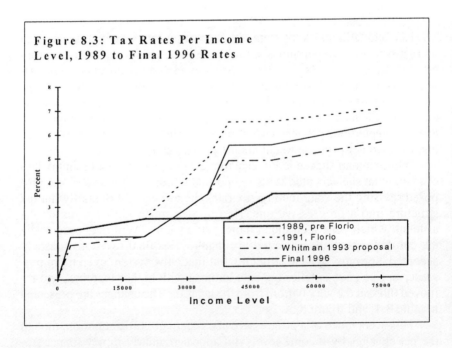

Figure 8.3: Tax Rates Per Income Level, 1989 to Final 1996 Rates

she render that accusation less plausible. The net changes in the tax system from 1991 to 1996 resulted in a more progressive tax system. The affluent got cuts worth more dollars, but their percentage cuts were smaller.

The legislative Republicans were also concerned about avoiding the accusation of being too sympathetic to the affluent. When asked how the party could avoid the Democratic criticism of being uncaring about the less fortunate while making these tax cuts, Chuck Haytaian, the Speaker of the assembly, answered:

> The answer is simple. We have cut taxes. We have cut the income tax to help middle-income families, and not the wealthy. We cut out the income tax for those [families] making less than $7,500. We did it deliberately. That kills the Democratic attack on Republicans. We cut the sales tax, which is the most onerous tax people face. The criticism of insensitivity should fall on deaf ears.[80]

REPUBLICANS AND TAX CUTS: NEWFOUND BELIEFS OR THE ENDURING ROLE OF CONDITIONS?

In prior years Republicans had control (1970) or significant power (1982), and had raised taxes. The legislative Republicans and Whitman followed a very different path in 1992 and 1994. They cut taxes. Did she embody a new resolve in the Republican Party to pursue a fiscally conservative route when in power? Do these choices reflect some newfound political will by Republicans to cut government?

In part, yes. Whitman did take on public interest groups—teachers, public employees, and municipal officials—who did not want aid cut back. As will be reviewed shortly, she did restrain the growth of the state budget. Growth ceased in the total budget and in state aid. She also articulated the belief that people should expect less out of state government. There was clearly less inclination to have the state play an increased role. But she was also successful because she did not challenge the role of the state too much. She did not propose cuts in state aid, but no growth in state aid. Her approach was to cut taxes, reduce pension obligations, and essentially maintain current spending levels.[81]

She was able to cut taxes and maintain aid because of an enduring condition that affects the decision-making of any governor: the economy. It grew steadily during her term of office. The country gradually emerged from a severe recession across the time, and experienced sustained and modest growth. State tax revenues increased steadily and significantly while she was cutting taxes. Previous Republican governors did not have the benefit of increasing revenues. Jim Florio had the opposite: declining revenues. She was able to make the final 15 percent tax cut in large part because the economy was growing.[82] She also benefited enormously from the decision to cut contributions to the state retirement system. In the welter surrounding her bold proposal to cut the income tax, that issue received little attention in the press. The reduction of required expenditures in that area meant she could at least maintain state aid to schools and municipalities.

Whitman's acceptance of the progressive tax structure also helped. A progressive tax structure, with smaller percentage cuts for the affluent, will continue to bring in substantial revenues. Those with lower incomes may experience a 30 percent cut in the taxes they pay, but they pay much less than the affluent to begin with, and cutting their taxes more means the overall cut in revenues is considerably less than 30 percent. These matters are crucial. Whitman followed a bold path, but it was made considerably easier by growing state tax revenues from an income tax system that was still very progressive.

Part V:
Republican Control and Choices

9

Grappling with State Responsibilities

THE 1991 ELECTION PUT REPUBLICANS IN CONTROL OF THE LEGISLATURE, AND they used that power to roll back the sales tax increase of 1990. The gubernatorial victory of Whitman in 1993 gave Republicans complete control of state government. Whitman did not hesitate to use that power to lower the state income tax. As noted earlier, however, while Republicans cut taxes, they did not choose to enact any significant reduction in state spending. The issue of what role state government would play relative to its local governments had not been resolved. The issue of what the state would do to address inequalities in finances among schools was still there. In addition, the gubernatorial campaign produced additional issues that involved state responsibilities.

The most immediate issue in 1994 was the school aid controversy. It reemerged on the agenda and presented Whitman and her legislative Republicans with a challenge of how to deal with inequality. Ironically, the issue was back on the agenda because of actions taken by Democrats. Following the tax increases enacted in 1990 by the Democrats, and the negative electoral reaction toward Democrats in the November 1990 elections, the Democratic leaders of the legislature attempted to reduce hostility to the tax increases. As previously mentioned, they took funds originally designated for state aid to schools, and reallocated $354 million to property tax rebates. Rather than send state aid directly to schools, and hope that local property tax increases would be restrained, the legislature specified that the funds should be used specifically to fund reductions in local property taxes. Property owners would receive a rebate (a check) from the state for some portion of local property taxes paid, so the benefit would go directly to individuals. The crucial matter was that the revenues for this came from diverting funds going largely to lower-income districts.

The reallocation prompted the Education Law Center to return to court to argue that there were not sufficient revenues going directly to schools. Their specific complaint was that the new formula widened the disparities between wealthier and poorer school districts rather than closed the gap.[1] In September 1993, a lower court ruled that the financing package adopted in 1991 did not go far enough in closing the gap between rich and poor districts. The case was then sent to the state supreme court for review.[2]

While that ruling was awaited, two state commissions tried to resolve the matter of distributing state aid to the schools. One, appointed amidst the 1993 campaign, was unable to reach agreement on a formula.[3] Another, appointed by Whitman after her election, reflected her philosophy and recommended that local schools, except the poorest, pick up a higher percentage of the costs of local education. The commission also recommended that the costs of pensions be shifted from the state level to local school districts.[4]

The Whitman administration sought to shape the court's decision about the new school finance case. The state argued that the state had made substantial progress in recent years in reducing inequities. The poor, urban districts spent 70 percent of the average of wealthier districts before 1990 and now were spending 84 percent of the average of the wealthier districts.[5] The Whitman administration also made a plea that they be given more time (unspecified) to resolve the problem.[6]

The court eventually ruled, in July 1994, after the legislative session, that the disparities between districts were still too large.[7] The court, however, granted Whitman's request that her administration be given more time. The court gave the state until September 1996 to enact financing legislation to give poorer districts equivalent financing and to respond to the special educational needs of children growing up in poor, urban areas. This meant dealing with issues such as preschool programs, health services, and smaller class sizes. The funding did not have to begin until the 1997–98 school year.[8]

While Whitman was preparing her response, a detailed study of school district finances was released. It concluded that the gap between the affluent and poor districts had narrowed since 1990,[9] lending support to those who argued that the state was moving in the right direction.

In formulating a response, Whitman faced a significant dilemma, one that at its core revolved around what responsibility the state should have for local education. She faced practical, political, and philosophical dilemmas in trying to decide what the response of state government should be. She had enacted significant tax cuts since winning reelection. The tax cuts reduced state revenue yields from the income tax, resulting in less state aid to less-affluent districts. If she was to respond to the court decision with more state aid, she had two difficult choices. She could reverse herself and propose a tax increase to pay for more state aid. Politically, that would be very harmful, as it would eliminate her most obvious accomplishment: lowering taxes. Her other alternative was to find more aid for schools by cutting other programs. That would also cause her considerable political problems. Further, if she took the route of responding by providing more aid to less-affluent districts, the demands would continue to escalate from other districts. The rural districts, for example, had felt for some time that they also needed money, and it was known that they were planning to sue the state for more aid on the grounds that they also lacked the tax base to provide adequate education.[10] Another possible response was to redistribute state aid from affluent districts to low-income groups. That was also dangerous politically, because the affluent areas of the state were a crucial part of her electoral base for a reelection effort in 1997. Republican legislators also came predominantly from these areas, so they were unlikely to accept any strict redistributive plans. Finally, there was the philosophical issue of whether she believed that the solution to the school finance issue was more money. She had made it clear that she was a fiscal conservative and that she did not think the answer to problems was more money and greater aid from the state. If Whitman did not somehow contain the growing demands for aid, it would require more taxes and a greater role for the state in supporting local education. Responding to that would require reversing her positions on taxes and state responsibility for funding.

Whitman's eventual response was to try to redefine the obligation of the state. While Florio had raised taxes and increased state aid, Whitman sought to redefine how the problem should be solved and what the role of state government should be. Her concerns were to reduce the expectation that the state would fund increased expenditures without restraint and to try to shift the focus to what schools should achieve and how well they were achieving those objectives. The shifts were important because they put much more focus on local decisions and actions. The introduction to her proposed legislation explained the logic of her proposal, and her view of state-local relations:

(1) Each student in New Jersey must be guaranteed access to a free public education based on rigorous standards which define the knowledge and skills all children must have to function in a contemporary setting as a citizen and competitor in the labor market, and each school district must be guaranteed access to resources to provide that education in an efficient manner;

(3) Prior school funding laws have not succeeded . . . in part because of the lack of specific definition of what constitutes a thorough and efficient education;

(4) Prior laws have also led to funding systems which have permitted high spending levels in many districts without reference to specific educa-

tional results, required State and local governments to seek ever-increasing levels of taxation and funding in order to keep pace with high-spending districts, and failed to generate measurable improvement in parity of academic achievement even in those districts in which funding has been increased to higher levels;

(5) Existing school budget development, approval and appeal processes ... have further encouraged a system that defines a thorough and efficient education as the sum of whatever elements each district determines to include in its own individual budget;

b. It is, therefore, necessary for the Legislature to provide, and the Legislature does hereby establish:

(1) A process for the establishment, and the periodic review and revision, of a clear and comprehensive definition of the substantive elements of a thorough and efficient system of education as required by the New Jersey Constitution, uniformly applicable to districts Statewide, specifying what students ought to learn and what academic standards they should meet in order to function as citizens and competitors in the contemporary world and workplace, as well as the types of programs and services that will accomplish these ends in a thorough and efficient manner;

(2) The level of fiscal support necessary to provide these programs and services;

(3) A funding mechanism that will ensure such support, shared by the state and local districts in a fair and equitable manner;[11]

The argument made here about state-local relations is important. This introduction acknowledges that each child is guaranteed an education and "access to resources." It acknowledges that "prior school funding laws have not succeeded." There is no attempt to back away from the right to an education or having sufficient resources for that education, *as defined in the legislation*. The problems with past approaches to resolving the problem are noted. The proposal was not an attempt to remove the state from playing a role in this area.

What is different is the interpretation of why past approaches had failed and what should be done to remedy the problem. The argument presented in the legislation is that the state had placed itself in a situation of having to continually react to the results of the actions of decentralized school districts, rather than trying to define and contain the state's obligation. In particular, state government was allowing the spending patterns of affluent districts to define the standard the state had to chase. With affluent districts continuing to spend more than other districts, the state was seeking "ever-increasing levels of taxation and funding to keep pace with high-spending districts. . . ." From this perspective, state government had been too passive in defining what needed to be done. The solution was not for the state to do less, but to do more in defining standards, and not just providing more revenue. In defining what school districts should accomplish, what personnel are necessary, and the range of costs necessary to achieve these goals, state government could seize the initiative to define its obligation.

This could limit the state's obligation, and by doing so shift the focus to making local school district officials explain why they needed more than the revenues currently available. This would shift the issue away from state elected officials continually having to explain why they were not providing more state aid, and allow state officials to raise the question of what was being done with existing levels of aid. State government would still play a very active role, but with less of an open-ended commitment of fiscal resources. The change involves a very different approach.

This general argument was accompanied by very specific proposals to reshape state-local relations in the area of school finance. First, with regard to local expenditures, Governor Whitman first proposed trying to contain the growth of specific local school expenditures. She proposed that any school district with noninstructional expenditures more than 30 percent above the statewide median for this category would not receive state assistance to support expenditures beyond the 30 percent level. Noninstructional expenses were defined as including administrators, librarians, school nurses, and guidance counselors. The argument was that too much state aid was going to support noninstructional expenses. "We are first in the country in costs and 49th in the proportion of money that goes into the classroom."[12] The penalty for exceeding the 30 percent limit would be a cut in state aid equivalent to the amount of overspending. She was following the principle that a district could spend much more than others, but that additional spending should be seen as a local decision that the state had no obligation to support. If current spending patterns were used as a guide, her proposal would result in state aid cuts in seventy wealthy districts.[13] An administrative spokesperson acknowledged that the proposal was part of an attempt to encourage small school districts to merge into larger ones and to press all of New Jersey's districts to cut back on overhead costs.[14]

Her proposal also provided a way for local districts to continue "excess" spending, but in a way that would increase the local scrutiny on school districts. For each year, that portion of a district's budget which was designated as excessive had to be taken to the voters for approval. If that portion passed, the district could continue spending at whatever level was approved. This made "excess" spending a local decision and not a state-endorsed decision. It would also increase local focus on why a school district had "excess spending." If local voters turned down the excess spending, the district could appeal to the local town government, but that decision could not be appealed to the state, as was currently the case. Local voters would decide what was acceptable, and local officials would decide appeals. State government would no longer be involved in sanctioning higher levels of spending.

Her brand of Republican conservatism was not just to seek cutbacks in redistributive efforts helping low-income districts. Republicans are often seen as conservative in the sense of representing middle- to upper-income constituents who are not supportive of redistribution. The emphasis of many Republicans is on accepting the outcomes of the private market and the current distribution of wealth and resources among people and across communities. Government actions to raise taxes from the affluent and redistribute funds to lower-income individuals and districts are opposed because they take from the achieving and distribute to the less achieving. Whitman's approach was to emphasize the logic of restraining state support, regardless of which individuals and communities that logic affected. She sought to restrain state support of local spending beyond some minimal level, even if it meant imposing harmful effects primarily on affluent districts, which were the ones that would be classified as having "excess" spending, and that had voted for her in 1993. It was conservatism driven by a sense that state fiscal obligations should be limited to some reasonable level, and not conservatism that reflected just class interests. She had staked out a new position: a state-level politician had chosen to confront school districts over costs and effectiveness and propose that the state draw a line on what it would support at the local level.

Much as with the tax cut, this approach made it more difficult for liberals, Democrats, and representatives of low-income districts to attack her for favoring the rich. Indeed, the reaction to her position created the interesting political situation that residents of affluent districts were angry with her because they would lose aid. It is difficult to attack a politician for favoring the rich when those very people are expressing anger toward her for cuts in state aid. It is also difficult to oppose an effort to contain administrative costs. While the public supports education, there is much less support for administrative costs.[15]

The second specific proposal was to have the state define what constitutes a "thorough and efficient" education.

> We need to define what we want to achieve in the school system. We have to give all our children parity in education, but until we know what it is, we can't determine if we've done that.[16]

The state would propose a core curriculum for students at each level. Then officials would figure out how much that education costs per student and devise a financing formula that would ensure each district receives that amount of money.[17] A preliminary report was issued in November 1995, so that interested parties could obtain an idea of what kind of plan was intended and so they could offer comments.

In her January 1996 annual message to the legislature, Whitman again emphasized that money was not the answer. "It has become increasingly clear that making a direct link between high spending and high achievement leads to a false conclusion. A great deal more goes into a successful education than an expensive education program."[18]

By May 1996, she had submitted several documents containing her proposals. As a first step, the administration issued the volume *Core Curriculum Content Standards*, which defined what should be achieved in each school district.[19] The document was filled with general objectives, such as:

- By grade 8, in social studies, a student should be able to examine the origins and continuing key principles embodied in the United States Constitution.

- By grade 12, in social studies, a student should be able to analyze the roles of the individual and the government in promoting the general welfare of the community under our Constitution.[20]

It was not at all clear what it would mean to fulfill each of these, and the document made it clear that "these standards are not meant to serve as a statewide curriculum guide." They define the results expected, but do not "limit district categories for how to ensure that their students achieve these expectations."[21]

This was accompanied by a final version of *Comprehensive Plan for Educational Improvement and Financing*, which contained total aid projections for specific forms of state aid. Perhaps the most important aspect of this report was that it specified the expenditure per student and the district personnel[22] necessary to achieve a thorough and efficient education. For 1997–98, for example, the amount was set at $7,200.[23] This level, which was below the amount most districts were currently spending, was crucial for several reasons. First, setting a specific level contained the obligations of state government. Second, setting a required amount below most current spending levels suggested that local districts could meet minimum requirements with less money than they were spending. The implication was that in many districts education cost too much or local districts were doing more than was needed. Third, this discrepancy between state requirements and local spending shifted the burden of proof for the discrepancy to local districts. If the state could get this level of spending accepted as the necessary amount, then the focus would shift to local officials having to justify the difference. This shifted focus would also direct attention to local budget processes and votes, rather than state aid increments.

This proposal did not neglect the issue of low-income districts. These districts, referred to as the "Abbott" districts, would receive the funding necessary to bring them to the minimal expenditures level. Those spending below the necessary level would not be required to raise local taxes to make up for any discrepancy, as that discrepancy would be made up by state aid.[24] This specification of a necessary level of spending per student was crucial for responding to the issue of the "Abbott" districts. It gave the state a targeted amount of spending in these districts to focus on, rather than an open-ended obligation. Once the state provided enough funding for low-income districts to get to that suggested spending level, the state's obligation should be less of an issue, and the local school district's use of the money more of an issue.

The last part of the package of proposals was *State Aid Projections for 1997–98*, which provided detailed amounts that each district would receive for each category of aid. The report indicated the increase or decrease in total state aid from the previous year. Whitman's aid proposal would increase state aid to schools by several hundred million dollars, with one-half of the increase going to the thirty special need districts that were at the center of the battle.

In summary, these proposals represented a significant state position. On one hand, the state was indicating what the general objectives of education should be and defining the expenditure the state deemed necessary to achieve those objectives. On the other hand, state government was telling school districts that they had the local autonomy to decide how much to spend on education and how to achieve educational objectives. If local school districts wanted to spend more than the state-defined norms for expenditure and staffing, each school district would have to fund that additional effort itself. State government was playing more of a role in trying to define the standards, vague as they might be, that school districts should achieve and be accountable for, and how money should be spent on specific positions to achieve the general objectives defined by the state. The crucial matter was that state government was making a statement that the answer to education problems was not just more money for districts.

ENACTING CHANGE

The political challenge for Whitman was to get the legislature to adopt her program. Her plan contained positives and negatives for Republicans in the legislature. It was attractive because a definition of a thorough and efficient education and a specified amount of spending necessary to achieve that, at the level her administration had proposed, would allow legislators to avoid future tax increases and preserve the tax cuts they had recently enacted. It would partially satisfy angry taxpayer groups who still thought that taxes were too high and that teachers' unions just wanted more money and no accountability.[25]

It was clear that the political climate had shifted sufficiently to make it legitimate to raise questions about whether local education was already receiving enough money and whether accountability was stressed enough. Newspaper series were appearing that asked whether the quality of teachers had improved as the state spent more on education,[26] that argued that methods of evaluating teachers had not improved,[27] and that bad teachers were not eliminated.[28] Stories were appearing that the pay of teachers was steadily increasing, sometimes by large amounts, with the highest-paid teachers making $80,000 a year.[29] From this perspective, the problem was not money, but effectiveness.[30] Some legislators may have felt that the time was ripe for asking for more accountability, and shifting the debate from more state aid to what school districts were doing with the aid. As one Republican senator expressed it:

> Since 1980, school spending in New Jersey has risen two and a half times the rate of inflation. Total state aid per pupil for the same period has also increased two and a half times as much as inflation.
> . . . despite this incredible support, there are still huge problems in some of our public school districts. The conclusion that can be drawn from this is that money alone will not solve the problem. [We need to consider] a comprehensive solution which stresses performance and accountability as strongly as it does money.[31]

But there were reasons to be very leery of the package. There were numerous criticisms, ranging from the specific to the very general. School district officials objected that the rules about what defines administrative expenses were changed without any advance notice. They also objected to the classification of librarians and guidance counselors as administrative costs.[32] Advocates for special education opposed the proposal because it provided a set amount for each special education student, regardless of the nature of the need. The proposal was opposed by the teachers' union, the New Jersey Education Association,[33] which created the possibility that the union would work against legislators voting for the proposal. The most critical criticisms came from the Education Law Center, which had regularly filed lawsuits challenging the school finance system.[34] They argued that there was no demonstrable link between the curriculum standards and the spending levels deemed adequate by the state. Indeed, the executive director, David Sciarra, charged that the designated amount was "an arbitrary, politically contrived dollar amount," which had been set at that level because it would not require any more state aid and would preserving the 30 percent tax cut of Whitman.[35] The argument persisted that resources still differed significantly among districts, and that resources needed to be equalized.[36]

Perhaps the most significant source of opposition came from school districts themselves. Numerous local superintendents and school boards opposed the plan.[37] There was support for the idea of standards, but there was considerable concern about the effects of the plan on districts currently spending relatively high amounts per student. The concern was that a state-specified amount set $3,000 or more below existing spending levels would mean that large parts of local budgets would have to be taken to voters every year, and negative votes could wreak havoc on the budgets of communities with strong educational programs. The Office of Legislative Services, in the legislature, published a list, based on existing spending levels in school districts, of which districts were currently above the suggested expenditure level and would have to take parts of their budgets to the voters for support. In the more-affluent counties, such as Morris County, where spending levels were higher, some argued that over one-half of districts would have to take the "excess" amounts of their budgets to voters, while in the less-affluent counties few budgets would have to go to a vote.[38] Superintendents and parents in affluent districts appeared at public hearings arguing that the state-suggested spending level was too low, and that too many district budgets would be exposed to local votes.[39]

Counties like Morris were also heavily Republican. The risk was that Republican legislators would vote for a proposition that could cause considerable turmoil in their districts if local voters turned down budgets.[40] Voters in affluent counties like Morris could, of course, regularly support local budgets above the state specified level (along with the corresponding local property levels), thus allowing affluent communities to spend more than less affluent districts. This would allow inequities among districts to continue. On the other hand, numerous negative votes on local school district budgets, even though they might be rationalized as reflecting the public's preferences, could cause considerable turmoil in local communities, with state legislators being blamed for creating the situation.

The proposal, therefore, was politically risky. It was fiscally attractive because it would reduce demands on state legislators for more state aid and more tax revenues. But the proposal was widely opposed by educators, and its long-term impact in Republican areas has been very unclear. In some ways, Republican legislators were in a situation similar to that of Democratic legislators under Governor Jim Florio. Democrats and their constituents were intended to be the prime beneficiaries of his proposals. The income tax increases and the distribution of state aid would help Democratic constituencies—low- and middle-income areas—more than others, but some of the most vociferous complaints about taxes came from the areas Democrats were trying to help.

There was an odd parallel in Whitman's proposal to the Democratic situation of 1990. Her proposal to curtail further increases in state aid, but give local areas the option to vote to exceed state spending standards, could ultimately benefit affluent, largely Republican areas more than less-affluent areas. Many affluent school districts were already not getting much state aid. They had wealthier tax bases and could support additional spending. If they voted to support "excessive" spending, this would legitimate, under the authority of state law, their spending more than lower-income districts. The state would not announce an official sanction for this divergence, but the law would allow it. Low-income districts, of course, could also vote to support excess spending. But with much more limited tax bases, they were much less likely to do so, and excess spending on their part would probably involve relatively limited spending amounts per student. If all this prevailed, state income taxes could be kept down, which would help affluent areas, and local variations in spending could continue. The problem that emerged for Republicans was that, despite this possible benefit, few of their constituents saw the plan as beneficial. Much as Democratic legislators had difficulty convincing their constituents that Florio's proposals would help them, few Republicans saw a clear advantage for their constituents.

Whether Whitman meant for her proposal to ultimately help affluent districts is unknown. Her proposal may have been constructed with the intent of restraining the continuing demands for state aid for schools, and shifting the focus to why local districts needed to spend more. Or the proposal may have been primarily an attempt to seek to maintain the tax cut, and offer a concession to legislators, so more-affluent districts could continue to spend more than others. Despite this possible benefit, the public hearings held on the legislation drew consistent complaints from those in affluent districts. Officials from districts that might benefit from this proposal, because of lower long-term state income taxes for their residents, saw only the potential for chaos for their local school budgets.

Not only was there very mixed support within affluent communities, but it did not appear that public opinion was supportive of cutting back state support for education or giving up on efforts to achieve more equality of school finance funding. A poll conducted in April 1996 by the Quinnipiac College Polling Institute provided some important results. Voters supported the approach of focusing on standards and accountability. Sixty-five percent of voters in New Jersey said they wanted state government rather than local communities to set standards of what students should learn, and only 35 percent wanted local communities to do so. Many voters sounded as if they were liberals who agreed with the Newark Law Center. Seventy-eight percent of voters agreed that public school spending should be equal throughout state. Seventy-seven percent said it was "very important" to improve the schools in the poorer districts, 55 percent said that the amount of state aid to poorer districts should be increased, and 51 percent would be willing to pay more taxes to improve the quality of schools in poorer communities. Support for taxes and spending as a solution was, to be sure, consistently higher among Democrats and lower among Republicans. On the other hand, 67 percent of voters also agreed that waste in New Jersey schools was a "big problem." The overall results, therefore, indicated some ambiguity among the public as to how to proceed. The public thought standards were important, but they also thought that money, and more of it for low-income districts, was important. [41] Yet they were not convinced all money was spent well.

The Republican legislators, concerned about the possibility for havoc if the requirement of voting for "excess" spending was adopted, chose to reject the portions of the governor's proposal that defined a standard spending level of $7,200 and would expose many local districts to votes. They did adopt the curriculum standards set forth by the Whitman administration. Rather than define $7,200 per student as the amount necessary to achieve these curriculum standards, however, they defined this amount as the minimum amount necessary.[42] They removed the characterization of "excess" spending, and the requirement of taking "excess" spending to the voters. This change, in effect, accepted all current district spending levels, with the hope that the court would focus on the required minimum of $7,200 per student and not on the higher levels of spending in affluent districts. The legislature allowed for growth with inflation and more students, and required a vote only for expenditure increases beyond any amount allowed by these provisions of the law. If voters turned down these increases, the district could ultimately appeal to the state education commissioner.[43] Finally, the legislature sought to placate the courts by adding $285 million in school aid to Whitman's proposal, with the majority of that increase going to the twenty-eight "Abbott districts."[44] The goal was to reduce the demand for more state aid by defining an amount necessary to achieve the new standards, and hope that the state courts would not focus on the continuing inequalities sanctioned by the legislation.

The difference from the original Whitman proposal was very important. Her proposal would make the state intrusive by setting a specified spending level, and making local expenditure beyond that suspect. The legislature, representing local constituents and governments, was unwilling to make such a definitive statement and risk disrupting local affairs. Her proposal said that $7,200 was all that was needed, while the legislature preferred to say that *at least* $7,200 was needed. Her proposal presumably gave the state a way out of having to match the spending of the affluent districts. It would contain future state obligations by saying spending levels beyond that amount were really not necessary. The legislature chose to stress the minimum, and fundamentally avoid the issue of what to make of the differences between the minimum-expenditure districts and the affluent districts. They left those differences intact, and chose to let the court react to the differences. The state would be responsible to support the low-income districts, but its responsibility for the overall state of affairs and inequities was simply avoided.

While Whitman and the Republicans in the legislature may have hoped this package of proposals would solve the school finance issue, the opposition continued. All but one Democrat opposed the package when the final vote was taken on December 19, 1996.[45] Democrats also made it clear that they saw the issue as continuing, and thought Whitman would be vulnerable about it during the gubernatorial campaign to be conducted during the next year.[46] They charged that the lack of increases in state aid would result in higher local property taxes, and that her plan would not satisfy the courts.[47] The partisan criticism was not about to end. The Education Law Center also argued that the plan was not satisfactory, and on January 6, 1997 they filed their sixth lawsuit in twenty-five years, contending that the package did not remedy the inequalities among school districts. David Scarria again argued that the Republican package had been proposed to preserve the income tax cut, and not to resolve the problem.[48]

The issue of what responsibility state government had, and how this could be fulfilled, was not resolved by the Republican package of 1996. The parties still differed on how the issue should be handled, and Democrats were prepared to criticize Whitman's proposals as avoiding the issue of equalizing opportunities. Another lawsuit had been filed for the courts to consider, and the issue remained to be resolved.

THE 1997 GUBERNATORIAL CAMPAIGN:
WHITMAN'S CASE FOR REELECTION AND A REDUCED STATE ROLE

The 1997 gubernatorial campaign provided another opportunity to continue the debate about the role of state government. Republicans had held power since winning veto-proof majorities in 1991. Party control had made a difference in the policies pursued, in the presumed role of state government, and in the concern for inequalities among local governments. The legislative leadership had repealed the 1 percent sales tax increase. Whitman had proposed and obtained a cut in the state income tax. She and the Republican leadership in the legislature had created a proposal intended to redefine the focus in the school finance issue away from money and toward meeting state standards. They had flinched on defining a limit to state support and creating mechanisms to make higher spending a local option not sanctioned by the state, but they had enacted a proposal that shifted the focus somewhat toward local responsibilities and away from state obligations.

The context was conducive for Whitman and the Republicans to be campaigning in 1997. The economy and jobs were growing, and, even with the tax cuts, state revenues were increasing such that the Republicans were able to maintain state aid. As the year began, her approval rating, at 62 percent, was at its highest. Her approval-disapproval ratings for handling the environment, crime, and welfare were all around 60–22, while her ratings for handling the state budget and education were less positive at 54–37.[49] The issue was how the electorate would react to her policies and Democratic criticism.

Whitman made her approach (and the case for her administration) clear in her 1997 state of the state address.

> For the past three years, we in state government have been unleashing those qualities [in the people of New Jersey] by turning government back to the supporting role that it was meant to play. We are curbing government's appetite for spending so people keep more of their own money to spend on their own needs. We are ensuring that government functions only where it needs to function and then as efficiently as possible. In short, we are giving citizens more choices and returning to them control over their own lives.
>
> At the same time, the dire predictions about skyrocketing property taxes have fizzled out. Over the past three years, the average increase in property taxes has been the lowest of any administration since 1982. Of course, property taxes won't ever be as low as we would like. But we should never give up trying. Government—at every level—must do what we have been doing in Trenton—control spending. That's how to keep property taxes down.[50]

Her presumption was not that state government could solve problems, but that local governments could. Less state government and lower taxes meant more freedom and choice were possible. Her views, while certainly presented in softer tones, and with less of the edge of an outright, hostile attack on government, were not very far from the growing libertarian movement that had developed in the national Republican party.[51] The solution to problems was not more money or an activist state government, but active citizens working within local settings. Inequalities among citizens and local governments in resources were not mentioned in her view of government. She had a clear approach to state government, a cut in the income tax, a proposal for how to solve the education issue, and strong poll ratings.

Her early moves in 1997 did much to enhance her strong position. With the economy growing, the state realized even more revenue, and she was able to propose a state budget with significant increases ($540 million) in state aid to schools.[52] She and the legislature agreed on legislation to conform to the new federal welfare program, passed by the Congress and accepted by President Clinton, in 1996. She chose to soften the impact of the change by opting to have the state continue benefits to legal immigrants, even though the law did not require the state to do so.[53] She opened her campaign on April 15, the day national taxes are due, touring the state and reminding voters that she had kept her promise to cut taxes and that she had made significant strides in dealing with property taxes and jobs.[54] Before the Democratic opponent was even decided in the June 3 statewide primary, she was running television ads reminding voters of her accomplishments.[55] The three Democrats seeking to oppose her were having trouble raising money and generating much interest in the primary campaign.[56] Her political position seemed as strong as one could hope for. Making an issue of the role of state government seemed unlikely.

The debate was not over, however. As is often the case when issues of the role of the state emerge, the impetus is not an abstract and philosophical debate about what role state government should play. The issue emerges because there are specific problems that citizens want state government to address. Philosophy matters less than specific problems. The issue of what role state government should play emerges policy by policy, with the abstract principle of government's role receiving less attention than actual problems. Four such issues emerged to plague Whitman in the campaign: state contributions to the state pension system, local education funding, local property taxes, and car insurance. Each raised the issue of whether state government should address problems, or whether it should just play a "supporting" restrained role. Each issue also appeared to play a significant role in affecting votes during the campaign. The continuing role of these issues in the campaign, and the final outcome of the election, indicated much about the public's desire for a reduced state role in the future.

THE PENSION OBLIGATION

State governments employ large numbers of workers, and they provide pensions to these workers. To fund the pensions, each state has established a pension fund, and state law requires regular contributions to the pension fund so the necessary funds will be there when workers retire. The estimation of the level of funds necessary is complicated, requiring estimating future inflation, the likely amount of money that the pension fund will earn in the future, how long workers will continue on the job, and how long they will live. Beginning in the 1970s, the state of New Jersey, like many other states, began to underfund its pension program. Part of the underfunding was an attempt to avoid tax increases that would have been necessary to provide the funding. Politicians also wanted to free up funds for other purposes. The prior governor, Jim Florio, had acknowledged the underfunding, and created a schedule of additional payments to the fund that would pay off the underfunded amounts by around the year 2005. By 1994 the cumulative unfunded obligation of the state was $800 million.[57]

Whitman had chosen to significantly cut the state's contribution to the pension fund in 1994. In 1993 the state was contributing approximately $1 billion a year to the pension fund. Whitman cut that obligation to $235 million. She argued that the pension fund was overfunded, and that many of the assumptions dictating the funding obligations needed to be revised. She argued that the state pension system was generating excess earnings each year, or returns beyond the minimum presumed in forming estimations of how much the fund would need in the future. State law prohibited using those additional earnings to pay part of each year's required contribution. She argued that the law should be changed to allow applying all earnings to the fund. More important, given her argument that the fund had enough money, she made several very specific changes to reduce the amount the state had to contribute. She postponed providing the money necessary to fund future cost-of-living obligations. If inflation occurs, retirees get increases in pension payments equal to those increases. She argued that funding for this was not necessary. She also chose to change from setting aside money for future medical care payments to just paying for them as they occurred. She also stretched out the time necessary for the state to fulfill its obligation to fully fund the pension fund. She made several other changes, all of them involving assumed changes over time in how long workers would stay in the workforce, and how long retirees would live.[58] Her proposals were heavily criticized by Democrats in 1994 as just a mechanism to fund her income tax cut, but the technical nature of the changed assumptions had made it difficult to gain much public attention for the changes, and the legislature had accepted her proposals. The unions had not, and filed a lawsuit in 1994 challenging the decision to reduce funding to the state pension system. As a result of the changes adopted in 1994, the state avoided $3.1 billion dollars in payments over the next three years, and the cumulative underfunding increased from $800 million to $4.2 billion.

Whitman chose to push the pension issue even further when she proposed her budget for 1997–98. In a move that surprised her own party, she proposed that she fulfill the cumulative underfunding by borrowing. Perhaps most surprising was that she also chose to borrow for the current year's contribution, which would give her $647 million to use for the current budget. She would borrow $3.4 billion. She would combine these borrowed funds with $1.3 billion of a "surplus" of earnings from the pension fund. The combined total would give her enough to pay off the obligated underfunded amount, and would leave her with enough to pay the $647 million for 1997–98. It would let her lower the contribution to the pension system, without raising taxes or cutting services.[59]

Her own party members in the legislature were surprised. The Democrats, and particularly those who were running in the primary to oppose her, began to say that Whitman had finally admitted that her income tax cut had been a bad idea, and that she had only been able to finance state operations by borrowing money. The proposal was controversial, and she eventually had to agree to cut the borrowed amount down to $2.9 billion, to shorten the length of time necessary to pay off the debt, and to make promises to unions about protecting their jobs and future benefits.[60]

Her plan was eventually adopted, but there was considerable critical commentary about it. It was the first time a state had borrowed to cover pension obligations, and the plan increased state debt by a third.[61] Her own party was reluctant to accept the plan and did so only when the opposition subsided. The Democrat who won the primary to oppose her, James E. McGreevey, a state senator, made it clear that he would keep up the criticism. At a time when she wanted to focus on how she had cut taxes and restrained the growth of government, attention was focused on how she had had to borrow money to fund state obligations.[62] While Whitman claimed that the proposal would ultimately save money by avoiding future borrowing, the plan made issues of state responsibility part of public discussions in ways she had not desired.

While conservatives were probably willing to cut state pensions, Whitman had not approached the issue in 1994 by proposing that state obligations be cut. Rather, she had retained state responsibility, but argued that they could be financed differently. Choosing that approach eventually lead to confrontation with a specific problem that had to be solved by state government. It was clear from the response of Republican legislators that they were unwilling to back away from the pension obligations. While Republican legislators were probably willing to argue for reduced state obligations in the abstract, they were much less inclined to do so about this specific obligation.

LOCAL EDUCATION AND PROPERTY TAXES

The issue of the state's obligation to schools also resurfaced during the year. In May 1997, the state supreme court rendered its decision about whether the package of bills passed in December 1996 met the requirements of the court's decision of 1994. The court ruled that "emphasizing standards rather than spending violated the state constitution." The court also directed the state education commissioner to conduct research on the needs of the twenty-eight special needs districts, and to prepare a plan to refurbish schools in the special needs districts. The judges praised the idea of new standards, and indicated they might someday be the foundation for a fair system, but they stated that $7,200 was inadequate for urban schools with special needs. They also pointed out that announcing standards did not address the problem of how those standards would be achieved. The court felt money was important, and the Education Law Center estimated that $200 million would be necessary to respond to the needs of the special districts.[63]

Whitman was equally specific in her response and in her signal to targeted constituents. She expressed clear disappointment in the ruling.

> I couldn't disagree more with the ruling that the funding formula that we devise does not provide sufficient funds. Dollar parity is not the solution to the education issue in the state of New Jersey.
> We are not going to try to allocate money away from the middle-income districts in order to achieve the court's decision. I want to make it very clear that I will not approve a single additional dollar to be spent in these districts [without assurance] that these dollars can be spent efficiently.[64]

It was clear that Whitman sought to contain the use of fiscal resources to the problems of low-income districts, and that she was opposed to redistribution.[65]

The court gave the state until the end of the year to conduct its study of the needs of the special needs districts and to come up with a plan for refurbishing schools. But the requirement for more money for the twenty-eight special needs districts was immediate. Whitman and the Republican leaders of the legislature, again the beneficiaries of a growing economy, were able to comply without tax increases or any redistribution. With more revenues rolling into the state treasury by June than had been expected in January, they were able to add almost $250 million to the budget for local education, with most of the money going to the twenty-eight special needs districts.[66]

The court ruling had the effect of pushing the issue of what the state should do for education back onto the political agenda. As in previous conflicts over education, the parties differed. While Republican governor Whitman sent a clear signal to affluent districts that she would oppose any reduction in their revenues, her Democratic opponent McGreevey responded to the ruling by applauding the court and criticizing her approach to handling the issue. There were now two issues, pension obligations and school funding, about which the parties differed on what to do.

The education finance issue also had relevance for one of the other enduring issues of New Jersey politics: local property taxes. New Jersey has relatively high local property taxes, and much of that burden is due to the high per capita spending on local education in the state. Whitman's approach to the issue was to try to shift the focus to local school district accountability and hope this would restrain continued education costs and local taxes. Even if this did not work to restrain growth, she could continue her argument that local spending decisions were beyond her control and not her fault. Indeed, local budget increases could be presented as decisions endorsed by local residents because they voted for school budgets.

Her case that higher taxes were a local decision was supported by the voting results in the annual school budget votes in April 1997. Overall, 76.2 percent of school budgets were approved, the highest rate since 1986. The new state law passed in 1996 required that any budgetary increase above a 3 percent increase had to be taken to the voters. There were 144 districts that exceeded this increase and had to have an additional vote. Voters in 100 of these districts, or 69.5 percent of them, voted to exceed the increase.

Those supporting the legitimacy of affluent local school districts spending more than Whitman's recommended $7,200 argued that it was proof that voters wanted spending levels higher than that. Whitman, on the other hand, said that her approach of making local districts decide what they wanted had worked. The results also gave her grounds for saying that tax increases were locally proposed and ratified, so the state was not responsible.[67]

While Whitman may have been able to make a principled argument that local taxes were locally imposed, and she should not be responsible, the public was, again, apparently less interested in principled arguments than in having the state solve the problem of taxes. Despite lowering the income tax 30 percent during her term, the public did not give her much credit for handling taxes. While it is difficult to know what logic was driving the assessments (were respondents thinking of state, local, or state and local taxes?), when asked if they approved or disapproved of how she was handling taxes, her approval ratings on this issue dropped from 49 percent in February to 42 percent in April and 39 percent in June. Disapproval ratings on this issue rose from 46 percent in February to 54 percent in April and 53 percent in June.[68] A significant tax cut should have been a clear source of strength for Whitman in a reelection bid, but would not be if voters were more interested in having lower property taxes and thought the state should somehow be able to solve the problem.

CAR INSURANCE

While Whitman was touting her record of reduced income taxes, another issue that involved how state authority would be used unexpectedly emerged to become significant in the election. Residents of New Jersey paid the highest premiums in the nation in 1997. State government regulates the rates that insurers can charge, and existing legislation provided for continuing increases. Insurers were allowed to have automatic annual increases as costs rose. Disputes about settlements in accidents were settled by hearing boards composed of lawyers, and insurers charged that the willingness of the lawyers to approve almost all claims led to the need for even further increases. The insurers argued that this approach did not involve enough investigation of fraud cases and that 20 percent of all costs were now due to fraud.

During her 1997 state of the state address Whitman promised to lower those rates. Her proposed remedy was to again use state authority to a limited extent, and allow car owners to make their own decisions. She proposed that drivers be given the chance to opt to have less coverage and receive rate reductions of almost 25 percent. Much as with education, change would come about in a decentralized fashion through choices made by car owners, and not state government. She abandoned this proposal in April after angry voters criticized her proposal as not doing enough.[69]

Surprisingly, the issue became more significant as the year wore on, and polls began to show that voters regarded car insurance as the most important issue facing the state. Under pressure to do something at the end of the legislative session in June, she and the Republican leadership took the fairly limited approach of proposing to limit automatic annual increases and creating a system for ranking drivers so that drivers with worse records would pay more. After much wavering, provisions to reform the process by which appeals were approved were removed. The result was that the "reform" package would not lower overall rates by any considerable amount.[70]

The issue quickly became a partisan issue, with Democrats arguing that the state should use its authority to roll back rates by 10 percent and to aggressively pursue fraud. The Democratic candidate for governor, James McGreevey, pledged to cut rates by 10 percent and charged that her idea of reform was a "charade."[71] Whitman, against the advice of her advisors, chose to continue discussing the issue as the summer wore on, because she thought she should address an issue of concern to constituents. Her opponent continued to criticize her record, arguing that she had not really brought about much change.[72] Finally, with polls showing that her ratings for handling the issue were very bad (in July 1997, 16 percent approved of her handling of this issue, and 75 percent disapproved),[73] Whitman decided to shift the campaign away from car insurance and back to tax cuts.[74] Her opponent resisted the shift. As often happens in campaigns, an opponent had found an opening for criticism, an unsolved problem that voters wanted solved. It involved active state involvement, and he was more willing to pursue that route.

THE CAMPAIGN

The campaign presented voters with candidates who took very different positions on the issue of state responsibility. A Republican governor claimed credit for cutting state taxes and slowing the growth of state government. The Democratic candidate for governor, McGreevey, focused on the irresponsibility of the pension borrowing, on the failure to resolve the school finance issue, on concerns about the still high local property taxes, and on the failure to aggressively reform car insurance.

The polls indicated there was considerable potential for the Democratic candidate to exploit these issues. Figure 9.1 indicates the electorate's assessment of how Whitman had handled several policy areas, as of September 1997.[75] She did well in the areas of the environment, crime, and welfare. Surprisingly, however, she did only fair in the areas of handling the economy and income taxes. Her ratings were very mixed with regard to the financing of public schools, and negative in the areas of property taxes and auto insurance. A cut in the state income tax of 30 percent and presiding over a growing state economy had not resolved these issues to the electorate. In areas in which she thought she could reverse public expectations, financing public schools and property taxes, she had not succeeded. The electorate apparently still expected more from the state. Finally, in an area that she had hoped she could handle with limited state intrusion, auto insurance, she received very negative ratings from the public.

Whitman had made a concerted effort over four years to lower expec-

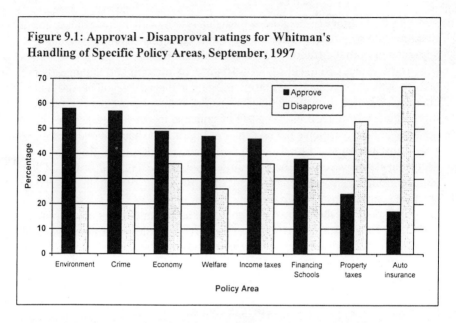

Figure 9.1: Approval - Disapproval ratings for Whitman's
Handling of Specific Policy Areas, September, 1997

tations of what state government could do to resolve problems, but considerable expectations were apparently still there. The campaign evolved with
the central difference between the candidates involving the willingness to
use state authority to address problems. Whitman emphasized her tax cut
and how that reduction in state taxes had helped spur growth in the state's
economy.[76] McGreevey criticized her for failing to deal with auto insurance, property taxes, and school finance, and implied he would be much
more willing to use state authority to address these issues.[77]

The polls indicated just how much a Democratic challenger could capi-
talize on frustrations with Whitman. As early as June, polls indicated the
race might be closer than expected. One June poll indicated a vote of 44
percent for Whitman versus 38 percent for McGreevey.[78] Polls in August,
September, and October continued to show the election to be close.[79] These
polls also indicated just how much Whitman had failed to lower expectations of state government and how effective McGreevey, the Democrat,
was in creating a focus on state responsibilities. When asked what problems the next governor should concentrate on, the most prominent issues
were auto insurance (46%), property taxes (21%), and education (11%).
When asked who would do a better job bringing down the cost of auto
insurance, voters indicated McGreevey, 40 percent to 27 percent. When
asked who would do a better job handling the problem of financing schools,
McGreevey was favored 40 percent to 39 percent. Fifty percent of voters
thought that if Whitman was elected, their local property taxes would go

up, while only 34 percent thought their property taxes would go up if McGreevey was elected.[80] The dissatisfaction with Whitman was evident in another way. As late as the week before the election, McGreevey's favorable-unfavorable rating was only 17 percent to 23 percent, yet he was consistently getting 40 percent of the vote in polls.[81] Many voters had no positive image of him, but were willing to vote for him.

The poll results indicated how difficult it is for a Republican to significantly lower expectations about state government. Whitman had cut the income tax by 30 percent, and made sure that low-income voters got a higher percentage cut. She had maintained state aid, though the use of borrowing for pension funds to keep money available for state aid had proved to be embarrassing. The state's economy was growing, though there were criticisms that high-paying jobs were not coming back as the economy grew.[82] But despite these successes, McGreevey's criticisms that she had not dealt with particular problems were harming her. Faced with continuing criticism and poll results indicating that people wanted problems dealt with, she reversed herself late in the campaign and ran a commercial in the closing days of the campaign in which she said, "You've sent me a message. Auto insurance and property taxes cost too much and people are hurting. I've heard you loud and clear."[83] She then promised to go after these costs if reelected. After four years of seeking to change expectations and faced with an election too close to call, she acknowledged the expectations for state government and promised to respond to them.

Whitman won by a small margin, about 20,000 voters out of 2.2 million votes cast. She received 46.9 percent of the vote to McGreevey's 45.8 percent. The presence of Murray Sabrin, running as a Libertarian, clearly hurt Whitman. He received 4.7 percent of the vote,[84] and with his conservative positions on abortion, gun control, and taxes, he clearly took conservative voters away from Whitman. But even if Sabrin had not been present, and Whitman had received his votes, she still would not have won an impressive share of the vote. What many thought would be an easy election was not.

COPING WITH EXPECTATIONS

The interpretation of elections is never simple, but the poll results suggest how unresolved the issue of the state was. On one hand, Whitman had fulfilled her campaign promise to cut taxes and the economy was doing well. Her reelection bid should have been easy, but she barely won. The polls showed that people were troubled by auto insurance, property taxes, and financing public schools. Whitman lost among those who were worried

about local property taxes and auto insurance rates, and won among conservatives and Republicans.[85] It would be easy to conclude that voters wanted
state government to resolve problems, and Whitman's philosophical commitment to restraining government was ultimately not that popular to voters. On the other hand, the election did not result in any shift to Democrats
in the legislative elections. In addition, it was possible to argue that the
only major issue was auto insurance rates, and it was ambiguous as to what
that opinions on that issue meant about general public preferences for an
active state government. The issue might have just been the desire for lower
insurance rates, and little more than that.

The Republican legislators, however, did not wait long to interpret the
results. On the Friday after the Tuesday election, the Republican legislative leaders held a press conference and announced that they would push
through major reforms of auto insurance, and that the program would be
theirs and not Whitman's.[86] Whitman followed that in December by appointing a commission to study how to bring down local property tax rates.
In her January 1998 state of the state address she offered proposals to reform education by making it more accountable and lowering costs. She
proposed eliminating tenure for principals, establishing pilot programs for
parents to choose schools for their children, and moving school elections
from April to November. She also suggested a statewide referendum to
have voters consider school district consolidation.[87] Just what the state would
do about these problems was not yet clear, but she and the Republican
legislators recognized that some sort of state action was necessary. The
voters had not communicated enthusiasm for the alternative of a state government that did not actively pursue solutions to problems.

During the 1998 session the Republicans sought to address the issues
that had emerged during the 1997 gubernatorial campaign. Legislation was
proposed and enacted in the areas of insurance and property taxes, and a
significant proposal was made in the area of financing education. In the
case of auto insurance, the legislature, after much wrangling over a proposal to give a bigger break to suburban drivers (the Republican constituency) and allow higher costs for urban drivers (the Democratic constituency),[88]
rejected that approach, and enacted a proposal that focused on lower costs.
The savings were projected to average about 15 percent and would come
from cracking down on fraud and changes in the rules governing lawsuits.[89]

In the area of property taxes, the actions were limited. No actions were
taken while the legislature waited until the Whitman-appointed commission reported in September 1998. The commission decided that its "recommendations should not result in an increase in the total State and local tax
burden."[90] They also "concluded that a significant shift of the revenue source
for local education from the property tax to a statewide tax could create

serious economic consequences for the state and would require New Jerseyans to forgo a degree of local control over the education of their children."[91] With the restraints that total taxes would not increase, and that the state would not pick up any more of the costs of local education, the result was a series of recommendations that focused on consolidation, costs savings, and better local assessment. The proposals were seen by many as not likely to significantly reduce local property taxes.[92] To Whitman, however, they maintained the focus on making local governments and school districts focus on how to save money and be more accountable to voters.[93] Finally, in September 1998, Whitman, acknowledging a surplus in the budge, offered a proposal to return $100 million as a property tax rebate, if revenue flows continued to meet certain expectations. The funds would be returned in the fall of 1999, prior to state legislative elections.[94]

The tax commission proposals, Whitman's acceptance of them, and her limited proposal for a property tax rebate indicated her continuing belief that the long-term solution to local property tax relief was cost reductions and not more state aid. As a Republican, her approach continued to be to try to make voters more attentive to local costs and the effort to contain them. The issue of local property tax rates was likely to persist, and remain a focus in future gubernatorial campaigns.

The approach of Republicans to local property tax rates was surely affected by the demands the state was likely to incur as it sought to resolve the school finance controversy. As noted earlier, in December 1996 legislation was enacted that sought to shift the focus to state standards and the performance of local school districts. The Education Law Center filed a lawsuit challenging the legislation as not providing enough funding. In May 1997, the state supreme court had declared her legislation unconstitutional. The court mandated that the state provide additional funding for the special needs districts and that studies be done by the state about what additional programs might be necessary to fully comply with the constitution. The court sent the issue of additional needs to a lower-court judge for review. Perhaps the most demanding aspect of the court ruling—one that did not receive as much attention in the press—was the mandate that the state come up with a plan to refurbish existing buildings in the special needs schools. While the focus in the school finance issue had usually been confined to issues of current operating revenues, the court was now requiring the state to be responsible for the condition of buildings, a capital budgeting issue. In a preliminary estimate, the state suggested that it would take at least $1.8 billion to refurbish these schools.[95] How this issue was resolved could have enormous consequences for the fiscal demands facing the state.

As the lower court reviewed the evidence on school finance in late

1997, the Whitman administration again chose to oppose the need for additional aid to the special needs districts, arguing before the lower-court judge that the emphasis should be on programs and their effectiveness, and not on spending. They argued that the state was already providing $2.3 billion to the special needs districts, which was almost one-half of all money spent in state aid for local education. The Education Law Center argued for additional state-supported programs for all-day preschool for three-year-olds and counseling for high school students in special needs districts.[96] In January 1998, the lower court ruled that the state needed to spend $312 million in additional funds for programs in special needs districts.[97] The decision then went to the state supreme court for a final decision. Given the prior decision that mandated more money for refurbishing buildings, and the reality that this expenditure could require more state revenue, the Whitman administration had little inclination to do anything but wait and see if the courts forced the state to spend more and raise more revenue.

In her state of the state address, Whitman argued that the court was overstepping its role, and that decisions of spending and taxing should be left to the governor and the legislature. The legislative leaders took the step of writing a letter to the supreme court's seven justices, stating that lawmakers "do not have a blank check when it comes to funding education."[98]

For whatever reasons, the supreme court finally accepted the argument that more money was not necessary. On May 21, 1998, the state supreme court rejected the decision of the lower court and accepted the plan of the Whitman administration for improving schools without spending more money. The court ruled that enough was being spent. The court also accepted the proposal to spend $2 billion on repairing schools as adequate.[99]

With that victory in hand, Whitman was able to focus on funding repairs of schools. In October 1998 she proposed a plan to spend $5.3 billion over ten years to rebuild local schools. A total of $2.6 billion would go to the special needs districts. In a move clearly designed to increase support for the program within the legislature, the public, and Republican districts, she went beyond assisting special needs districts and proposed an additional $2.7 billion in spending for other schools in the state. After a considerable delay, the legislature finally accepted her plan in July 2000.[100] It was presumed that this would satisfy the earlier court decision.

WHITMAN'S CHALLENGE TO STATE RESPONSIBILITY

Whitman's goal was to change the debate about state and local government responsibilities. Whether she succeeded will be indicated by future political debates and decisions. But she did force some questions onto the agenda that some had been reluctant to advocate. She cut back on state taxes and revenue raising, and did so while preserving a progressive tax system. She also challenged local governments and schools to be more accountable in how they spend money. Her approach to education was very different from that pursued by Democrats. She sought to define more clearly the obligations of local governments and school districts and focus attention on how existing funds were spent. The presumption was not just that local governments and education needed more money. The issue was how money was used.

The central issue that Republicans had to grapple with was how much of a role they would carve out for state government. How much would they reduce expectations, state aid, and state intrusion? The Republicans and Whitman acquired power in 1991 and 1993, respectively, because of a powerful resentment of taxes imposed by Democrats. In repealing the tax increases of 1991, Republicans then had to grapple with the issue of expectations of what state government should do. To return to one of the central questions of this study, their policy choices indicate something about what Republicans do when they acquire power, and the problems they face in seeking to achieve "less government."

In some areas they were clearly aware of and anticipated the criticisms of Democrats in making their choices. They cut the sales tax first, rather than the income tax, so the benefits would be seen as going to everyone. When they cut the income tax, they made sure lower-income families received a higher percentage reduction. On the crucial issue of state aid, they did not seek to redistribute state aid to affluent school districts. To be sure, their situation was constrained in an unusual way in that they faced a state supreme court that was continually pressuring them to distribute more to low- income districts. Nonetheless, their policy choices on major issues of the distribution of tax burdens and state aid suggest a pattern of anticipating partisan criticism and trying to render it less effective. Whitman did not pursue an explicit antiredistributive agenda so much as she pursued an agenda of restrained state government growth and greater local government accountability. Because her policies did not clearly and specifically favor the affluent, it was difficult for Democrats to attack her.

With regard to the crucial issue of the size of state government, the Republicans ultimately were unwilling to make significant cuts. Rather than reduce state spending and state aid, and be accused of being uncaring and draconian, the Republicans took advantage of a growing economy and increasing state revenues, and the ability to postpone pension fund obligations, and chose to slow growth rather than to significantly cut the state budget. Late in her first term, Whitman and the Republicans ultimately choose to borrow money rather than increase taxes or cut state aid. Apparently the image of seriously cutting state support was seen as politically too dangerous to Republicans. Faced with demands to deal with auto insurance and local property taxes, Whitman capitulated just before the election, and promised to use state powers to address the issues.

In some ways, it would seem plausible to accept the claim of those who argue that parties did not differ much. Parties in New Jersey, however, did differ significantly in how they addressed the issue of the role of state government. While Democrats were willing to raise taxes and aggressively address problems, Republicans, even faced with criticism, were willing to cut taxes and announce that future expectations for state aid increases should be reduced. They were willing to take on the teachers' union, local governments, and school districts and argue that they should be more accountable for how they spend money. They were willing to adopt pursue the idea of establishing standards for schools, and argue that more money was not the solution. Finally, they were willing to argue this case forcefully to the supreme court, and ultimately were able to convince it that the state was doing enough for local education and the special need districts, and that their plan deserved a trial. They may have even been able to alter the sense that state government should always do more.

Whether that expectation has really been altered will be seen in future events. Expectations are difficult to alter, but Republicans did articulate the position that less state aid should be expected, and they survived in office. The condition of a growing economy had helped bring about their survival. They were able to cut taxes and advocate principles without having to significantly cut the size of government because of revenue growth and borrowing. As always, political choices are highly dependent on conditions, and conditions were favorable to the Republicans. A real test of Republican commitments would have to wait for some future time when they would be faced with a sluggish or declining economy.

Part VI:
Conclusion

10

The State, Parties, and Public Policy

State and local roles and relations in New Jersey are now very different than they were in 1950. State government was a minor source of revenues for local governments, and it is now a major source. The state enacted a sales tax (1966) and raised it three times (1970, 1982, and 1990). An income tax was enacted (1976) and made more progressive twice (1982 and 1990). State government now provides local government with more aid. The state's role in funding local education has increased dramatically. As in many other states, more state aid was accompanied by more regulations. The state also assumed responsibility for programs once handled by local governments, such as welfare, and added new responsibilities, such as Medicaid.

State "politics" also changed. In the 1950s state government was not regarded as the arena in which major policy decisions were made. By the 1990s state government was the arena where major policy issues were consistently debated. State politics debates were presumed to be important because state government was important.

This case study of the emergence of state government in New Jersey offers the opportunity to explore three crucial questions about change. First, how and why do issues of a greater state role get on the political agenda? What makes this issue a major focus of political debate? Second, how does the decision to increase the role of state government get enacted, and what role do parties play in this decision? Reallocating political authority from local governments to the state is a contentious issue, with many opponents and supporters. Amidst all this disagreement, public officials, who are ultimately partisan, must enact change. What role do parties play in this process? Do parties propose clear policies and are they able to create unity

among members to enact change? Do Democrats have a clearly less affluent electoral base, do they make the case for addressing issues of opportunity, and can they enact change responding to such issues? Did Democrats
play the role we presume? Third, do policy enactments ultimately have
much impact? Does increasing the state's role affect the distribution of
resources in society? Changing the role of the state creates such intense
fights because it involves redistributing resources from local populations
and communities to state coffers. Does state action actually result in redistributive change?

The changes in New Jersey reflect just one of fifty state situations, and
no presumption is made that the answers to these questions in this state
will be identical to those in other states. But the situation in New Jersey
does provide some initial conclusions about these questions. Only studies
in other states will indicate how much similarity in patterns prevails across
states.

GETTING ISSUES ON THE AGENDA:
PROGRAMMATIC PARTIES?

For an issue to be considered, it first has to get on the agenda. It has to
be a concern that politicians feel the need to at least address, and perhaps
act on. Political parties might be central to getting this issue on the agenda.
Party members can play the crucial role of calling attention to problems
and inequities and serving as advocates for responsive policies. The party
might emphasize their concern for issues in an attempt to differentiate themselves from the other party. This will allow the electorate to discern differences between parties and vote for the party they prefer. Campaigns would
then provide a mandate for those in power. The parties, in this model, put
issues on the agenda and actively shape public debate.

That model has only limited relevance for New Jersey politics for the
time period analyzed here. Changes in the role of state government were
generally not a part of campaigns, and change did not stem from promises
made in political campaigns. Major tax increases, to be sure, were enacted
by Democratic governor Hughes and the Democratic legislature (the 1966
sales tax), Democratic governor Byrne and the Democratic legislature (the
1976 income tax), and Democratic governor Florio and the Democratic
legislature (the 1990 sales and income tax increases). Lesser tax increases
were adopted in 1970 by Republican governor Cahill and a Republican
legislature and in 1982 by Republican governor Kean and a Democratic
legislature. In all these cases a gubernatorial election, with its heightened
focus on state issues and legislative elections, preceded the tax enactment.

In no case, however, did the campaign prior to the enactment involve a focused debate about taxes and the obligations of state government. During the campaigns the legislative parties issued no statements of support for a greater state role or for a tax increase. Gubernatorial candidates did not campaign on the issue of the need for tax increases. While governors eventually proposed tax increases, they did not use their campaigns as means to solicit support for positions they may or may not have intended to eventually adopt.

Indeed, gubernatorial candidates generally avoided discussions of tax increases during their campaigns. Hughes, Cahill, and Byrne would not rule them out, but did not talk much about them. Kean said he did not need to raise taxes, and proposed business tax cuts. Florio talked only vaguely about the issue, but said he did not definitively rule them out. Gubernatorial candidates who were winning saw no need to raise an issue that might harm them. The strongest statement that can be made about discussions of tax increases is that Democrats were less adamant in saying they saw no need to raise taxes.

The only campaigns involving explicit tax pledges were in 1991 and 1993. In 1991 legislative Republicans campaigned against the tax increases of 1990 and, after winning a majority, they interpreted their victory as a mandate and cut taxes. Christie Whitman, running in a close gubernatorial campaign in 1993, pledged an income tax cut of 30 percent, and after winning, she fulfilled that pledge. These campaigns, however, did not focus on cutting back the role of state government. That issue was largely avoided.

If the question is, "Do politicians propose policies to get elected, or do they try to get elected so they can enact policies,"[1] it is clear that, at least for the set of issues involving the role of state government, the answer is not the former.

But it is not clear that the answer is the latter, either. Do politicians have clear agendas that they wish to pursue once in office? Hughes, Byrne, and Florio may simply have had activist agendas that they chose not to articulate. Perhaps so, but the answer to what shapes political agendas is more complicated than the simple dichotomy of whether politicians propose policies to win, or try to win to enact policies. The answer seems to be, rather, that politicians have differing political dispositions that affect how they react to arguments about recessions or other events that must be dealt with. Those dispositions shape the responses to problems. A liberal Democrat, faced with a recession, worries about cuts in programs for the less affluent if more state revenues are not found. A conservative Republican worries more about deficits, restraining the growth of state government, and the negative effects of enacting tax increases.

The primary source of change appears to be that events trigger party dispositions and reactions. The norm over this time period was not (with the exception of Whitman, to be discussed later) for politicians to tackle the issue of the role of state government in policy proposals during campaigns. Rather, events prompted responses. Partisanship matters in that Democrats and Republicans differ in what they think should be done about problems. If a problem is put on the agenda, these partisan dispositions then become relevant. The statement might be rephrased to: politicians get elected to get elected, and then their dispositions shape their reactions to events. The first goal of any politician is to get elected. Then they can worry about the issues they may face and what policies they may be able to pursue. They may have clear agendas, but the first step is to get elected. Policy proposals are presented during campaigns, with varying degrees of sincerity and commitment, but the first goal is to get elected.

GETTING ISSUES ON THE AGENDA:
THE ROLES OF EVENTS AND IDEAS

If campaigns are not vehicles for presenting and discussing the issue of what state government should do, then how do these issues get on the public agenda? Their consideration stems largely from "events," which present politicians with choices. Only in the case of the Hughes election in 1965 did a governor propose major changes without a precipitating event. Only in his case was there even the semblance of a mandate, which provided some basis for making major policy proposals. Otherwise, events—recessions, new federal programs, and court decisions—created situations that presented politicians with choices. It is when politicians are presented with a pressing problem that parties and the dispositions they embody become relevant.

Of all the events that might present state politicians with the need to make choices, some played minor roles while others were regular sources of decision junctures. Despite the common view that the federal government intrudes into state politics, federal pressures were not a significant factor in prompting change in New Jersey. The only occasion when a federal program had an apparent relationship to state taxes and the role of state government was when Medicaid was adopted by the state. Adopting this program as a state program meant the state would need greater revenues, and that played a role in creating pressure to raise revenues. But there was not direct pressure from the federal government. The state chose to adopt the program, underestimated the future financial obligations, as most states did, and then had to deal with the need for greater revenues.

That, coupled with the need for revenues to cope with a recession, resulted in an increase in the sales tax from 3 to 5 percent in 1970.

Perhaps the most persistent problem requiring state politicians to make a choice about taxes and the state's role was recessions. There were major recessions in 1969–70, 1981–82, and 1989–90. In each case, politicians were forced to decide whether they would cut state programs and aid or increase taxes. In every case, the decision was to raise taxes. Republican governor Cahill proposed an income tax, but settled for a sales tax increase. Republican governor Kean sought to maintain the role of the state, but with regressive taxes. Democrat Florio, faced with a recession and a court decision, responded with progressive taxes and an increased role for the state. All governors sought to maintain state programs and revenues, but the parties differed about the means of responding. Republican governors accepted more regressive taxes, while the Democrat pursued and enacted a progressive tax increase.

The other major stimulus state politicians had to contend with was court decisions about school finance. Four different administrations—two Democratic and two Republican—were presented with court decisions declaring the existing system of school finance unconstitutional. Byrne, a Democrat, responded by accepting the decision and proposing an income tax. His legislative party responded only when forced to respond. Florio, a Democrat, responded, even before the court decision was announced, with an increase in the sales and income tax, and a state aid program to provide much more money to middle- to lower-income school districts. His legislative party, with enormous reluctance and fear, accepted his proposal.

Republicans responded very differently. Kean opposed the plaintiffs' case about inequality at every turn. Whitman opposed the decision, and sought to redefine and reduce the obligation of the state to address problems of finance. Both Republican governors chose to focus on holding schools and teachers more accountable for how they were spending money and for their effectiveness in using resources. They consistently argued that more money was not the answer, and that more emphasis needed to be placed on what was being achieved with existing funds. They were not antieducation, but they were less sympathetic to just spending more money as the answer. Partisan dispositions again shaped the reactions to situations.

Partisanship matters, but not, in these cases, in the sense that party politicians take the initiative to propose policies. Party matters in that it shapes the proposals formed as responses to specific events. Differences in party dispositions exist, but in many ways these dispositions are latent. They become specifically relevant when a situation emerges that requires a choice to be made. Even then, party dispositions do not immediately result in a unified party response. Rather, a situation requiring a choice begins the process whereby the party assesses the extent of consensus within the party. In some cases that consensus is limited, which limits the ability of the party to form a coherent response. Despite this diversity, Democrats and Republicans differ significantly in their responses to situations.

While specific events, such as a recession or a court decision, are sometimes an obvious source of issues getting on the agenda, in other cases the source is more amorphous. Ideas—broad changes in conceptions of the sources of inequality and in the role of government—also play a very significant role. Ideas shape whether we see problems in society. In New Jersey, the issue of inequality of school finance illustrates the impact of ideas. It was not an issue in the 1950s, but it dominated the 1990s. Why did this issue become so powerful? Two changes in particular are important. First, the extent of inequality among municipal tax bases did actually increase. Reality changed. Second, and perhaps more important, this increase was accompanied by changing societal notions about inequality and the importance of equality of opportunity. Perceptions changed.

As discussed in chapter 2, from 1950 through the 1990s New Jersey, like most states, experienced a significant growth in its suburbs and decline in the central cities.[2] Tax bases were redistributed as population growth evolved. Cities like Newark were relatively affluent in 1950. When movement out of the city occurred, it was primarily by the more affluent. Those moving were not rich, but they had greater resources than those staying in central cities. The more affluent sought to live in communities where there would be similar populations and where homogeneity would be preserved and their property values would be preserved.[3] These preferences combined with zoning laws that allow communities to shape the size and expense of housing and resulted in communities segregated by income. The process of creating enclaves of wealth was probably accentuated in New Jersey by the enormous number of municipalities of limited geographical size in the state. As the population spread across the state, municipalities emerged with wealthy homes and highly valued commercial properties while other municipalities experienced less growth or even declines and had much lower valued properties. Inequality among areas developed.

The growth in this inequality can be seen in the previously discussed sample of sixty New Jersey municipalities over time. Figures 10.1 and 10.2 present indicators of the degree of diversity among tax bases and tax rates for these municipalities in 1952, 1969, and 1995. The important matter is not the average or absolute tax base or tax rate per municipality in any year, but the diversity among districts. Again, the coefficient of variation for school tax bases (assessed value per student, figure 10.1) increased from

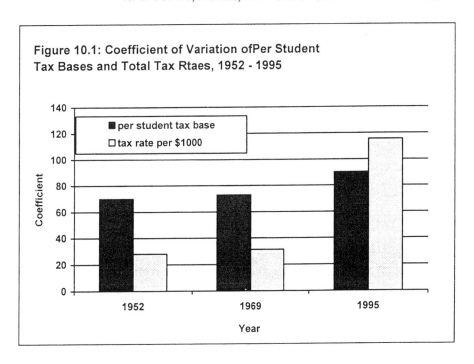

Figure 10.1: Coefficient of Variation ofPer Student Tax Bases and Total Tax Rtaes, 1952 - 1995

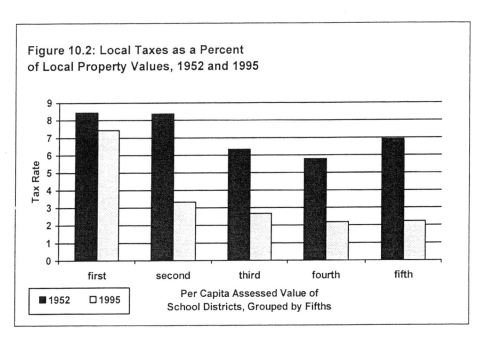

Figure 10.2: Local Taxes as a Percent of Local Property Values, 1952 and 1995

1952 to 1995. For figure 10.2, the municipalities are again grouped by fifths, ranging from the set with the lowest average per student tax base to the group with the highest average per student tax base. The tax rate is the average rate for those municipalities falling within each quintile.

Municipal tax rates (figure 10.2) decreased for all groups of municipalities from 1952 to 1995. Municipalities with wealthier tax bases, however, were able to lower their tax rates more than those municipalities with less-affluent tax bases. The result was that inequality of tax bases and of tax rates among municipalities increased over time.

These changes became crucial matters in public debates. The distribution of local property wealth, which finances schools and government services, was steadily becoming more unequal as populations relocated themselves. The spatial segregation of wealth increased, and that became a persistent issue in public debates. Critics of the inequality conducted studies, and developed indexes of the extent of inequality and of how much less wealth low-income school districts had relative to affluent districts. Critics pressured state commissions into gathering the same kinds of information. They persistently filed lawsuits about the degree of inequality.[4] In the case of schools, the fact that those harmed by these inequities were children made opposition more difficult. Within American individualism it is easy to blame adults for their poverty, but it is not easy to blame children. They do not choose to be poor, and their poverty is more difficult to justify or ignore. The unequal education opportunity they face creates a powerful issue of whether equality of opportunity is a fundamental principle of American society, and whether deviations from it will receive a response. The fact that the state plays a fundamental role in creating municipalities and granting them the power to zone, which leads to this inequality, also makes it difficult for the state to claim it has no responsibility for the resulting situation.

While reality—the equality of tax bases—was changing, this drew a response because beliefs changed. There was a growing belief that educational environment matters, and that government can and should do something about inequality. Without those changed beliefs, there would be little basis to react to inequality. Opportunities have always been unequal to some degree, but it is how we react to it that is important. The combination of greater inequality and the growing belief that inequality should be addressed made this an issue. Once the public perceives the existence of inequality and accepts the argument that it matters, the issue lingers even while many politicians would rather avoid it.[5] The existence of a sympathetic state court, willing to take on such a difficult policy issue, made it possible to translate this issue into an agenda item to put before politicians.

Without these court rulings the governor and the legislature would prob-ably have avoided the issue of inequality.

Change, therefore, stemmed largely from reactions to events such as recessions or court decisions. Parties were important because they consti-tuted collections of politicians with, on average, different dispositions as to how to react to events. Democrats were more willing, but generally not very willing, to respond by raising taxes and increasing the role of state government. Republicans were less inclined to respond in a way that would enhance the role of state government.

While the school finance issue was the most visible manifestation of this issue, and has received the most attention in New Jersey and in this analysis, it was not the only policy area in which issues of inequality and fairness played a role. In the 1950s there was concern about local varia-tions in the assessment of property. In the 1960s there was the emergence of concern about urban areas lacking the resources of other areas, while having more problems than other areas. The issue of housing opportunities surfaced in the 1970s and 1980s. Over time the general issue of variations in opportunities by area of the state persisted, gaining more prominence in some eras and less in others. Throughout, the interaction of actual social conditions and beliefs about inequality and opportunity became more im-portant.

DEMOCRATS AND THE HAVE-NOTS

V. O. Key once argued that without sustained representation, the have-nots lose in the political process.[6] He argued that the party of the have-nots must make a persistent case for their needs if there is to a public policy response to their problems. Over the long run—almost fifty years in this case—the situation of the have-nots was responded to with a progressive state tax system, adoption of Medicaid, greater state aid for central cities, state assumption of most welfare program costs, and a redistributive school aid program. Is the response in New Jersey a result of a sustained case made by a party of the have-nots? And what role did Republicans play as the opposition party?

Key was articulating a variant of the responsible-party model. This presumes that two parties with clearly different constituency bases will articulate contrasting policy concerns. In this model the party of the have-nots, the Democrats, will call attention to perceived injustices, and seek policies to benefit their constituencies. Their sustained representation of the have-nots will, in the long run, result in more favorable policies than would otherwise occur. New Jersey appears to fit that pattern. Major tax and policy changes came about when Democrats were in power, and those tax and state aid programs helped the less affluent.

The difficulty is that actual changes in New Jersey do not suggest a scenario quite like the responsible-party model. Change did occur, the Democrats played a major role, and redistribution has occurred. But Democrats certainly did not behave like a programmatic party seeking to help the have-nots. They did not announce programmatic positions during campaigns or at the beginning of new legislative sessions. The legislative party waited for governors to take the initiative on change, fought over whether to follow him, and only reluctantly voted for change. Further, they often distributed benefits widely, rather than targeting benefits for the less affluent, so that they significantly diminished the advantage for the less affluent from what it might have been. It would be difficult to characterize their actions as focused or sustained on behalf of the have-nots.

But as erratic as their focus on the have-nots was, they still were the party that enacted almost all the major changes in the role of state government. The difference from any simple model of party behavior is that party engagement in seeking to affect policy for their constituency was triggered by events, rather than being expressed as a sustained pursuit of a program. In contemporary terms, they were not proactive. Party dispositions emerge when events trigger them. If this study suggests anything about parties, it is that we should seek to assess them by how they react to situations requiring choice, and not by the norm of how much they offer programmatic policies when they attain political control. Party control may or may not coincide with events that create a decision juncture, and our efforts to understand parties should involve how they respond to the flow of conditions and events. Parties may engage in occasional statements of policy positions, but the serious announcement of their positions is done when necessary, and not as a steady set of pronouncement of policy positions. The disposition to represent the have-nots may be ever-present, but it needs to be activated.

When Democrats had power and sought to formulate policy proposals, their ability to play the role of advocate for the less affluent was complicated by their electoral base. When the Democrats achieved the governorship and a majority in both houses, they did so by winning significant votes and seats in the suburbs. While the wing of the party representing the poorer, urban areas was able to work for the less affluent without hesitation, suburban Democrats were constrained by anxiety about how redistributive positions would be received by the electorate. To the extent the Democratic Party depends on suburban seats, the role of the Democratic Party as an advocate for the less affluent is likely to be inhibited.

This situation is not unique to New Jersey. The suburban population has steadily increased in the United States,[7] and suburban areas have come to dominate many states.[8] State Democratic parties vary in how much they divide the electorate along class lines,[9] and in many states the Democratic Party can achieve a majority only by winning seats in suburban, middle-income areas. In such situations Democrats are more likely than Republicans to be the vehicle to challenge inequalities and the status quo, but their efforts will be erratic, and will be pursued with the same anxiety and reluctance as found in New Jersey. Democrats will have to contend with how their arguments and policies will play in the suburbs. Each venture in advocating change is likely to play out with some hesitation because of the enormous uncertainty of how an issue will play in the suburbs.

REPUBLICANS AND THE ISSUE OF THE STATE ROLE

Finally, there is the much-neglected political question of the policy impact of Republicans. Much of our attention is on Democrats as vehicles of change. Republicans are often seen as opponents of a greater state role and of redistributive programs. What do they do with power? Do they repeal changes? Republicans gained complete power only in 1970, which was after Democrats had enacted the sales tax in 1966. They gained partial power in 1982 (when Kean won as governor) and in 1985 (when Republicans took the assembly). In neither situation did Republicans seek to repeal changes. Indeed, they accepted the new status quo and, when faced with a recession, were willing to enact new taxes to maintain the state role.

The only case in which they did repeal prior enactments was in 1992, when the legislature repealed the 1 percent sales tax increase, and in 1994 - 95, when Whitman and the Republican legislature cut the income tax. But even in that situation, they did not cut back on state aid. The party was the beneficiary of strong and continuing growth in the economy, which resulted in increases in state revenues even as state taxes were being cut. They also financed much of the tax loss by dramatically cutting state contributions to the pension system and eventually borrowing money to pay back that obligation. What the party would have done if faced with a weak economy is mere speculation. The point is that the party accepted much of the current state obligation to provide state aid. They chose to cut contributions to the state pension system to avoid cutting the state's role.

Why do Republicans generally avoid cuts?[10] The effects of alternations in party control could be that state taxes and aid rise *and* fall as Democrats raise taxes and Republicans cut them. Republicans did not pursue that path in New Jersey. There are several possible reasons why they did not enact cuts in the role of government. One is that New Jersey is a relatively liberal Northeast state, with a higher percent of voters who support spending.[11] New Jersey may simply be a more activist state because of the general political dispositions of its population, and Republicans may simply be unwilling to support cuts in a relatively liberal context.

This relatively liberal disposition has surely been reinforced by the general growth of the belief that people are affected by their environment. This development coupled with the value that equality of opportunity should exist creates more of a sense that government should do something about social inequalities. While there are always groups that oppose government action, there is now more general support for government action than prevailed fifty years ago. Issues of how much government should do are a continual part of political debates. Some specific government programs may, of course, decline in legitimacy while others rise over time. Welfare has, for example, lost some of its legitimacy in this debate, because many argue it places too little emphasis on individual responsibility. Education does not appear to have lost any legitimacy over time. While these fluctuations occur, the general sense that government should somehow address issues of equality of opportunity persists.[12] This general political climate acts to restrain Republicans from making serious cuts in programs. Whitman, for example, while seeking to cut taxes, faced an electorate that supported greater equality of school finance, and was reluctant to appear unconcerned about inequality.

But the most serious source of restraint is likely to come from Democrats. As Key argued, Democrats can play the role of making a sustained case for the have-nots and portraying Republicans as catering to the affluent and being uncaring about equality. Changes in beliefs make this role a little easier, because they provide a basis for Democrats to raise issues of equity. The crucial matter is whether Democrats play that role and act to inhibit Republican actions. If the Democratic Party has a clear electoral base among the less affluent, they are more likely to play this role.

The three situations in which Republicans acquired power in New Jersey illustrate the impact Democrats can have on Republican actions. The first time Republicans acquired power was in 1969. This was during a time when liberal inclinations to enact social programs were arguably at their peak in the 1950–99 time period. Faced with a this general political climate, a shortfall in state revenues, and the demands of new programs, Republicans were inclined to continue increasing state taxes to support state government activities. They imposed new taxes to maintain state government activity levels, and Democrats did not have to mount a sustained criticism of Republicans.

The role of Democratic criticism became evident the next two times Republicans acquired a measure of power. In 1982, when Republican Tom Kean became governor, he faced a complicated situation. It is generally argued that there was declining support for government, as embodied by Ronald Reagan, and Kean had campaigned on cutting taxes. He had not, however, won a substantial majority and had no mandate. He was faced with a recession and a Democratic legislature. Kean tried to entangle Democrats in his proposed solution by indicating he would cut programs unless they gave him some regressive taxes. The situation was complicated, with much of the focus on trying to assign political blame, but Democrats were able to use the argument about fairness to achieve a maintained state effort and a more progressive tax system. Eventually he capitulated to their claims of fairness and approved an increase in the income tax on the affluent. The ability of the Democratic Party to make issues of fairness central to the budget discussions was crucial to restraining the actions of Republicans.

The most prominent case of Democratic criticism of Republican goals occurred in 1994. Christie Whitman, faced with a campaign promise to cut taxes, the consequence of reduced revenues for state aid, and persistent Democratic criticism that she was favoring the rich, chose to maintain state aid by cutting the state payment to the state pension system. This cut in contributions to the state workers' pension fund affected a group few would like to defend. In addition, and perhaps in anticipation of likely Democratic criticisms, she made sure her tax cut gave the affluent a smaller percentage cut, and she continued a progressive state income tax structure. A growing economy allowed her to deflect the Democratic criticism of cuts to favor the rich because there were no visible cuts in programs. The Democratic criticism, and the awareness that the attacks would grow more intense, and might be listened to if aid was cut, provides an example of how significant the Democratic role can be even when a party is out of power. In a society that worries about equality of opportunity, those attacks can have considerable impact. When effective, they inhibit Republicans from enacting significant cutbacks.[13]

Parties ultimately can matter a great deal. Democrats were willing to enact the major taxes to increase the state role. They were also willing to lead the attack on cuts in those few times that serious consideration was given to reducing the state role. That opposition may have prevented a cycle of an increasing state role under Democrats and a decreasing role under Republicans. Instead of such a cycle, over time there has been a significant net increase in the role of state government, and a significant increase in redistribution within the state.

Summarizing the Argument:
State Conditions and Party Debates

The argument presented in chapter 2 is that the Democratic Party is crucial to make a sustained argument on behalf of the less affluent and to keep Republicans hesitant about repealing programs and appearing uncaring. For Democrats to play this role, several specific conditions must prevail within a state. First, the state party must be fairly cohesive. As noted before, states differ in how well Democrats do among middle- to lower-income individuals,[14] and whether that also occurs across districts.[15] The greater the reliance of the party on the less affluent, the more likely the party will advocate their interests. On the other hand, the greater the proportion of votes and seats won among moderates and suburbs, the less adamant Democrats will be in their advocacy for the less affluent.

The behavior of Democrats will also be affected by the general political context. States vary considerably in the extent to which their population is liberal or conservative.[16] As conservatives increase in dominance, Democrats are likely to curtail their positions accordingly. To the extent that the state is liberal, Democrats are more likely to push a liberal agenda, and Republicans are more likely to be hesitant about repealing any redistributive policies that Democrats enact. Table 10.1 presents a summary of these conditions.

Table 10.1. State Political Conditions and
the Impact of Democrats

| | | Dominant Political Attitudes in the State | |
		Conservative	Liberal
Reliance of Democratic Party on less affluent	Low	Limited concern with equality and redistribution issues	
	High		High concern with equality and redistribution issues

By the 1980s and 1990s New Jersey had evolved to be closer to the lower-right cell than the upper-left cell. The population is relatively liberal. The Democratic Party did not have a clear electoral base in the 1950s, but by the 1980s and 1990s it clearly had consistent and high rates of success in legislative elections in less-affluent districts. The party had to win in suburban districts to attain a majority, which created strong tensions within the party. When a decision about a greater state role had to be made, however, the party, with considerable reluctance, came together three times across three decades to enact higher taxes and increase the role of state government. The combination of a relatively liberal population and a reluctantly cohesive Democratic Party resulted in enactment of policies that increased the role of state government and generated more redistributive policies. This situation has also restrained the Republicans from repealing these policies, with the consequence that the increase in the state role has not been reversed.

In other states, with a more conservative population, and a Democratic Party with less reliance on the less affluent and less cohesion about redistributive issues, there is likely to be very limited redistributive policy enacted. Texas, for example, has a Democratic Party that has only recently acquired either clarity or cohesion,[17] and it is also a relatively conservative state.[18] The consequence has been that the state has not enacted an income tax, and the fiscal role of state government has expanded little in recent decades.[19] The combination of conditions that prevail in other states and their effect can only be assessed after conducting case studies in those states. The New Jersey experience does provide suggestions, though, about what conditions must prevail for change in the state role to occur.

CRISIS AND PUBLIC ACCEPTANCE

The New Jersey experience also suggests something about what creates public acceptance of tax increases and a greater state role. Democrats Hughes and Florio interpreted their elections as providing the authority to enact change. They each sought to do so in a relatively rapid way. Hughes initially proposed an income tax, lost, and then had to return to the legislature to finally obtain a sales tax. Florio plunged in and got enactment of his proposed tax increase and greater state aid package relatively quickly. In both cases Democrats lost the legislature in the next election. Hughes lost just one house, and Florio lost both. Democrats may have lost in 1967 anyway, as the negative impact of Barry Goldwater on the Republican Party faded in the electorate's mind. But it is still the case that Democrats gambled and lost in the 1967 elections. Byrne and the legislative Democrats, on the other hand, did not lose following their enactment of an income tax in 1976. After a protracted battle over taxes, they enacted the income tax and survived in the 1977 elections.

These cases suggest something important about the dynamics of enacting change and gaining acceptance for change in the electorate. The public generally pays little attention to politics. Political conflicts that consume the state capital are often only dimly perceived by the electorate, even if numerous state commissions have published dramatic statements about the need for action and newspapers have printed numerous stories. For change to be accepted, it may be valuable for politicians to "allow" a crisis to emerge before casting votes. A crisis generates more media coverage, and makes it appear that politicians are reluctantly forced into enacting change. A protracted crisis also provides a politician with a justification for enacting a major change. This is particularly important when the change involves taxing people and redistributing wealth. Indeed, supporters of more money for low-income school districts in 1991 urged Jim Florio to drag the process out to convince everyone that he was somewhat forced into making change.[20] He was unwilling to do that, and his policies were subsequently rejected by the bulk of the electorate.

If the change is accepted, it then becomes the status quo, and creates a new level of state responsibility that is difficult to challenge and repeal. In the case of tax increases, the new tax system will also yield higher revenues when growth in the economy occurs. This, given acceptance of the new tax structure, allows the state to provide even more aid to local governments.

The legitimacy of an increased state role then creates a dynamic in which the state is likely to be drawn into further involvement. The increase in state aid in the 1950s created the issue of whether the state was then going to have to supervise local assessment practices—a sacred local prerogative—because state officials recognized varying local assessment practices and worried about how they were affecting the distribution of state aid. The increased state aid for local welfare and a state bureaucracy that generated studies documenting varying practices among jurisdictions created the issue of whether state government should do something to reduce these variations. The decision by state government to establish minimum standards for local education led to the issue of what state officials should do about local failures. That led to state takeover of several school districts in the 1980s and 1990s. With the enactment of the sales and income taxes, the state became a greater source of local government revenues. When the national economy declines and state revenues decline, the issue is generally whether the state will find some way to replace declining revenues. When state government provided little aid, the issue of maintaining state aid did not emerge with as much force as it does now. Every increase in the state role as a revenue provider makes it difficult to decrease that responsibility when the economy declines. Continuing increases in aid further entangle the state with local issues, and that is unlikely to change.

THE CONSEQUENCES OF CHANGE: THE STATE'S ROLE AND REDISTRIBUTION

Finally, there are the crucial questions of who wins and loses over the long run as these decisions are made, and what role parties, and particularly Democrats, played in shaping long run outcomes. Did all these confrontations and changes really achieve any redistribution? Did Democrats play a major role or does change flow from both parties in response to broad societal changes in notions of fairness and equity?

Three policy areas have involved fundamental questions of equity and redistribution: tax policy, school finance, and access to affordable housing. The state's intrusion into forcing the creation of affordable housing in more municipalities was relatively limited. While Republicans put up the greatest resistance, members of both parties were reluctant to get involved in an issue that involved affecting people's achievements and their right to shape with whom they lived. The result was very little change in this area. The Democrats did not act as a cohesive party seeking to significantly increase low-income housing opportunities, and little changed.

In the area of tax policy, some very fundamental and progressive changes were made. State efforts in raising tax revenue displaced local tax efforts. The state enacted an income tax, and twice made it more progressive. This greater reliance on the income tax as a source of state revenue has enormous consequences for equity. First, it means that a smaller percentage of state and local taxes are raised from the regressive property tax. Second, as conservatives have noted, the collection of this revenue at the state level has enormous potential for further redistribution. More tax revenue is collected from affluent suburbs than from central cities. That revenue is then available for distribution through the political process. This potential for redistributive activities is not present in states where large portions of all tax revenues are collected at the local level within communities that vary in affluence.

The important matter is how these additional revenues are distributed. Over time the state assumed responsibility for more welfare costs and adopted the Medicaid program. These are programs that primarily benefit lower-income residents of the state. The combination of the state playing a greater role in raising taxes and in funding these programs creates significant redistribution. In addition to these programs, there is also the issue of whether the distribution of state aid affects inequality. Did all the battles over state aid reduce inequality within the state? The next four charts provide a simple overview of what happened in the area of school finance, the area that received the most attention over the years. As noted before, inequality of local tax bases increased over time. Over time the state also increased aid to local schools. Figure 10.3, using the same sixty municipalities as analyzed before, indicates the percent of local school revenue, per student, that came from local and state sources in 1952. Again, districts are arrayed from those with the lowest tax base per student (the "first" category) to those with the highest tax base per student (the "fifth category). In 1952 the state provided minimal resources to all districts, and what was provided had only a slight redistributive effect, with the poorer districts getting a higher percentage of their resources from the state. The situation by 1995 is shown in figure 10.4. The state contribution increased significantly, and the extent of redistribution was much greater. Whether there is enough redistribution is something that will be argued about in the political process and the courts for some time. What is clear, however, is that there is now much greater reliance on state aid than in the 1950s, and districts with poorer tax bases receive a substantial portion of their resources from the state. The data from the studies used by the Education Law Center in Newark (see chapter 6) suggest that if the focus is on all districts, arrayed from poorest to wealthiest, the state role in redistribution is now even greater than this random sample suggests.

Another important indicator is the equality of spending among school districts. Figures 10.5 and 10.6 present the total per student spending, and the amount from local and state sources, for the sixty districts. In 1952 there was considerable variation in spending levels, and state aid played a minor role in remedying those inequities. By 1995, state aid had come to play a major role, with that role greater in districts with a poorer tax base. As suburbanization shifted tax bases, the distribution of state aid has played a major role in offsetting some of the developing inequality in tax bases. While critics, and to some extent the courts, are not satisfied with the degree of equality that has been achieved, the long-term impact of higher taxes and how those revenues are distributed indicates that the response of the state has clearly helped the less affluent. The battle over taxes and aid resulted in redistribution of resources within the state. In the end, the party battles over state government have mattered a great deal. A decentralized system would entail much more inequality in resources than prevails now.

The New Jersey experience suggests that Democrats are often reluctant to lead the battle over inequality. It also appears that it is crucial to have the presence of a state court willing to push the issue. The ultimate effect on public policy of even a reluctant Democratic Party is, however, very significant.

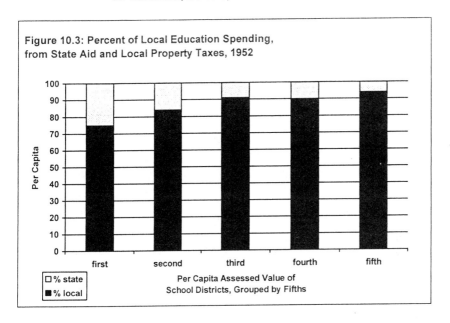

Figure 10.3: Percent of Local Education Spending, from State Aid and Local Property Taxes, 1952

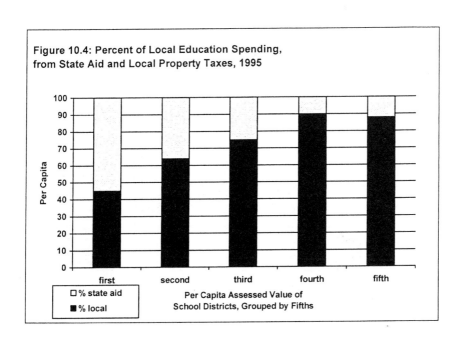

Figure 10.4: Percent of Local Education Spending, from State Aid and Local Property Taxes, 1995

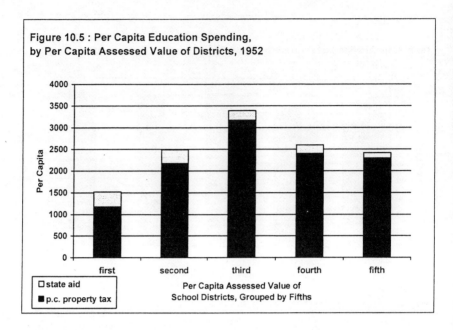

Figure 10.5 : Per Capita Education Spending,
by Per Capita Assessed Value of Districts, 1952

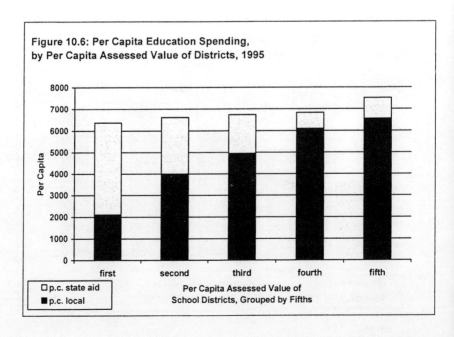

Figure 10.6: Per Capita Education Spending,
by Per Capita Assessed Value of Districts, 1995

Notes

PREFACE

1. Ann Bowman and Richard Kearney, *The Resurgence of the States* (Englewood Cliffs, N.J.: Prentice-Hall); and David B. Walker, *The Rebirth of Federalism* (Chatham: Chatham House, 1995), 251–57. For a different perspective on the states, see Morton Keller, "State Government Needn't Be Resurrected Because it Never Died," in *State Government: CQ's Guide to Current Issues and Activities, 1989–90,* ed. Thad L. Beyle (Washington, D.C.: Congressional Quarterly, 1989), 174.

2. William H. Flanigan and Nancy H. Zingale, *Political Behavior of the American Electorate*, 9th ed. (Washington, D.C: CQ Press, 1998), 12–15.

3. David M. Hedge, *Governance and the Changing American States* (Boulder, Colo.: Westview Press, 1998).

4. Alice M. Rivlin, *Reviving the American Dream* (Washington, D.C.: Brookings Institution, 1992), 85–109.

5. Ballard C. Campbell, *The Growth of American Government* (Bloomington: Indiana University Press, 1995), 68–70, 180–96; and David C. Nice and Patricia Frederickson, *The Politics of Intergovernmental Relations*, 2d ed. (Chicago: Nelson-Hall, 1995), 161–66.

6. The major change in state roles in the 1930s occurred when local property taxes were cut significantly and state taxes were increased. See Susan Hansen, *The Politics of Taxation: Revenue without Representation* (New York: Praeger, 1983), 154; and Jeffrey M. Stonecash, "The Reluctant Emergence of State Governments: Property Tax Revolts and State Tax Increases," Department of Political Science, Maxwell School, Syracuse University, 2000.

7. Jeffrey M. Stonecash, "Fiscal Centralization in the American States: Similarity and Diversity," *Publius* 13, no. 4 (Fall 1983): 123–37; and Jeffrey M. Stonecash, "The Politics of State-Local Relations," in *Governing Partners,* ed. Russell L. Hanson (Boulder, Colo.: Westview Press, 1998), 81.

8. Nancy Burns, *The Formation of American Local Governments* (New York: Oxford University Press, 1994).

9. These issues are reviewed in Dennis R. Judd and Todd Swanstrom, *City Politics: Private Power and Public Policy* (New York: Longman, 1998), 259–315. For the battle over federal and state responsibility for responding to local governments with varying tax bases, see Richard Child Hill, "Federalism and Urban Policy: The Intergovernmental Dialectic," in *The Changing Face of Fiscal Federalism,* ed. Thomas R. Swartz and John E. Peck (Armonk, N.Y.: M. E. Sharpe, 1990), 35–55.

10. V. O. Key, *Southern Politics* (New York: Knopf, 1949), 307.

11. Barbara G. Salmore and Stephen A. Salmore, *New Jersey Politics and Government: Suburban Politics Comes of Age* (Lincoln: University of Nebraska Press, 1993), 8

12. For a summary of the national debate, see Jeffrey M. Stonecash, *Class and Party in American Politics* (Boulder, Colo.: Westview, 2000), chaps. 3 and 4.

Chapter 1. The Role of the State

1. Advisory Commission on Intergovernmental Relations, *State Limitations on Local Taxes and Expenditures* (Washington, D.C.: U.S. Government Printing Office, 1977); Jeffrey M. Stonecash, "State Policies Regarding Local Resource Acquisition," *American Politics Quarterly* 9, no. 4 (October 1981): 401–25; Burns, *Formation of Local Governments.*

2. For a review of these issues, see the chapters in Russell L. Hanson, ed., *Governing Partners* (Boulder, Colo.: Westview Press, 1998).

3. For a discussion of this controversy, see Martha Derthick, *The Influence of Federal Grants* (Cambridge: Harvard University Press, 1969).

4. Kenneth T. Jackson, *Crabgrass Frontier: The Suburbanization of the United States* (New York: Oxford University Press, 1985); Douglas S. Massey and Nancy A, Denton, *American Apartheid* (Cambridge: Harvard University Press, 1993); Thomas J. Sugrue, *The Origins of the Urban Crisis* (Princeton: Princeton University Press, 1996).

5. Michael Danielson, *The Politics of Exclusion* (New York: Columbia University Press, 1976).

6. E. Blaine Liner, "Sorting Out State–Local Relations," in *A Decade of Devolution: Persepectives on State–Local Issues,* ed. E. Blaine Liner (Washington, D.C: Urban Institute Press, 1989), 21–22.

7. Jonathon Kozol, *Savage Inequalities* (New York: Crown, 1991).

8. Alan Rosenthal, *The Decline of Representative Democracy.* (Washington, D.C.: CQ Press, 1997).

9. Barbara G. Salmore and Stephen A. Salmore, *Candidates, Parties, and Campaigns,* 2d ed. (Washington, D.C.: Congressional Quarterly Press, 1989).

10. Advisory Commission on Intergovernmental Relations, *Significant Features of Fiscal Federalism, 1987 Edition* (Washington, D.C., June 1987), 31.

11. Ibid., 37.

12. All fiscal data are taken from the annual report of the Census of Governments, *Governmental Finances,* GF 5. This was issued as a printed report until 1991. Subsequent reports are taken from the web page of the Census of Governments.

13. This index is explained in , G. Ross Stephens, "Fiscal Centralization in the States," *Journal of Politics* 36 (February 1974): 52–66; and Jeffrey M. Stonecash, "Centralization in State–Local Fiscal Relationships," *Western Political Quarterly* 36 (1981): 301–9.

14. Jeffrey M. Stonecash, "Fiscal Centralization in the American States: Findings from Another Perspective," *Public Budgeting and Finance* 8, no. 4 (Winter 1988): 81–89.

15. For analyses that address the issue of the nature of change, see: Robert B. Albritton, "Measuring Public Policy: Impacts of the Supplemental Social Security Income Program," *American Journal of Political Science* 23 (1979): 559–78; and Jeffrey M. Stonecash, "Incremental and Abrupt Change in Fiscal Centralization in the American States, 1957–1983," in *The Politics of Intergovernmental Relations,* ed. David R. Morgan. (Westport, Conn: Greenwood Press, 1985), 189–200.

16. For examples of studies that seek to assess long-term changes or short-term changes, see: James C. Garand "Explaining Growth in the U.S. States," *American Political Science Review* 82 (September 1988): 837–49; Gregory R. Weiher and Jon Lawrence, "Growth in

State Government Employment: A Time Series Analysis," *Western Political Quarterly* 44 (June 1991): 373–88; and Frances Stokes Berry and William D. Berry, "Tax Innovation in the States: Capitalizing on Political Opportunity," *American Journal of Political Science* 36 (August 1992): 715–42.

17. Key, *Southern Politics*, 298–311.

18. Jeffrey M. Stonecash, "Inter-Party Competition, Political Dialogue, and Public Policy: A Critical Review," *Policy Studies Journal* 16, no. 2 (Winter 1987–88): 243–62.

19. Frances Stokes Berry and William D. Berry, "Tax Innovation in the States: Capitalizing on Political Opportunity," *American Journal of Political Science* 36, no. 3 (August 1992): 735.

20. For examples of such efforts, see Richard E. Dawson, and James A. Robinson, "Inter-Party Competition, Economic Variables, and Welfare Policies in the American States," *Journal of Politics* 25 (1963): 265–89; Thomas R. Dye, *Politics, Economic, and the Public: Policy Outcomes in the American States* (Chicago: Rand McNally, 1969), chaps. 1, 2, and 11; Michael Lewis-Beck, "The Relative Importance of Socio-Economic and Political Variables for Public Policy," *American Political Science Review* 71 (1977): 559–65; Thomas R. Dye, "Party and Policy in the American States," *Journal of Politics* 46, no. 4 (November 1984): 1097–1116; James D. King, "Interparty Competition in the American States: An Examination of Index Components," *Western Political Quarterly* 42, no. 1 (March 1989): 83–92; Joseph A. Aistrup, "State Legislative Party Competition: A County–Level Measure," *Political Research Quarterly* 46, no. 2 (March 1993): 433–46; Thomas M. Holbrook and Emily Van Dunk, "Electoral Competition in the American States," *American Political Science Review* 87, no. 4 (December 1993): 955–62.

21. Gerald C. Wright, Robert C. Erikson, and John P. McIver, "Measuring State Partisanship and Ideology with Survey Data," *Journal of Politics* 47 (1985): 47, 469–89; Robert S. Erikson, John P. McIver, and Gerald C. Wright, "State Political Culture and Public Opinion," *American Political Science Review* 81, no. 3 (September 1987): 797–813; Gerald C. Wright, Robert S. Erikson, and John P. McIver, "Public Opinion and Policy Liberalism in the American States," *American Journal of Political Science* 31, no. 4 (November 1987): 980–1001; and Robert S. Erikson, Gerald C. Wright, and John P. McIver, *Statehouse Democracy* (New York: Cambridge University Press, 1993).

22. Robert D. Brown and Gerald C. Wright, "Elections and State Party Polarization," *American Politics Quarterly* 20, no. 4 (October 1992): 411–26; and Robert D. Brown, "Party Cleavage and Welfare Effort in the American States," *American Political Science Review* 89, no. 1 (March 1995): 23–33.

23. Berry and Berry, "Tax Innovation in the States," 735.

24. This is the primary limitation of diffusion studies. They provide valuable information about how policy adoption (change) was diffused through the states, and what state traits are associated with early or late adoption, but these studies provide no information about the dynamics of decision-making within states. For examples of these studies, see Jack L. Walker, "The Diffusion of Innovations among the American States," *American Political Science Review* 63, no. 10 (September 1969): 880–99; Virginia Gray, "Innovation in the States," *American Political Science Review* 67, no. 10 (December 1973): 1174–85; Robert L. Savage, "Policy Innovativeness as a Trait of American States," *Journal of Politics* 40, no. 10 (February 1978): 212–24; and Robert L. Savage, "Diffusion Research Traditions and the Spread of Policy Innovations," *Publius* 15, no. 4 (Fall 1985): 1–28.

25. Alexander L. George, "Case Studies and Theory Development: The Method of Structured, Focused Comparison," in *Diplomacy: New Approaches in History, Theory and Policy,* ed. Paul G. Lauren (New York: Free Press, 1979), 44.

26. Jeffrey M. Stonecash, "The State Politics Literature: Moving Beyond Covariation Studies and Pursuing Politics," *Polity* 28, no. 4 (Summer 1996): 561–81.

27. For a general discussion of case study research, see Robert K. Yin, *Case Study Research: Design and Methods*, 2d ed. (Thousand Oaks, Calif.: Sage, 1994).

28. Case studies have been used to examine single states, states within a region, or sets of states. As examples, see: John Fenton, *Midwest Politics* (New York: Holt, Rinehart, and Winston, 1966); Earl Black, *Southern Governors and Civil Rights: Racial Segregation as a Campaign Issue in the Second Reconstruction* (Cambridge: Harvard University Press, 1976); Jennings, "Some Policy Consequences of the Long Revolution"; Richard Winters, "Political Choice and Expenditure Change in New Hampshire and Vermont," *Polity* 12, no. 4 (Summer 1980): 598–621; Diana Dwyre, Mark O'Gorman, Jeffrey M. Stonecash, and Rosalie Young, "Disorganized Politics and the Have-nots: Taxes and Politics in New York and California," *Polity* 27, no. 1 (Fall 1994): 25–47; and Thad Beyle, ed., *Hard Times* (Washington, D.C: Congressional Quarterly Press, 1992). In recent years the University of Nebraska has published a series of books on single states.

29. George, "Case Studies and Theory Development," 43–45.

30. Arend Lijphart, "The Comparable-Cases Strategy in Comparative Research," *Comparative Political Studies* 8, no. 2 (July 1975): 159–61.

31. Harry Eckstein, "Case Study and Theory in Political Science," in *Strategies of Inquiry,* ed. Fred Greenstein and Nelson Polsby (Reading, Mass.: Addison-Wesley, 1975), 80; and George, "Case Studies and Theory Development," 43–45.

32. Donald T. Campbell, "'Degrees of Freedom' and the Case Study," *Comparative Political Studies* 8, no. 2 (July 1975): 178–86.

33. Eckstein, "Case Study and Theory in Political Science," 113–23.

34. Stonecash, "Fiscal Centralization in the American States," 81–89; and Stonecash, "The Reluctant Emergence of State Governments."

35. For an excellent recent example, see Salmore and Salmore, *New Jersey Politics and Government.*

CHAPTER 2. POLICY CHANGE AND THE ROLE OF PARTIES

1. Studies differ in the extent to which they assume contextual traits are a cause or source of change. The diffusion studies track the speed of policy adoption (change) across states, and what state traits are associated with early or late adoption. The limit of these studies is that within-state decision processes are never probed, so we never know why there are patterns of association or nonassociation. This study of New Jersey, in contrast, is focused on why actors within the state were willing to adopt new tax policies. For examples of these studies, see Walker, "Diffusion of Innovations among the American States," 880–99; Gray, "Innovation in the States," 1174–85; Savage, "Policy Innovativeness as a Trait of American States," 212–24; and Savage, "Diffusion Research Traditions and the Spread of Policy Innovations," 1–28.

2. Key, *Southern Politics*, 307.

3. Frank Levy, *Dollars and Dreams: The Changing American Income Distribution.* (New York: W. W. Norton, 1988); Sheldon Danziger and Peter Gottschalk, *America Unequal* (Cambridge: Harvard University Press, 1995), 39–66.

4. For discussions of inequality as a political issue, see Kevin Phillips, *The Politics of Rich and Poor: Wealth and the American Electorate in the Reagan Aftermath.* (New York: Random House, 1990); Kevin Phillips, *Boiling Point: Republicans, Democrats, and the Decline of Middle-Class Prosperity* (New York: Random House, 1993); and John E. Schwarz, *Illusions of Opportunity* (New York: W. W. Norton, 1997).

5. Gary Orfield, *The Closing Door* (Cambridge: Harvard University Press), 205–34.

6. Kenneth T. Jackson, *The Crabgrass Frontier* (New York: Columbia University

Press, 1985); and Dennis R. Judd and Todd Swanstrom, *City Politics* (New York: HarperCollins, 1994).

7. Salmore and Salmore, *New Jersey Politics and Government,* 3–6.

8. The year 1955 is used because this is the first year that the state published estimates of the true or full value of assessed property within each state. This move to estimate the full value of property—taking account of the different assessment ratios across the state—was a product of the state's concern about varying assessment practices and reliance on these estimated property values in distributing state aid. This development is discussed in chapter 3.

9. The full value property wealth for each county for 1955 and 1994 was taken from Annual Reports released by State of New Jersey, Department of the Treasury, Division of Taxation, Local Property Branch, "Table of Equalized Valuations," for the indicated years.

10. To put tax bases in constant dollar amounts (adjusting for or eliminating inflation), the standard approach is to divide dollar figures by the Consumer Price Index for that year. The CPI index is first adjusted by multiplying it by .01, so an index of, say, 200 is expressed in terms of the ratio of prices to a base of 1. If the ratio is 2 then prices are twice as high. If a tax base is $50,000 per student and goes to $100,000, and the index goes from 100 (1.0) to 200 (2.0), then the real value of the tax base is $50,000 in each year. One further adjustment is made in this case. To make sure all figures are expressed in contemporary values, the index is set to have the current year equal 100. This is done by dividing the index of 1955 by the index for 1994. If the index were 200 now, then division by 200 will give the current year a value of 1.0. If the index were 100 twenty years ago, then dividing by 200 will give an index for twenty years ago of .5. Dividing values from twenty years ago by .5 will double their real value. This should occur, since inflation has lowered the real value of current tax bases, and tax bases prior to inflation were really worth more twenty years ago.

11. The role of education as a source of equality of opportunity is fundamental to elites and to the mass public. For the former, see Grant Reeher, *Narratives of Justice: Legislator' Beliefs about Distributive Justice* (Ann Arbor: University of Michigan Press, 1996), 63, 127. For the latter see Jennifer Hochschild, *Facing Up to the American Dream: Race, Class, and the Soul of the Nation* (Princeton: Princeton University Press, 1995).

12. Kenneth Newton, "Feeble Governments and Private Power: Urban Politics and Policies in the United States," in *The New Urban Politics,* ed. Louis H. Masotti and Robert L. Lineberry (Cambridge: Ballinger, 1976), 37–58; and Michael Danielson, *The Politics of Exclusion* (New York: Columbia University Press, 1976).

13. Rusk, *Cities without Suburbs;* Gary Orfield, *Closing Door;* and Douglas S. Massey and Nancy Denton, *American Apartheid* (Cambridge: Harvard University Press, 1993).

14. The sample was derived as follows. There were 567 municipalities in New Jersey in 1996. Financial data on each municipality is contained in the *Annual Reports of the Division of Local Government Services,* for various years. The municipalities are also summarized in *The New Jersey Municipal Data Book,* various editions. The 1992–93 edition had all the municipalities listed alphabetically. This order is presumably random, since size, place, time of origin, or wealth play no role in the ranking. To minimize the data collection necessary, every tenth municipality was selected. For each municipality, the total tax base (nominal and full value) was recorded, along with the population size, the number of students enrolled in the accompanying school district, and the total tax rate per $100 and the school tax rate per $100. This sample includes significant diversity in size and tax bases. To obtain equivalent information on the same set of municipalities for prior years, the *Financial Statistics of New Jersey Municipalities and Schools* was used. For recent years I employed the *Annual Reports of the Division of Local Government Services* for various years, to be indicated in the text. The *Annual Report* focuses on school districts, but it contains the tax base for the accompanying municipality, student enrollment, and the school

and total tax rate. The total population for the municipalities for the relevant years was acquired from census documents.

15. The reports indicate that the assessed values for each municipality are the equalized values, which suggests that the state had adjusted the values for the differences in assessment rates across communities, such that it is possible to compare assessed valuations across communities.

16. An example may help illustrate how the coefficient of variation captures changing diversity even as mean scores are changing. In this example, one set of numbers will have changing means over time, but constant real diversity. In the second set of cases the degree of diversity increases as mean values increase over time. Assume, in the first case, that in three different years there are three municipalities. In each year there is a mean score, a score 25 percent above the mean and another 25 percent below the mean. The mean changes over time, but the relative dispersion of cases around the mean (25 percent plus or minus) does not change. The scores are: year 1: 7.5, 10, 12.5; year 2: 15, 20, 25; year 3: 22.5, 30, 37.5. The standard deviation for the three years is 2.5, 5.0, and 7.5, but the coefficient of variation for the three years is 25, 25, and 25. For the second set of numbers, the numbers are: year 1: 7.5, 10, 12.5; year 2: 13, 20, 27.5; year 3: 18, 30, 42. In both sets of cases the mean values increase by the same amount over time, but there is greater dispersion around the mean in the second set of numbers. The coefficient of variation increases from 25 to 35 to 40 over the three years. This increasing coefficient of variation indicates a real increase in the degree of dispersion around the mean value.

17. See note 10.

18. The grouping into fifths is done according to the distribution within each year. The concern is the differences between the top and bottom fifth in any given year, and not to track how a specific municipality moves over time. There is a limitation to the method employed here, which should be noted. Income distribution data have all income recipients and can classify all recipients within any year into fifths. In this case a set sample is tracked. It is possible that just this set of sixty municipalities became more divergent over time, and that the overall population of municipalities did not. That appears to be unlikely, because, as will be discussed throughout the book, those who filed suit charging inequality of school finance continually produced evidence of growing inequalities.

19. The role of these beliefs is discussed by Robert Wuthnow, *The Consciousness Reformation* (Berkeley: University of California Press, 1976); and Grant Reeher, *Narratives of Justice* (Ann Arbor: University of Michigan Press, 1996).

20. Jacob Weisberg, *In Defense of Government: The Fall and Rise of Public Trust* (New York: Scribner, 1996), 49–81.

21. James T. Patterson, *America's Struggle against Poverty* (Cambridge: Harvard University Press, 1994), 78–96.

22. Robert Weisbrot, *Freedom Bound: A History of the Civil Rights Movement* (New York: Penguin, 1991).

23. Patterson, *America's Struggle against Poverty*, 99–114.

24. Judd and Swanstrom, *City Politics*, 179–214.

25. Robert Jay Dilger, "The Expansion and Centralization of American Governmental Functions," in *American Intergovernmental Relations Today,* ed. Robert Jay Dilger (Englewood Cliffs, N.J.: Prentice-Hall, 1986), 18–22.

26. William H. Flanigan and Nancy H. Zingale, *Political Behavior of the American Electorate,* 8th ed. (Washington, D.C: CQ Press, 1994), 8–11.

27. Charles Murray, *Losing Ground* (New York: Basic Books, 1984).

28. Thomas B. Edsall and Mary D. Edsall, *Chain Reaction: The Impact of Race, Rights, and Taxes on American Politics* (New York: W. W. Norton, 1991), 198–214; and Stanley B. Greenberg, *Middle-Class Dreams* (New York: Times Book, 1995).

29. For reviews of the development of the conservative movement over the last several decades, see Paul Gottfried and Thomas Fleming, *The Conservative Movement* (Boston: Twayne Publishers, 1988); Jerome L. Himmelstein, *To the Right: The Transformation of American Conservatism* (Berkeley: University of California Press, 1990); and Godfrey Hodgson, *The World Turned Right Side Up* (Boston: Mariner Books, 1996).

30. Robert Dilger, *National Intergovernmental Programs* (Englewood Cliffs, N.J.: Prentice-Hall, 1989), 20; and see Jeffrey M. Stonecash, *American State and Local Politics* (Fort Worth, Tex.: Harcourt, 1995), 35–37, for an overview of reimbursement rates for different programs.

31. Donald F. Kettl, *The Regulation of American Federalism* (Baltimore: Johns Hopkins University Press, 1987).

32. Edwin Amenta and Bruce G. Carruthers, "The Formative Years of U.S. Spending Policy: Theories of the Welfare State and the American States during the Great Depression," *American Sociological Review* 53 (1988): 661–78; and Edwin Amenta, Elisabeth S. Clemens, Jefren Olsen, Sunita Parikh, and Theda Skocpol, "The Political Origins of Unemployment Insurance in Five American States," *Studies in American Political Development.* 2 (1987):: 137–82.

33. Martha Derthick, "Intercity Differences in Administration of the Public Assistance Program: The Case of Massachusetts," in *City Politics and Public Policy,* ed. James Q. Wilson (New York: John Wiley, 1968), 243–66.

34. Martha Derthick, *The Influence of Federal Grants* (Cambridge: Harvard University Press, 1970); and Susan Welch and Kay Thompson, "The Impact of Federal Incentives on State Policy Innovation." *American Journal of Political Science* 24, no. 4 (November 1980): 715–29.

35. Advisory Commission on Intergovernmental Relations, *State Limitations on Local Taxes and Expenditures* (Washington, D.C.: U.S. Government Printing Office, 1977); Advisory Commission on Intergovernmental Relations, *State Mandating of Local Expenditures* (Washington, D.C.: U.S. Government Printing Office, 1977).

36. Jeffrey M. Stonecash, "State Responses to Declining National Support: Behavior in the Post 1978 Era," *Policy Studies Journal* 18, no. 3 (Spring 1990): 214–26.

37. Key, *Southern Politics,* 307.

38. The ideal is based on the "responsible party" model, which was articulated in American Political Science Association, "A Report of the Committee on Political Parties," *American Political Science Review* 44 (September 1950): 1–99; and American Political Science Association, *Toward a More Responsible Party System* (New York: Holt, Rinehart, and Winston, 1950).

39. For national elections, see Paul Allen Beck and Frank J. Sorauf, *Party Politics in America* (New York: HarperCollins, 1992), 159–68; Jeffrey M. Stonecash, *Class and Party in American Politics* (Boulder, Colo.: Westview Press, 2000); and for state legislatures, see: Jeffrey M. Stonecash, "Political Cleavage in State Legislative Houses," *Legislative Studies Quarterly* 24, no. 2 (May 1999): 281–302.

40. Jonathan Kozol, *Savage Inequalities* (New York: Crown, 1991).

41. For some time in state politics the approach was to assume that state party electoral bases differed as the national parties did. See Stonecash, "Inter-Party Competition, Political Dialogue, and Public Policy," 243–62. In recent years, there have been studies that employ survey data to assess differences in the bases of state parties. Several analyses have been done with this focus. See the works associated with the project culminating in Robert S. Erikson, Gerald C. Wright, and John P. McIver, *State House Democracy* (New York: Cambridge University Press, 1993); and Robert D. Brown and Gerald C. Wright, "Elections and State Party Polarization," *American Politics Quarterly* 20 (October 1992): 411–26. It is also possible to assess the differences in the electoral bases of state political parties

by using the demographic traits of state legislative districts to examine how Democratic and Republican success varies as the income of districts varies. See Stonecash, "Political Cleavage in State Legislative Houses."

42. See evidence of state variations in Stonecash, "Political Cleavage in State Legislative Elections."

43. The only recent study of state party platforms is Joel Paddock, "Inter-Party Ideological Differences in Eleven State Democratic Parties," *Western Political Quarterly* 45, no. 3 (September 1992): 751–60.

44. Salmore and Salmore, *Candidates, Parties, and Campaigns.*

45. David Morgan, *The Capitol Press Corps* (Westport, Conn: Greenwood Press, 1978); Phil Brooks and Bob W. Gassaway, "Improving News Coverage," *State Legislatures,* March 1985, 29–31; and William T. Gormley, "Coverage of State Government in the Mass Media," *State Government* 52, no. 2 (1979): 45–51.

46. Willaim H. Flanigan and Nancy H. Zingale, *Political Behavior of the American Electorate,* 9th ed. (Washington, D.C.: CQ Press, 1998), 35–37.

47. Martin Wattenberg, *The Decline of American Political Parties, 1952–1994* (Cambridge: Harvard University Press, 1996), 36–49.

48. Among those studies finding mixed evidence for the impact of party control are Terrence Jones, "Political Change and Spending Shifts in the American States," *American Politics Quarterly* 2 (1974): 414–29; Thomas R. Dye, "Party and Policy in the States," *Journal of Politics* 46, no. 4 (November 1984): 1097–1115; and James A. Garand "Partisan Change and Shifting Expenditure Priorities in the American States," *American Politics Quarterly* 13 (October 1985): 355–91. These studies share the approach of assuming all state parties have the same electoral bases, and find that sometimes state party control matters and sometimes it does not. The variation in found impact is to be expected, since states were not differentiated based on any evidence. The studies which do seek to differentiate the electoral bases of states find that a clear difference (cleavage) between the parties does result in clear policy effects when party control shifts. For these studies, see Edward T. Jennings, "Competition, Constituencies, and Welfare Policies in American States," *American Political Science Review* 73 (1979): 414–29; and Robert D. Brown, "Party Cleavages and Welfare Effort in the American States," *American Political Science Review* 89, no. 1 (March 1995): 23–33.

49. E. J. Dionne, *Why Americans Hate Politics* (New York: Touchstone, 1991).

50. Donald T. Campbell, "'Degrees of Freedom' and the Case Study," *Comparative Political Studies* 8, no. 2 (July 1975): 178–86.

51. Harry Eckstein, "Case Study and Theory in Political Science," in *Strategies of Inquiry,* ed. Fred Greenstein and Nelson Polsby (Reading, Mass.: Addison-Wesley, 1975), 80.

52. Eckstein, "Case Study and Theory in Political Science;" and George, "Case Studies and Theory Development," 43–45.

53. These presumptions were made in many of the early state level studies of political parties. The differentiation presumption is evident in the coding for party control. Democratic control (1 in a dummy variable) could be coded as different from Republican control (0 in a dummy variable). The unitary presumption was evident in that a party was simply treated as unified or an entity without having to examine the composition of the party. It was assumed that a party that acquired control would act in a unified way. More accurately, the approach was to inquire if the party acted in a unified way, and then not explore why a party did not fit the presumption. These presumptions existed in the works cited in note 36 above, such as Jones and Garand. Later works by Jennings (1979) and Dye (1984) made an effort to distinguish states according to whether the parties in a state represented differing groups. These studies assumed invariance of party behavior by assuming that party inclination to enact change would be constant over time.

54. Technically, this occurs when an analysis is run in which Democrats are coded as 1 and Republicans as 0, and the question is whether the presence of Democrats leads to higher taxes or higher spending in a particular area.

55. For a study that documents that among state legislative party candidates Republicans are more conservative than Democrats, see John Frendreis, Alan R. Gitelson, Gregory Flemming, and Anne Layzell, "State Legislative Elections: Choices or Echoes," in *Do Elections Matter?*, ed. Benjamin Ginsberg and Alan Stone (Armonk, N.Y.: M. E. Sharpe, 1991), 190–204. For an analysis indicating that Democratic state party officials are more liberal than Republican state party officials, see Gerald Wright, Robert Erikson, and John McIver, "Political Parties, Public Opinion, and State Policy in the United States," *American Political Science Review* 83, no. 3 (September 1989): 729–50.

56. This argument is made in Jeffrey M. Stonecash, "The State Politics Literature: Moving Beyond Covariation Studies and Pursuing Politics," *Polity* 28, no. 4 (Summer 1996): 561–81.

57. The idea that the policy pursuits of parties are contingent on their internal coherence has been discussed extensively regarding national parties in David W. Rohde, *Parties and Leaders in the Postreform House* (Chicago: University of Chicago Press, 1991), 46–47, 82, 124–27; and John H. Aldrich, *Why Parties* (Chicago: University of Chicago Press, 1995).

58. Salmore and Salmore, *Candidates, Parties, and Campaigns.*

59. Joseph Schlesinger, "On the Theory of Party Organization," *Journal of Politics* 46, no. 2 (May 1984): 383. The original quote was in Anthony Downs, *An Economic Theory of Democracy* (New York: Harper and Row, 1957), 28.

60. Jeffrey M. Stonecash, *American State and Local Politics* (New York: Harcourt, Brace, 1995), 288–94.

61. Jeffrey M. Stonecash, "'Split' Constituencies and the Impact of Party Control," *Social Science History* 16, no. 3 (Fall 1992): 455–78.

62. Stonecash, "Political Cleavage in State Legislative Parties."

63. This may explain why some studies, such as Dye, "Party and Policy in the States," have found cases where changes in party control did not lead to policy changes. Studies in which the focus is whether control is or is not associated with change are interesting, but without pursuing why associations are found, we have no idea what the associations or lack of them mean.

64. J. R. Pole, *The Pursuit of Equality in American History* (Berkeley: University of California Press, 1978).

65. For discussions of how attacks about unfairness and favoring the rich affected Republicans in Congress in 1995 and 1996, see David Maraniss and Michael Weisskopf, *Tell Newt to Shut Up* (New York: Touchstone, 1996).

Chapter 3. The Emergence of Democrats and the State, 1950–67

1. This means that tax burdens in 1953 were converted to 1994 values. Inflation since 1953 has eroded the value of dollars, so 1953 tax dollars were worth more, compared to 1994. To increase the value of 1953 tax dollars, they were divided by the CPI.

2. All data are taken from *Government Finances*, the GF-5 series, published by the Bureau of the Census. Expenditures are adjusted using the Consumer Price Index, using the index of 1967 = 100. To put all dollars in terms of 1994 values, the 1967 index is recalculated with 1994 set as 100. This is done by converting all indexes to a ratio of the 1994 value.

3. Salmore and Salmore, *New Jersey Politics and Government*, 11.

4. The Commission on State Tax Policy, *The Fifth Report of the Commission on State Tax Policy: Taxation and Public Policy* (Trenton: State of New Jersey, 14 April 1950), 34–50.

5. Ibid., 87.

6. Ibid., 27.

7. Ibid., 90.

8. Ibid., 2.

9. Salmore and Salmore, *New Jersey Politics and Government*, 47–48.

10. Ibid., 58.

11. Thomas J. Anton, "The Politics of State Taxation: A Case Study of Decision-Making in the New Jersey Legislature" (diss., Princeton University, 1961), 83.

12. From Morris Beck, "Government Finance in New Jersey," in *The Economy of New Jersey*, edited by Solomon J. Fink et al. (New Brunswick, N.J.: Rutgers University Press, 1958), 560, cited in Salmore and Salmore, *New Jersey Politics and Government*, 245.

13. Salmore and Salmore, *New Jersey Politics and Government*, 244–45.

14. Anton, "The Politics of State Taxation," 91.

15. "Balanced Budget Offered in Jersey," *New York Times*, 14 February 1950, 27.

16. Warren Moscow, "Driscoll Attacks Federal Spending," *New York Times*, 18 January 1950, 1; and "Economies in Jersey Hailed by Driscoll," *New York Times*, 19 April 1953, 73.

17. "Jersey May Stay within Revenues," *New York Times*, 28 December 1951, 19. "This was not the first time governors boasted of the low taxes imposed on citizens. In 1905 Governor Stokes declared "Of the entire income of the state, not a penny was contributed by the people." This was possible because of railroad taxes and corporate charges. Salmore and Salmore, *New Jersey Politics and Government*, 26.

18. "Leaders in Jersey Oppose New Taxes," *New York Times*, 11 January 1950, 30.

19. George C. Wright, "Jersey Leadership Taken by Mayner," *New York Times*, 15 May 1953, 1.

20. "Jersey Issues Set for Fall Election," *New York Times*, 11 May 1951, 22.

21. "Money Measures Voted," *New York Times*, 27 March 1951, 30; and "Jersey's Fund Law Signed by Driscoll," *New York Times*, 20 April 1952, 64.

22. George C. Wright, "Jersey Leadership Taken by Mayner," *New York Times*, 15 May 1953, 1.

23. "Text of Governor Meyner's Inaugural Address in Trenton," *New York Times*, 20 January 1954, 12.

24. George C. Wright, "$89,500,000 Levy for New Jersey Seen," *New York Times*, 2 April 1954, 50:1.

25. "George C. Wright, "Meyner's Budget Averts Tax Rises," *New York Times*, 1 February 1955, 1:6.

26. George C. Wright, "Budget in Jersey Asks $315,452,130," *New York Times*, 7 February 1956, 7:7

27. "George C. Wright, "Meyner Appeals to Legislature," *New York Times*, 16 September 1956, 54.

28. George C. Wright, "Meyner to Offer a Record Budget," *New York Times*, 4 January 1957, 13; and George C, Wright, "342 Million Budget Sets Jersey Record; Tax Rises Averted," *New York Times*, 19 February 1957, 1 .

29. George C. Wright, "Meyner Wins in Jersey, Takes Assembly," *New York Times*, 6 November 1957, 1.

30. George C. Wright, "Meyner Asks Rise of 1C in 'Gas' Tax to Finance Roads," *New York Times,* 15 January 1958, 1.

31. "Geroge C. Wright, "Meyner Budget Sets 399 Million Mark; Seeks New Taxes," *New York Times*, 18 February 1958, 1.

32. George C. Wright, "Jersey Advances Business Tax Bill," *New York Times*, 22 April 1958, 45; and George C. Wright, "GOP Acts to Cut Meyner's Budget," *New York Times*, 6 May 1958, 37.

33. George C. Wright, "Meyner and Legislative Chiefs Agree on Record Jersey Budget," *New York Times*, 27 May 1958, 33.

34. Anton, "Politics of State Taxation," 53.

35. Ibid., 23.

36. Ibid., 1–89.

37. Ibid., 40.

38. State of New Jersey, *Sixth Report of the Commission on State Tax Policy: The General Property Tax in New Jersey: A Century of Inequities* (Trenton, N.J., 1953), 39–52; and Anton, "Politics of State Taxation," 33.

39. Anton, "The Politics of State Taxation," 30.

40. Ibid., 42–43.

41. For an indication of the disparities in school finance, see State of New Jersey, *Seventh Report of the Commission on State Tax Policy: Public School Financing in New Jersey: Public School Financing in New Jersey: A Problem of More Money Where It Is Most Needed* (Trenton, 22 March 1954), 41–75.

42. Archibald S. Alexander, "Just Taxation through Assessment Equalization," *New Jersey Municipalities* 33, no. 1 (January 1956): 5–7; and Alfred N. Beadleston, "Equalization and Revaluation at the Local Level," *New Jersey Municipalities* 34, no. 1 (January, 1957): 5–10.

43. Anton, "Politics of State Taxation," 56–57.

44. Ibid., 59.

45. Ibid., 61.

46. Ibid. 65.

47. Ibid., 70–77.

48. Ibid., 79–89.

49. Ibid., 139–42.

50. Ibid., 155–56.

51. Ibid., 235–64.

52. Division of Taxation, Local Property Branch, State of New Jersey, Department of the Treasury, "Table of Equalized Valuations" (Trenton, N.J., 1987), 370.

53. Salmore and Salmore, *New Jersey Politics and Government*, 251. A commission was formed to propose changes that would reduce the inequalities derived from assessment practices: New Jersey Property Tax Assessment Study Commission, *Report of Property Tax Assessment Commission* (Trenton, N.J., October 1986).

54. Richard C. Leone, "The Politics of Gubernatorial Leadership: Tax and Education Reform in New Jersey" (diss., Princeton University, 1969), 23–24.

55. For an overview of these changes, see Dennis R. Judd and Todd Swanstrom, *City Politics: Private Power and Public Policy* (New York: HarperCollins, 1994), 107–213. The situation in New Jersey is discussed in George Sternlieb and James W. Hughes, "Demographic and Economic Dynamics," in *The Political State of New Jersey,* ed. Gerald Pomper (New Brunswick, N.J.: Rutgers University Press, 1986), 27–44.

56. Michael Harrington, *The Other America* (Baltimore: Penguin Books, 1971).

57. In the 1920s in the Northeast many traditional Republicans deserted the party to

vote for Progressives who backed several reforms in how government should work. The Progressive Party pulled many relatively liberal Republicans away from the party, and left many Democrats with enough votes to win in three-way races. After the rift among Republicans was repaired, Republicans in the Northeast returned to their dominant position.

58. Counties are classified on the basis of the percentage urban, density, and the percent minority. The counties are classified as following using 1960 census data: urban: Essex, Hudson, and Union; suburban: Bergen, Camden, Mercer, Middlesex, and Passaic; rural or transitional to suburban: Atlantic, Burlington, Cape May, Cumberland Gloucester, Hunterdon, Monmouth, Morris, Ocean, Salem, Somerset, Sussex, and Warren.

59. Results taken from State of New Jersey, Results of the General Election, Held November 8th, 1955. Compiled from records on file in the Secretary of State's Office. No date or place of publication.

60. Much of this change was reflective of a secular decline of Republican strength in the North. The Civil War and the realignment of 1896 had left the North with a strong alignment with the Republican Party. As the historical legacy of these earlier events faded in memory, and the Democratic Party came to be seen as more reflective of relatively moderate to liberal concerns in the North, the population gradually shifted to the Democratic Party. See Jeffrey M. Stonecash and Anna Agathangelou, "Trends in the Partisan Composition of State Legislatures: A Response to Fiorina," *American Political Science Review* 91, no. 1 (March 1997): 148–56

61. Results taken from State of New Jersey, Results of the General Election, Held November 3rd, 1959. Compiled from records on file in the Secretary of State's Office. No date or place of publication.

62. Maureen Moakley, "New Jersey," in *The Political Life of the American States,* ed. Alan Rosenthal and Maureen Moakley (New York: Praeger, 1984), 221–27.

63. Gerald Pomper, "Political Parties," in Pomper, *Political State of New Jersey,* 46–51; David R. Mayhew, *Placing Parties in American Politics* (Princeton: Princeton University Press, 1986), 46–55; and Maureen Moakley, "Political Parties," in Pomper, *Political State of New Jersey,* 45–49.

64. Richard P. McCormick, "An Historical Overview," in *Politics in New Jersey,* ed. Richard Lehne and Alan Rosenthal, rev. ed. (New Brunswick, N.J.: Eagleton Institute of Politics, 1979), 18.

65. Maureen Moakley and Gerald Pomper, "Party Organizations," in Lehne and Rosenthal, *Politics in New Jersey,* 88–93.

66. "Jersey Sales Tax Nearing Reality," *New York Times,* 5 April 1966, 30; and Ronald Sullivan, "Jersey Sales Tax Signed by Hughes," *New York Times,* 28 April 1966, 47.

67. McCormick, "Historical Overview," 23.

68. Anton, "Politics of State Taxation," 95–98.

69. Salmore and Salmore, *New Jersey Politics and Government,* 29–45.

70. Alvin S. Felzenberg, "The Impact of Gubernatorial Style on Policy Outcomes: An In-Depth Study of Three New Jersey Governors" (diss., Princeton University, 1978), 186.

71. Leone, "Politics of Gubernatorial Leadership, " 173–74.

72. Ibid., 189.

73. Ibid., 23–24; and Salmore and Salmore, *New Jersey Politics and Government,* 261.

74. Leone, "Politics of Gubernatorial Leadership," 173.

75. Based on a review of the legislative history of the legislation, taken from the *Journal of the Senate* and *Minutes of the General Assembly.*

76. Ibid., 53.

77. Walter H. Waggoner, "Jersey Passes Districting Plan; Senate Will Have 29 Members," *New York Times,* 13 April 1965, 41.

78. Walter H. Waggoner, "Republican Rule Ended in Jersey," *New York Times*, 3 November 1965, 31.

79. Carl Leone, "The Politics of Gubernatorial Leadership," 37. Leone served as administrative assistant to Hughes from February 1965 to January 1967. He was an active participant in many of the events he describes in his dissertation.

80. Ronald Sullivan, "Hughes Calls Victory a Mandate for Program Equaling Johnson's," *New York Times*, 4 November 1965, 51:2; and .Felzenberg, "Impact of Gubernatorial Style on Policy Outcomes," 181.

81. Leone, "Politics of Gubernatorial Leadership," 15.

82. Ibid., 37–38, 53.

83. Ibid., 66.

84. Ibid., 51.

85. Ibid., 39.

86. Ibid., 37.

87. Telephone interview with Richard C. Leone, 16 July 1997. Dr. Leone is currently the president of the Twentieth Century Fund, New York City, New York. He said it was widely perceived that Hughes had not received a mandate to pursue any particular set of policies, but he felt that Hughes really felt that the state should respond to the growing social and urban problems in the state, and he saw this as his opportunity to respond.

88. Leone, "Politics of Gubernatorial Leadership," 28–29.

89. Ibid., 58.

90. Ibid., 43, 66, 73.

91. Ibid., 104.

92. Ibid., 99, 115.

93. Ibid., 145.

94. Ibid., 152.

95. Ibid., 87

96. Ibid., 165–69.

97. Ibid., 149.

98. Ronald Sullivan, "Jersey Sales Tax Signed by Hughes," *New York Times*, 28 April 1966, 1.

99. Leone, "Politics of Gubernatorial Leadership," 210–14.

100. Ibid., 216–18.

101. Ibid., 183–208.

102. Ibid., 282–92.

103. Ibid., 300–320.

104. Dye, "Party and Policy in the States," 1024.

105. Leone, "Politics of Gubernatorial Leadership," 18–19.

106. As with figures at the beginning of the chapter, all fiscal data are expressed in terms of constant purchasing dollars, in 1994 values.

107. Ronald Sullivan, "A New Tax Needed, Hughes Asserts," *New York Times*, 11 January 1967, 23; and Ronald Sullivan, "Jersey's Budget Is Near $1–Billion," *New York Times*, 15 February 1967, 24.

108. The argument about the mistakes the Democrats were making is probably best expressed in Edsall and Edsall, *Chain Reaction*.

109. "Hughes Says G.O.P. Bids for Backlash," *New York Times*, 28 July 1967, 12.

110. Ronald Sullivan, "Hughes Says G.O.P. Is Injecting Racial Issue Into Its Campaign," *New York Times*, 28 October 1967, 31; and Ronald Sullivan, "Busing of Pupils a Top Jersey Issue," *New York Times*, 29 October 1967, 72.

111. Ronald Sullivan, "Hughes and Case Take to Stump as Jersey Campaign Nears End," *New York Times*, 6 November 1967, 25.

112. Ronald Sullivan, "A Hughes Setback," *New York Times*, 8 November 1967, 1:6.

113. It might well be that rural legislators were able to survive because the sales tax was seen as a way to reduce reliance on the property tax, which was seen as an onerous tax by farmers in rural areas. See Anton, "Politics of State Taxation," 244. It might also be that Republicans were in safe districts in rural areas and were not threatened by Democrats, regardless of how they voted on the sales tax.

114. Stonecash and Agathangelou, "Trends in the Partisan Composition of State Legislatures."

115. Surprisingly, there are few studies at the state level of areal redistribution of wealth. Almost all studies focus on the incidence of taxes by income level, but there is almost no attention to how various taxes redistribute resources among communities.

CHAPTER 4. THE RETURN OF REPUBLICANS

1. Ronald Sullivan, "Hughes Is Warned of Tax Increase," *New York Times*, 14 January 1968, 16.

2. Ronald Sullivan, "Hughes Says Urban Need May Dictate Budget Rise," *New York Times*, 16 February 1968, 1.

3. For how welfare programs developed nationally from 1900 until the 1960s, see James T. Patterson, *America's Struggle Against Poverty, 1900–1994*. (Cambridge: Harvard University Press, 1994). For the early history of welfare in New Jersey, see: Ellen C. Potter, "The County as a Public Welfare Unit," *Social Service Review* 6, no. 3 (September 1932): 452–95; and Paul T. Stafford, *State Welfare Administration in New Jersey* (Trenton, N.J.: Department of Institutions and Agencies, 1934).

4. Governor's Task Force on Welfare Management, *A State Welfare System for the Poor* (Trenton: State of New Jersey, 2 June 1971), 4.

5. Ibid., 6.

6. The same issues had developed in other states. Massachusetts faced similar issues, with the added pressure that the federal government wanted the state to assume responsibility to reduce the effects of local administration on benefits and treatment of clients. See Martha Derthick, *The Influence of Federal Grants* (Cambridge: Harvard University Press, 1970).

7. Ibid., 79; and Governor's Task Force, *State Welfare System*, 12.

8. Governor's Task Force, *State Welfare System*, 24–25.

9. Ronald Sullivan, "Hughes Asks Rise in Tax to Aid Cities," *New York Times*, 23 April 1968, 1.

10. Ronald Sullivan, "Hughes Asks Income Tax," *New York Times*, 26 April 1968, 1.

11. Ronald Sullivan, "Jersey Spending of $2 Billion Asked," *New York Times*, 28 April 1968, 38.

12. Sullivan, "Hughes Asks Income Tax," 49.

13. Ronald Sullivan, "Republicans Cut Hughes Program," *New York Times*, 23 May 1968, 38.

14. Ronald Sullivan, "Hughes Says G.O.P. Aid Cuts 'Could Provoke Civil Disorder'," *New York Times*, 24 May 1968, 24.

15. Ronald Sullivan, "Jersey 'Very Ill,' Hughes Declares," *New York Times*, 5 May 1968, 17.

16. Ronald Sullivan, "Republicans Revolt in Jersey: Lean to Hughes on Urban Aid," *New York Times*, 28 May 1968, 1.

17. Ronald Sullivan, "Jersey Senate Backs a Budget of $1.15 Billion," *New York Times*, 18 June 1968, 27.

18. Ronald Sullivan, "Hughes Appeals for Aid to Cities," *New York Times*, 16 June 1968, 41.

19. Ronald Sullivan, "Hughes Vetoes 32 Bills in Jersey; G.O.P. to Fight for Aid Plans," *New York Times*, 10 September 1968, 43.

20. Ronald Sullivan, "Hughes Defeated on Aid Programs," *New York Times*, 14 September 1968, 17.

21. Ronald Sullivan, "Jersey Senate Backs a Budget of $1.15 Billion," *New York Times*, 18 June 1968, 27.

22. Ronald Sullivan, "Hughes' Budget Asks $1.36 Billion," *New York Times*, 11 February 1969, 1.

23. Walter H. Waggoner, "Trenton Session Reopening Today," *New York Times*, 2 July 1969, 43.

24. Walter H. Waggoner, "Jersey Approves Anticrime Bills," *New York Times*, 3 July 1969, 1.

25. Ronald Sullivan, "Cahill Proposes a 5% Sales Levy in Budget Crisis," *New York Times*, 13 January 1970, 1.

26. Robert Stevens and Rosemary Stevens, *Welfare Medicine in America: A Case Study of Medicaid* (New York: Free Press, 1974), 260–81.

27. Walter H. Waggoner, "Cahill Says Rising Relief Costs May Bring Need for New Taxes," *New York Times*, 2 November 1970, 82.

28. Sullivan, "Cahill Proposes a 5% Sales Levy,'" 1.

29. Ibid., 34.

30. Salmore and Salmore, *New Jersey Politics and Government*, 134–35.

31. Ronald Sullivan, "Cahill and Meyner Clash in Angry Debate," *New York Times*, 20 October 1969, 1.

32. His situation was similar to that of Nelson Rockefeller, who drew well in urban areas, was more liberal than his legislative party, and supported tax increases in New York. See Jeffrey M. Stonecash, "Political Cleavage in Gubernatorial and Legislative Elections: The Nature of Inter-Party Competition in New York Elections, 1970–1982," *Western Political Quarterly* 42, no. 1 (March 1989): 69–81; and Stonecash, "'Split' Constituencies and the Impact of Party Control," 455–77.

33. Salmore and Salmore, *New Jersey Politics and Government*, 247.

Chapter 5. Schools, Democrats, and the Income Tax

1. C. Gerald Fraser, "Blacks on Patrol at Asbury Park," *New York Timres*, 9 July 1970, 1.

2. Walter Waggoner, "Cahill Says Rising Relief Costs May Bring Need for New Taxes," *New York Times*, 20 November 1970, 82.

3. Ronald Sullivan, "$50 Millin Newarek Aid Plan Is Voted by New Jersey Legislature," *New York Times*, 19 December 1970, 20.

4. Thomas Ronan, "Governor Hails Aid Idea but Asks More U.S. Funds," *New York Times*, 24 January 1971, 1.

5. Ronald Sullivan, "Cahill Presents Austerity Budget," *New York Times*, 17 February 1971, 26.

6. Ronald Sullivan, Now Cahill Inherits a Few Disasters," *New York Times*, 18 January 1970, sec. iv, 6.

7. *Robinson v. Cahill*, 287 Atlantic Reporter 2d 187, 1973, 198.

8. Walter Waggoner, "Cahill Sees Ruling as Proving the Need to Find A New Way to Pay for Schools," *New York Times*, 4 April 1973, 91.

9. Harold J. Rudvolt, "The Right to Learn," *New Jersey State Bar Journal,* vol. 51 (January 1970).

10. Richard Lehne, *The Quest For Justice* (New York: Longman, 1978), 27.

11. Ibid., 27–30.

12. "Arguments Are Heard in School-Aid Case," special to *New York Times*, 10 January 1973, 86.

13. *Robinson v. Cahill*, 189–202.

14. *Robinson v. Cahill,* appendix A and 200.

15. *Robinson v. Cahill*, 194–96.

16. Lehne, *Quest for Justice,* 32.

17. *Robinson v. Cahill,* pp 202–3.

18. *Robinson v. Cahill*, 205.

19. Ibid.

20. Ibid.

21. Lehne, *Quest for Justice*, 52.

22. Ronald Sullivan, "High Court Refuses to Hear Plea by Jersey Defending School Tax," *New York Times*, 24 October 1973, 97.

23. Walter Waggoner, "Senate Bids Court Rehear Tax Case," *New York Times*, 14 January 1975, 72.

24. Mary C. Churchill, "School Crisis May Stop Aid to Ratable Rich Towns," *New York Times*, 10 February 1975, 84.

25. "Byrne Asks July Deadline for School-Aid Legislation," *New York Times*, 26 February 1975, 84.

26. Waggoner, "Senate Bids Court Rehear Tax Case."

27. Ronald Sullivan, "Byrne's Tax Defeat," *New York Times*, 29 July 1974, 51.

28. Mary Churchill, "Assembly Democrats to Sift State Fiscal Woes," *New York Times*, 27 October 1974, 81.

29. "Deadlock Foreseen on State Fiscal Woes," special to the *New York Times*, 3 November 1974, 91.

30. Ronald Sullivan, "Byrne Tax Proposal Appears in Trouble; G.O.P. Is Opposed," *New York Times*, 14 June 1974, 69 and 71.

31. Walter H. Waggoner, "Byrne Presses Late Drive For a Jersey School Tax," *New York Times*, 24 December 1974, 43.

32. "Education Board Seeks Court Help," *New York Times*, 7 January 1975, 71.

33. "Byrne Asks July Deadline for School-Aid Legislation," special to the *New York Times*, 26 February 1975, 84.

34. Ronald Sullivan, "Byrne to Seek Income Tax and Cut in the Sales Levy," *New York Times*, 28 January 1975, 1.

35. Ronald Sullivan, "66 Million Withheld from Jersey Budget," *New York Times*, 17 January 1975, 1.

36. Ronald Sullivan, "Byrne Takes Tax Fight to the People," *New York Times*, 27 June 1975, 75.

37. "Senate Passes a Measure Guaranteeing 'Thorough and Efficient' Education," special to the *New York Times*, 28 May 1975,87.

38. Joseph F. Sullivan, "Plan Reached to Finance Schools Till End of Year," *New York Times*, 16 July 1975, 79

39. Ronald Sullivan, "Legislature to Give All 'Efficient Schooling'," *New York Times,* 23 September 1975, 79.

40. Lehne, *Quest for Justice*, 147–53.

41. "New Jersey Briefs: Pennsylvania Seeks Return of Taxes," *New York Times*, 30 September 1975, 80.

42. Ronald Sullivan, "Byrne Says Defeat of Bond Proposals Creates New Crisis," *New York Times*, 6 November 1975,1.

43. Ronald Sullivan, "Byrne Says an Income Tax Is Now Up to Legislature," *New York Times*, 14 November 1975,79 .

44. "Byrne Calls on Teachers to Press for Tax Reform," *New York Times*, 15 November 1975, 59.

45. Ronald Sullivan, "Byrne to Ask High Court to Order New School Plan," *New York Times*, 27 November 1975, 71.

46. Martin Waldron, "Byrne's Tax Plan Draws Union Fire," *New York Times*, 6 February 1976, 61.

47. Ronald Sullivan, "New Jersey Had 18 Months, and Still No School Plan," *New York Times*, 12 January 1975, sec. 4, 6

48. Ibid.

49. Associated Press, "Byrne Orders Cut of 5% in Jersey Payroll Costs," *New York Times*, 3 January 1976, 45.

50. Lehne, *Quest for Justice*, 61.

51. Ibid., 65, 72–73.

52. Martin Waldron, "School Equality Upheld in New Jersey," *New York Times*, 31 January 1976, 1.

53. Martin Waldron, "New School Taxes Unlikely in New Jersey," *New York Times*, 3 February 1976, 65.

54. Martin Waldron, "Jersey Assembly Passes an Income Tax Measure," *New York Times*, 16 March 1976, 1.

55. Martin Waldron, "Schools in Jersey Face July Closing," *New York Times*, 14 May 1976, 19.

56. "Byrne Cautions Trenton on Schools," *New York Times*, 26 May 1976, 84.

57. Martin Waldron, "High Court Lets Stand the Order That Could Close State Schools July 1," *New York Times*, 11 June 1976, 23.

58. Alfonso A. Naravaez, "Jersey Senate Approves 1.5% State Income Tax," *New York Times*, 18 June 1976, 1.

59. Alfonso A. Naravaez, "Jersey's Assembly Rejects Income Tax," *New York Times*, 22 June 1976, 73.

60. Joseph F. Sullivan, "School Closings in Jersey Jeopardize the Handicapped," *New York Times*, 7 July 1976, 37.

61. Lehne, *Quest for Justice*, 151.

62. Alfonso A. Naravaez, "Jersey Assembly, Ending Deadlock, Votes Income Tax," *New York Times*, 8 July 1976, 1.

63. These negative votes were from Jersey City, where the mayor requested that they not support the bill because he believed that Jersey City would be better off with a court-imposed budget.

64. Salmore and Salmore, *New Jersey Politics and Government*, 307–8.

65. Alvin Maurer, "The Pattern of Politics in Jersey Is Crazy Quilt," *New York Times*, 24 April 1977, sec. 4, 53.

66. Martin Waldron, "Income Tax Fails as Issue in Legislative Primaries, Dugan and Mrs. Ammond Defeated in Senate Race," *New York Times*, 9 June 1977.

67. Alfonso A. Naravaez, "2 Candidates for Governor Clash on Education and Are Booed," *New York Times*, 28 October 1977, part 2, 17.

68. Joseph F. Sullivan, "Bateman Is Routed: Govenor Sweeps Bergen, Key G.O.P. Area—Gets Big Blue-Collar Vote," *New York Times*, 9 November 1977, 1.

69. Joseph F. Sullivan, "Imperiale, Withdrawing, Backs Bateman," *New York Times*, 20 September 1977, 87.

70. Figures 5.2 through 5.5 are based on information compiled by the Census on Governments

71. While the level of state aid increased, it has been argued that the increase may not have been much greater than it would have been without the controversy. Lehne, *Quest for Justice*, 168–73, demonstrates that the increase in state aid to education for the 1976–1977 school year was not that much higher than what would have been predicted using the average annual increase of 14.7 percent between 1966 and 1977. For the 1974–75 school year the state gave $782 million to local school districts. Had the average annual rate of increase applied to 1975–76 and 1976–77 years, the expected state contributions would have been $897 million and $1030 million respectively. In reality the controversy over responding to Robinson froze the budget in 1975–76 and spending was reduced to $777 million. In 1976–77 the state contribution was $1103 million, only 7 percent higher than the estimated expenditure without *Robinson*.

72. Martin Waldron, "Income Tax Fails to Help State's Cities," *New York Times*, 16 October 1977, sec. 11, 1.

73. Ibid.

74. Margret E. Goertz "Where Did the 400 Million Dollars Go? The Impact of the New jersey Public School Education Act of 1975," Education Policy Research Institute Educational Testing Services, Princeton, N.J., March 1978, 33.

75. Robert Hanley, "T and E Problems Persist as New School Year Begins," *New York Times,* 9 September 1979, sec. 11, 1.

76. Ibid.

77. David E. Weischadle, "T and E: Is the Act an Asset or Not?" *New York Times*, 12 December 1978, sec. 11, 46.

CHAPTER 6. THE RETURN OF REPUBLICANS' INFLUENCE

1. Richard J. Meislin, "Kean: G.O.P. Candidate with Liberal Tendency," *New York Times*, 28 October 1981, B1.

2. Joseph F. Sullivan, "Kean and Florio Evaluate Education," *New York Times*, 23 October 1981, B2.

3. Joseph F. Sullivan, "Kramer and Kean: A Shift in Emphasis," *New York Times*, 1 February 1981, sec. 2, 8.

4. "Excerpts from the Debate Between Candidates for Governor," *New York Times*, 13 October 1981, B6.

5. Sullivan, "Kean and Florio Evaluate Education," B2.

6. Joseph F. Sullivan, "Jersey Race to Test President's Policies," *New York Times*, 7 June 1981, 1.

7. Joseph F. Sullivan, "Florio and Kean Get the Race into High Gear," *New York Times*, 30 August 1981, sec. 11, 1.

8. Richard J. Meislin, "Jersey Economy Dominates Second Florio-Kean Debate," *New York Times*, 2 October 1981, B2.

9. Richard J. Meislin, "Taxes Are a Crucial Question in Race for Governor in New Jersey," *New York Times*, 27 October 1981, sec. 2, 1.

10. Sullivan, "Kean and Florio Evaluate Education," B2.

11. Richard J. Meislin, "Jersey Poll Indicates Voters' Background Overshadows Issues," *New York Times*, 21 October 1981, A1; and Richard J. Meislin, "Poll Finds It's Still a Kean-Florio Toss-Up," *New York Times*, 25 October 1981, sec. 11, 1.

12. Adam Clymer, "A Warning for the G.O.P.," *New York Times*, 18 November 1981, B18.

13. Joseph F. Sullivan, "Kean Gives Vow He Won't Raise Tax on Income," *New York Times*, 2 December 1981, B1.

14. Robert Hanley, "Kean Asks Rise in Consumer Taxes and Fares," *New York Times*, 11 March 1982, A1; and Joseph F. Sullivan, "40 Percent of Towns Found Hit by Cutback," *New York Times*, 20 June 1982, sec. 11, 1.

15. Robert Hanley, "Alter Tax Plan, Democrats Tell Kean," *New York Times*, 12 March 1982, B3.

16. Robert Hanley, "Democrats Gird to Battle Kean on First Budget," *New York Times*, 14 March 1982, sec. 11, 1.

17. Joseph F. Sullivan, "Legislature Survives a Stormy Session," *New York Times*, 1 August 1982, sec. 11, 1.

18. Alfonso A. Narvaez, "Jersey Assembly Votes Death-Penalty Bill, 54–19," *New York Times,* 22 June 1982, B2.

19. "New Tobacco Tax Advances in Jersey," *New York Times*, 25 May 1982, B1; "Kean and Democrats Agree on Budget Cuts," *New York Times*, 26 June 1982, B4.

20. Joseph F. Sullivan, "Tomorrow Is a Big Day for the Budget," *New York Times*, 12 December 1982, sec. 11, 1.

21. Joseph F. Sullivan, "Kean Rejects Income-Tax Rise," *New York Times*, 16 December 1982, B3.

22. Joseph F. Sullivan, "Jersey Democrats to Seek a Compromise on Taxes," *New York Times*, 17 December 1982, B4; and Vincent R. Zarate, "Kean Backs Sales Tax Hike as Alternative to Gas Levy," *Star-Ledger*, 8 December 1982, 1.

23. Joseph F. Sullivan, "Jersey Lawmakers Approve Tax Rise, but Kean Vetoes It," *New York Times*, 21 December 1982, B1.

24. Joseph F. Sullivan, "Showdown on Budget Is Set by Karcher," *New York Times*, 19 December 1982, sec. 11, 1.

25. Ibid.; and Vincent R. Zarate, "Legislators to Vote on Income Tax Hike for 'Rich'," *Star-Ledger*, 16 December 1982, 22.

26. Sullivan, "Jersey Lawmakers Approve Tax Rise," B1; Vincent R. Zarate, "Dems Ready to Defy Kean on Income Tax Hike Vote," *Star-Ledger*, 19 December 1982, 1; and Vincent R. Zarate, "Governor Vetoes Boost in the State Income Tax," *Star-Ledger*, 21 December 1982, 1.

27. Joseph F. Sullivan, "Tax Rises Proposed in Jersey; Kean to Work for Both Bills," *New York Times*, 28 December 1982, B3.

28. Joseph F. Sullivan, "Jersey Considers Tax Compromise to Raise Funds," *New York Times*, 31 December 1982, B2; and Richard S. Remington, "Kean Gives Final Approval to Income, Sales Tax Hikes," *Star-Ledger*, 1 January 1983, 1. The votes on each bill are taken from Vincent R. Zarate, "Kean Says Tax Increases Will Balance Books Till '84," *Star-Ledger*, 2 January 1983, 1, 10–11.

29. Joseph F. Sullivan, "Kean Proposes Income Tax Cut of 10% for 1985," *New York Times*, 10 May 1985, B2.

30. Joseph F. Sullivan, "Jersey Assembly Votes Income Tax Relief," *New York Times*, 4 January 1985, B2.

31. Joseph F. Sullivan, "Kean Signs Bill Providing Cuts on Income Tax," *New York Times*, 27 August 1985, B2.

32. Joseph F. Sullivan, "Kean Shift to the Left Sets Stage for Race," *New York Times*, 3 February 1995, sec. 11, 1.

33. In 1983 Kean proposed an increase in school aid of $186 million (Joseph F. Sullivan, "Austerity Budget of $6.8 Billion Sought by Kean," *New York Times*, 30 January 1984, A1); in 1984 he proposed an increase of $194 million (Joseph F. Sullivan, "Kean Budget Plan Seeks No Tax Rise," *New York Times*, 29 January 1985, A1); in 1986 Kean proposed

an increase in school aid of $271 million (Joseph F. Sullivan, "Kean Will Propose $8.8 Billion Budget, Including Tax Relief," *New York Times*, 27 January 1985, A1); in 1986 he proposed an increase of $213 million (Joseph F. Sullivan, "Kean Proposes Study of Funds for Education," *New York Times*, 11 February 1986, B2); In 1987 Kean proposed an increase in school aid of $248 million (Joseph F. Sullivan, "Kean to Propose a Rise of 9.6 % in Jersey Budget," *New York Times*, 1 February 1987, A1); in 1988 he proposed an increase of $300 million (Joseph F. Sullivan, "Kean to Propose a $11.8 Billion Budget," *New York Times*, 31 January 1988, A36); in 1989 Kean proposed an increase in school aid of $171 million (Joseph F. Sullivan, "Kean Urges Spending Cuts in Budget Plan," *New York Times*, 26 January 1988, B1).

34. Joseph F. Sullivan, "Taxes Resolved, Kean Addresses Other Problems," *New York Times*, 9 January 1983, sec. 11, 1; Joseph F. Sullivan, "Legislature Divided over Kean Budget," *New York Times*, 31 January 194, B2.

35. Joseph F. Sullivan, "2 Bills Facing Vetoes Pressed by Democrats," *New York Times*, 25 March 1984, sec. 11, 1.

36. Joseph F. Sullivan, "Kean Will Propose $8.8 Billion Budget, including Tax Relief," *New York Times*, 27 January 1985, A1.

37. Richard Kamin, "A Rational Plan for Needy Cities," *New York Times*, 5 June 1998, sec. 12, 30.

38. Joseph F. Sullivan, "Aid to Cities Splits Kean and G.O.P. in Assembly," *New York Times*, 1 March 1987, sec. 11, 1; and Joseph F. Sullivan, "Hardwick and Kean Split on Aid to Localities," *New York Times,* 10 April 1988, sec. 12, 1.

39. Peter Kerr, "To Cut Local Taxes, Kean Urges Shifting Some Costs to State," *New York Times*, 27 January 1989, B1.

40. The chronology of events involved in *Mt. Laurel* are taken from David L. Kirp, John P. Dwyer, and Larry A. Rosenthal, *Our Town: Race, Housing, and the Soul of Suburbia.* (New Brunswick, N.J.: Rutgers University Press, 1995).

41. In New Jersey municipalities are not necessarily cities; they can be any local government unit.

42. Kirp, Dwyer, and Rosenthal, *Our Town,* 46.

43. Ibid., 44.

44. Ibid., 53.

45. Ibid., 2.

46. Ibid. 55.

47. Ibid., 198–202.

48. Ibid., 65–72.

49. Ibid., 72.

50. Ibid., 74.

51. Ibid., 81.

52. John C. Pittenger, "The Courts," in Pomper, *Political State of New Jersey*, 165.

53. Kirp, Dwyer, and Rosenthal, *Our Town*, 89.

54. Ibid., 102–3.

55. Ibid., 109–10.

56. Ibid., 104.

57. Salmore and Salmore, *New Jersey Politics and Government*, 198.

58. Kirp et al., *Our Town*, 119–21.

59. Ibid., 123–29.

60. Ibid., 130–33.

61. Ibid., 126–30.

62. Ibid., 134–35.

63. Ibid., 137.

64. Ibid., 153–62.

65. Ronald Smothers, "Mt. Laurel Votes to Build Homes for Poor," *New York Times*, 12 April 1997, B1.

66. Kirp, Dwyer, and Rosenthal, *Our Town*, 123.

67. Salmore and Salmore, *New Jersey Politics and Government*, 298–300.

68. Margaret E. Goertz, *Money and Education: Where Did the 400 Million Dollars Go?* (Princeton, N.J.: Education Policy Research Institute, Educational Testing Service, March, 1978).

69. Joseph F. Sullivan, "Census Dramatizes Changes in Jersey Life During the 1970s," *New York Times,* 26 January 1981, 3.

70. Edward H. Salmon, "Public School Finance Reform in New Jersey" (diss., University of Delaware, 1991), 48–66.

71. This argument is presented in detail in Kozol, *Savage Inequalities*. The specific response of the State of New Jersey is presented by Salmon, "Public School Finance Reform," 75–84.

72. Priscilla Van Tassel, "Poor Districts Gain in Battle on School Funds," *New York Times*, 27 May 1984, sec. 11, 1.

73. Salmon, "Public School Finance Reform," 92.

74. Priscilla Van Tassel, "School Financing Challenged at Trial," *New York Times*, 5 October 1986, sec. 11, 1.

75. Joseph F. Sullivan, "Jersey's Funds for Schools Found Flawed," *New York Times*, 26 August 1988, B1.

76. Peter Kerr, "Jersey System of School Aid Is Ruled Fair," *New York Times*, 24 February 1989, B1.

77. Salmon, "Public School Finance Reform," 94.

78. At the last step, in 1989, he did propose in a joint proposal with Democratic leaders additional for all local governments, but Republican leaders in the legislature rejected the package. See Kerr, "Jersey System of School Aid Is Ruled Fair," B1. For an overview of Kean's education policies, see Priscilla Van Tassel, "As Schools Open, Kean's Impact Is Assessed," *New York Times*, 3 September 1989, sec. 12, 1.

Chapter 7. Schools, Democrats, and Taxes
(and Electoral Retribution)

1. Salmore and Salmore, *New Jersey Politics and Government*, 251.

2. See New Jersey State and Local Expenditure and Revenue Policy Commission, "State and Local Finances, 1974–1984: A Background Report" (Trenton: State of New Jersey, 1987), and the complete report, New Jersey State and Local Expenditure and Revenue Policy Commission, "State and Local Finances" (Trenton, 1988).

3. Interview, 16 July 1996, law offices of Jim Florio.

4. Allan R. Odden and Lawrence O. Piscus, *School Finance: A Policy Persepctive* (New York: McGraw-Hill, 1992), 173–82.

5. Salmore and Salmore, *New Jersey Politics and Government*, 273.

6. Interview, 16 July 1996, law offices of Jim Florio.

7. Ibid.

8. Ibid.

9. Peter Kerr, "Read His Lips: More Taxes," *New York Times Magazine*, 20 May 1990, 32.

10. Interview, 16 July 1996, law offices of Jim Florio.

11. Peter Kerr. "Florio Urges Taxing Rich," *New York Times*, 20 March 1990, B1.

12. Robert Hanley, "Florio Urges Added Aid in City Schools," *New York Times*, 25 May 1990, B1.

13. Numerous books and articles had appeared documenting these trends. For examples, see: Frank Levy, *Dollars and Dreams: The Changing American Income Distribution* (New York: W. W. Norton, 1988); Sylvia Nasar, "Even Among the Well-Off, The Richest Get Richer," *New York Times*, 5 March 1992, A1; and Jason DeParle, "Democrat's Invisible Man Specializes in Making Inequity of Poor Easy to See," *New York Times*, 19 August 1991, A12; Edsall and Edsall, *Chain Reaction;:* and Sylvia Nasar, "Fed Gives New Evidence of '80s Gains by Richest," *New York Times*, 21 April 1992, A1.

14. Kevin Phillips, *The Politics of Rich and Poor* (New York: Random House, 1991).

15. Kerr, "Read His Lips," 32.

16. Peter Kerr, "Florio Woos a New Kind of Coalition," *New York Times*, 13 June 1990, B2.

17. Ibid., B2.

18. Ibid., B1.

19. Robert Hanley, "The New Math of Rich and Poor," *New York Times*, 10 June 1990, E6.

20. 575 A. 2d 359 (NJ 1990), 363.

21. Ibid., 409.

22. Ibid., 359.

23. Kerr, "Florio Woos a New Kind of Coalition," B2.

24. Peter Kerr, "Florio School-Aid Package Gains Final Approval," *New York Times*, 22 June 1990, A1.

25. Kerr, "Florio Urges Taxing Rich," B1.

26. Kerr, "Florio School-Aid Package Gains Final Approval," B2.

27. Kerr, "Florio Woos a New Kind of Coalition," B2.

28. Interview with Thomas Paterniti, 10 July 1996.

29. Attempts were made by numerous advisors, friends, and legislators to persuade Jim Florio to stall on the issue to create a public perception that there was a serious problem that had to be resolved. Interview with Steve Block, 13 January 1996.

30. Interview with Thomas Paterniti, former New Jersey senator, 10 July 1996, via telephone.

31. Interview with Chuck Haytian, 16 July 1996, Trenton, New Jersey. Mr Haytian was a state assembly member and the minority leader in 1990. At the time of the interview he was the chair of the Republican State Committee.

32. Interview with Thomas Paterniti, former New Jersey senator, 10 July 1996, via telephone.

33. Interviews with Gerald Stockman, 17 July 1996, Trenton, New Jersey.

34. Interview with Thomas Paterniti, former New Jersey senator, 10 July 1996, via telephone.

35. Peter Kerr, "As Florio Changes Politics, His Foes are Overwhelmed and His Allies are Nervous," *New York Times*, 24 June 1990, sec. 4, 22.

36. Interview with Joe Doria, 11 July 1996, via telephone. Mr. Doria was the Speaker of the assembly in 1991 and is currently a member of the assembly.

37. Peter Kerr, "New Jersey Confused Over Taxes," *New York Times*, 27 June 1990, B1. Gerald Stockman, another Democratic legislator, also reported in an interview that he encountered the same thing.

38. Wayne King, "New Jersey Democrats Wary of Tax Issue," *New York Times*, 28 July 1990, A28.

39. Ibid., B4.

40. Robert Hanley, "New School Aid in '91? Toms River Isn't Cheering," *New York Times*, 17 September 1990, B4.

41. Peter Kerr, "To Poor, Florio's Plan Is Just Another Promise," *New York Times*, 23 November 1990, A1.

42. Interview with Jim Florio, 16 July 1996, and interview with Joe Doria, 11 July 1996.

43. Peter Kerr, "Florio's Popularity Crashes in Survey," *New York Times*, 15 July 1991, A15.

44. Interview with Chuck Haytian, 16 July 1996, Trenton, New Jersey.

45. King, "New Jersey Democrats Wary of Tax Issue," A28; and Wayne King, "Threats of Deficit and Tax Revolt Make Trenton Noisy," *New York Times*, 17 September 1991, A1.

46. Joseph F. Sullivan, "Leaders of New Jersey Tax Rebellion Take Aim at Legislature," *New York Times*, 23 November 1990, B6.

47. Peter Kerr, "Florio's Gamble," *New York Times*, 9 January 1991, B2.

48. Peter Kerr, "Democrats Urge Big Shift in Florio Plan," *New York Times*, 8 January 1991, B1; and Robert Hanley, "Plan for Property-Tax Relief to Cut Urban School Money," *New York Times*, 25 January 1991, B2.

49. Wayne King, "G.O.P. Runs against Florio, Who's Not Running," *New York Times*, 25 September 1991, B2.

50. Salmore and Salmore, *New Jersey Politics and Government*, 82; and King, "G.O.P. Runs against Florio."

51. Wayne King, "Florio Urges Democrats to Fight Back," *New York Times*, 24 October 1991, B1.

52. Joseph F. Sullivan, "Florio Calls for Election to Be a Referendum on Bush," *New York Times*, 30 October 1991, B1.

53. King, "G.O.P. Runs against Florio."

54. Wayne King, "With Anti-Florio Voting Wave, Republicans Win the Legislature," *New York Times*, 6 November 1991, A1.

55. Kerr, "New Jersey Confused over Taxes," B5.

56. Interview with Jim Florio, 16 July 1996.

57. For discussions of this pattern, see Edsall and Edsall, *Chain Reaction;* Phillips, *Politics of Rich and Poor;* and Greenberg, *Middle-Class Dreams,* 23–54.

CHAPTER 8. THE RETURN OF REPUBLICANS AND TAX CUTS

1. It should be noted that legislative Democrats came close to repealing their tax increases before the Republicans took office. The Democrats, stung by criticisms that they had enacted all these increases, sought to repeal them in December, 1991, so they could claim credit for the repeals. They also thought this would leave Republicans without the needed revenues for a balanced budget and with the responsibility to govern without that revenue. They could not mobilize enough votes, however, and the attempt failed in late December. See: Wayne King, "Assembly to Begin Debating Rolling Back Tax Package," *New York Times*, 16 December 1991, B7; Jerry Gray, "Senate Democrats Delay Tax Vote as Assembly Stalls," *New York Times*, 17 December 1991, B6; Jerry Gray, "New Jersey Democrats Say the Bill Is Due," *New York Times*, 19 December 1991, 30; Jerry Gray, "Trenton Senate Votes to Repeal Most of Tax Package," *New York Times*, 20 December 1991, B5; Jerry Gray, "Assembly Democrats Weigh Foes' Tax Repeal Bills," *New York Times*, 21 December 1991, 25.

2. Wayne King, "New Jersey G.O.P. Vows to Roll Back Millions in Taxes," *New York Times*, 6 November 1991, A1.

3. Wayne King, "All Is Scarce in Trenton Except Republicans," *New York Times*, 15 January 1992, B4.

4. Wayne King, "Legislature in New Jersey Cuts Sales Tax," *New York Times*, 3 April 1992, B1.

5. Wayne King, "Another in a Series: New Jersey Republicans Propose a Revised School Aid Plan," *New York Times*, 13 March 1992, B5.

6. King, "Legislature in New Jersey Cuts Sales Tax," B6.

7. Wayne King, "Trenton May Dance a Two-Step Tax Shuffle," *New York Times*, 27 March 1992, 28.

8. Wayne King, "Sales Tax Cut a Step Closer in Trenton," *New York Times*, 24 March 1992, B4; and King, "Legislature in New Jersey Cuts Sales Tax," B1.

9. Wayne King, "Democrats Stalk Out of Budget Hearing," *New York Times*, 29 April 1992, B6.

10. Republicans, following their argument that tax cuts would generate economic growth, wore "Jobs Now!" buttons. King, "Another in a Series" B5.

11. Jerry Gray, "Florio Says He Will Veto Republicans' One-Cent Cut in Sales Tax," *New York Times*, 16 May 1992, 25; and Wayne King, "Florio Vetoes 1-Cent Cut in Sales Tax," *New York Times*, 19 May 1992, B1.

12. Wayne King, "Some Back Florio on Tax; Others Side with G.O.P.," *New York Times*, 20 May 1992, B6.

13. Jerry Gray, "Tax Vote Was Easy Part for G.O.P.," *New York Times*, 23 May 1992, A29.

14. Wayne King, "Homestead Rebate Cuts Won't Include Elderly," *New York Times*, 19 June 1992, B4.

15. Jerry Gray, "GOP Cuts Florio's Plan on Its Budget," *New York Times*, 19 June 1992, B4.

16. Jerry Gray, "G.O.P. Details Sweeping Cuts in New Jersey," *New York Times*, 12 June 1992, B1; and Wayne King, "Republicans Budget Plan Repudiates 2 Decades of Tradition," *New York Times*, 19 June 1992, A1.

17. Wayne King, "Errors Cited for Budget in New Jersey," *New York Times*, 24 June 1992, B1.

18. Wayne King, "Senate in Trenton Passes Budget with Sharp Reductions," *New York Times*, 26 June 1992, B5.

19. Wayne King, "G.O.P. Vows Budget Fight with Florio," *New York Times*, 28 June 1992, A23.

20. Jerry Gray, "G.O.P. Votes to Override Budget Veto," *New York Times*, 1 July 1992, B5.

21. Wayne King, "Shift in School Fund Gains in Trenton," *New York Times*, 30 June 1992, B4.

22. Jerry Gray, "G.O.P. Is Told Not to Alter Constitution," *New York Times*, 14 July 1992, B6.

23. Wayne King, "Quality Education Act Reconsidered," *New York Times*, 21 July 1992, B6.

24. Wayne King, "Trenton G.O.P. Shifting School Aid to Suburbs," *New York Times*, 28 August 1992, 40.

25. Wayne King, "Florio Seeks $15.6 Billion in New Budget," *New York Times*, 9 February 1993, B1.

26. Jerry Gray, "Add, Subtract," *New York Times*, 31 January 1992, B4; and Joseph F.

Sullivan, "Fight on Trenton Aid to Poor School Districts Goes to Court, Again," *New York Times*, 9 July 1992, B8.

27. Jerry Gray, "Judge Says Trenton Spending Fails Mandate to Aid Schools," *New York Times*, 1 September 1993, A1.

28. Michael Aron, *Governor's Race* (New Brunswick, N.J.: Rutgers University Press, 1994), 28.

29. The other responses were "poor" or "no opinion."

30. Jerry Gray, "Florio Gains in Popularity, New Poll Says," *New York Times*, 28 February 1993, 4.

31. Aron, *Governor's Race*, 57.

32. Ibid., 117.

33. Ibid., 166.

34. Ibid., 32.

35. Ibid., 95–97.

36. Ibid., 127.

37. "Using His Right, Florio Moves from Dead to Dead Heat," *New York Times*, 20 September 1993, A1.

38. Iver Peterson, "Poll Indicates Florio Is Winning Approval of 1990 Tax Increases," *New York Times*, 28 September 1993. A1.

39. Aron, *Governor's Race*, 179–80, 227.

40. "How Whitman Sees the Bottom Line," *New York Times*, 22 September 1993, B6.

41. Aron, *Governor's Campaign*, 224.

42. Interview in Jim Florio offices, 16 July 1993.

43. Jerry Gray, "Florio Attacks Whitman's Tax-Cut Proposal," *New York Times*, 23 September 1993, B1.

44. Aron, *Governor's Race*, 223–24.

45. Kimberly J. McLarin, "Tax-Cut Temptation," *New York Times*, 8 October 1993, B6.

46. Aron, *Governor's Race*, 226.

47. Ibid.

48. Joseph F. Sullivan, "'90 Tax Rise Overshadows Trenton Races," *New York Times*, 18 October 1993, B1.

49. "The Ad Campaign," *New York Times*, 30 September 1993, B7; and Jerry Gray, "Whitman and Florio Issue Hard-Edged Ads," *New York Times*, 30 October 1993, 40.

50. Aron, *Governor's Race*, 230–31.

51. Ibid., 241.

52. Ibid., 243, 258, 263.

53. Ibid., 270, 282.

54. In contrast, when the assembly Democrats, the majority party, were battling with Governor George Pataki, the Republican, over a tax cut in 1995, many newspapers presented graphs in which the focus was on the dollar cuts by income levels. Those graphs consistently showed that Pataki's cuts would give large cuts to upper-income families. This made it easier for Democrats to argue that his cuts were a giveaway to the rich. The original Pataki cuts had been presented as percentage cuts, much as Whitman had done, but the newspapers generally presented the charts in terms of dollar cuts.

55. Iver Peterson, "Whitman Pledges to Cut Taxes by Next Budget," *New York Times*, 4 November 1993, A1.

56. Iver Peterson, "Inaugural Surprise: Whitman Wants Tax Cut Now," *New York Times*, 19 January 1994, A1.

57. Jerry Gray, "Whitman's Tax Pledge: A Bold, Risky Surprise," *New York Times*, 20 January 1993, B7.

58. Iver Peterson, "As Whitman Nears Inaugural, Debt Complicates Tax-Cut Pledge," *New York Times*, 16 January 1994, A1.

59. Iver Peterson, "State Aid and Whitman Tax Plan," *New York Times*, 30 November 1993, B6.

60. Todd S. Purdum, "Whitman Concedes Chance of Higher Property Taxes," *New York Times*, 22 January 1994, 27.

61. Teachers' unions have become, in most states, the best-financed interest group in the state. They have also become more concerned over the last decade with bread-and-butter issues of salary and benefits. See Clive S. Thomas and Ronald J. Hrebenar, "Interest Groups in the States," in *Politics in the American States: A Comparative Analysis*, ed. Virginia Gray, Russell L. Hanson, and Herbert Jacob, 7th ed. (Washington, D.C.: CQ Press, 1999), 113–43.

62. Iver Peterseon, "Whitman Challenges the Teachers," *New York Times*, 6 February 1994, 39.

63. There is little survey data available on public opinion on teachers' pay. There is, however, indirect evidence that the salaries of teachers have become an issue. More and more newspapers have taken to printing the salaries of teachers. I gave an address to the New York State NEA annual convention in 1993, and asked those in attendance (approximately 100) if the newspapers in their community were printing their salaries. Most said it was now an annual event, and that they sensed considerable hostility to their salary levels. The fact that New Jersey has among the highest paid teachers, on average, in the country is a regular part of stories about education and education finance.

That statistic, however, does not accurately capture the real compensation of teachers. In New York newspapers there have been stories about total compensation, including pay for conferences, training sessions, lunchroom duty, committees, and extracurricular responsibilities, and the total compensation is often much higher than the base salary. I do not know how much those types of stories have appeared in New Jersey, but the reaction in New York has generally been surprise among the public that teachers made that much.

The important point is that it appears that teachers have gone from being seen as underpaid to a situation in which there is much less support for increasing their compensation.

64. Iver Peterson, "Commission Urges Curbing Pay in New Jersey Schools," *New York Times*, 9 April 1994, 23.

65. Ibid.

66. Iver Peterson, "Schools Are Target of Budget Ire After Cuts by Trenton," *New York Times*, 21 April 1994, B7.

67. Peterson, "State Aid and Whitman Tax Plan," B6; Peterson, "Inaugural Surprise," B6.

68. Jerry Gray, "G.O.P. Plans on Surpluses to Make Up for Tax Cuts," *New York Times*, 1 February 1994, B5.

69. Jerry Gray, "Whitman's Plan for a 5% Tax Cut Passes in Senate," *New York Times*, 4 March 1994, A1.

70. Joseph F. Sullivan, "Battered Democrats Try a New Direction," *New York Times*, 6 February 1994, 44.

71. Iver Peterson, "Whitman Calls for Tax Cut Aimed at the Middle Class," *New York Times*, 16 March 1994, B1.

72. Jerry Gray, "Whitman Goal: Cut Taxes without Wounding Voters," *New York Times*, 17 March 1994, B1.

73. Iver Peterson, "New Jersey Teachers Flex Muscles, but Carefully," *New York Times*, 19 April 1994, B1; "Huge Protest by State Unions Threatens Whitman Budget," *New York Times*, 13 June, 1994, B1.

74. Joseph F. Sullivan, "Learning the Power of Tax Cuts," *New York Times*, 20 June 1994, B5.

75. Jerry Gray, "Legislature Agrees to Whitman Budget Request," *New York Times*, 22 June 1994, B7.

76. Iver Peterson, "Whitman Pledges Early Completion of 30% Tax Cut," *New York Times*, 24 January 1995, A1.

77. Ibid.

78. Kimberly J. McLarin, "Budget's Losers Display a Touch of Resignation," *New York Times*, 24 January 1995, B5.

79. Iver Peterson, "In Rare Accord, Leaders in Both Parties Say Public Employees' Salaries Are Rising Too Fast," *New York Times*, 24 February 1995, B6.

80. Interview with Chuck Hytaian, Trenton, New Jersey, 16 July 1996.

81. Jonathan Walters, "The Whitman Squeeze," *Governing* 9, no. 2 (November 1995): 18–25.

82. Art Weissman, *Christine Todd Whitman* (New York: Birch Lane Press, 1996), 206, 257; and interview with Chuck Haytaian, 16 July 1996.

Chapter 9. Grappling with State Responsibilities

1. Joseph F. Sullivan, "Fight on Trenton Aid to Poor School Districts Goes to Court, Again," *New York Times*, 9 July 1992, B1.

2. Jerry Gray, "Judge Says Trenton Spending Fails Mandate to Aid Schools," *New York Times*, 1 September 1993, A1.

3. Kimberly McLarin, "Trenton Committee Snags on School Spending Plans," *New York Times*, 31 March 1994, B6.

4. Iver Peterson, "Trenton Panel Offers Plan on School Aid," *New York Times*, 8 April 1994, B1.

5. Kimberly McLarin, "Financing of Poor Schools Back in New Jersey Court," *New York Times*, 10 May 1994, B5.

6. Joseph F. Sullivan, "Whitman Asks for Time to Solve School Aid Gap," *New York Times*, 25 May 1994, B6.

7. Joseph F. Sullivan, "Top New Jersey Court Orders New Plan for School Funds," *New York Times*, 13 July 1994, 1.

8. Iver Peterson, "Court's Decision Gives a Grateful Whitman Some Breathing Space," *New York Times*, 13 July 1994, B6.

9. Jerry Gray, "Gap Narrowing for Poor School Districts, Study Finds," *New York Times*, 12 October 1994, B6.

10. There had even been consideration of adding rural districts to the suit filed by the Education Law Center in the late 1980s, but the center had chosen to focus instead on the lawsuit. The rural districts continued with their plans to sue. The enactment of the new state education requirements in December, 1996, prompted these districts to argue even more strenuously that they needed more money. See the stories: Abby Goodenough, "Rural Schools Feel Ignored by Trenton Aid to Poor," *New York Times*, 23 June 1997, A1; and Abby Goodenough, "New Jersey Schools Planning to Sue State," *New York Times*, 21 September 1997, A45.

11. Senate Bill No. 40, introduced 27 June 1996, pp. 1 and 2.

12. Iver Peterson, "Overspending School Districts Facing $11 Million Penalty," *New York Times*, 22 February 1995, B5.

13. Clifford J. Levy, "In a Wealthy District, Opposition to Whitman's Cuts in School Aid," *New York Times*, 3 February 1995, A1.

14. Peterson, "Overspending School Districts," B5.

15. In polling I have done in upstate New York for various local candidates, I have

often asked questions about whether too much is spent on education, on teachers' salaries, and on administrators. The answers are consistently that we spend too much on administrators, but not that we spend too much on education or teachers' salaries.

16. Kimberly J. McLarin, "Whitman Plans Change in School-Fund Formula," *New York Times*, 17 February 1995, B4.

17. Peterson, "Overspending School Districts," B5.

18. Iver Peterson, "Whitman Puts Standards Above Money for Schools," *New York Times*, 12 January 1996, B3.

19. Leo Klagholz, Commissioner of Education, *Core Curriculum Content Standards* (Trenton: The New Jersey Department of Education, May 1996).

20. Ibid., 6-5, 6-6.

21. Ibid, i.

22. Assumptions for the aid were also presented, including the assumed number of students in, for example, a typical middle school, the assumed class size, the number of administrators, teachers, aides, security guards, clerical workers, guidance counselors, and any other personnel. The assumed salaries for each title were also presented.

23. New Jersey Department of Education, *Comprehensive Plan for Educational Improvement and Financing* (Trenton, N.J.: May 1996), 10.

24. Ibid., 12.

25. For example, see the testimony of representatives of the Concerned Taxpayers Association, 29–36, and United Taxpayers of New Jersey, 97–101, at 17 July 1996 Public Hearing on Senate Bill No. 40, Morris Plains, New Jersey; the testimony of Ira Marks, from Hands Across New Jersey, Inc., at 25 July 1996 Public Hearing on Senate Bill No. 40 and Assembly Bill No. 20, Trenton, New Jersey, 97–101; and the testimony of Steven Napoliello, speaking for the Burlington Chapter of New Jersey Hands '91, at the 29 July 1996 Public Hearing at Voorhees, New Jersey, 132–34.

26. David Glovin, "Efforts Produce No Measurable Result," *Bergen Record*, 24 December 1995, n.p. This and subsequent *Bergen Record* stories were taken from the web page (www.bergen.com) of the newspaper. None of the stories had accompanying dates.

27. John Mooney, "Evaluation of Teachers Inconsistent in New Jersey," *Bergen Record* (web page), 31 December 1995, n.p.

28. David Glovin and John Mooney, "The Teacher Performance Factor," *Bergen Record* (web page), 31 December 1995, n.p.

29. David Glovin, "Salary Guide Pushes Teachers Up the Scale," *Bergen Record*, 24 December 1995, np; and David Glovin and John Mooney, "An Advancing Class: Many Teachers Making $70,000," *Bergen Record* (web page), 24 December 1995, n.p.

30. John Mooney, "Finding a Way to Better Schools," *Bergen Record* (web page), 8 December 1996, n.p.

31. Comments by Senator Robert J. Martin (R), at 17 July 1996 Public Hearing on Senate Bill No. 40, Morris, New Jersey, 5.

32. Joseph F. Sullivan, "For Whitman and Senate, Agreement on School Aid," *New York Times*, 19 May 1995, B5.

33. Comments by Dennis Testa, president, New Jersey Education Association, at 25 July 1996 Public Hearing on Senate Bill No. 40 and Assembly Bill No. 20, 27–31, Trenton, New Jersey.

34. Comments by David Sciarra, executive director, Education Law Center, at 17 July 1996, Public Hearing on Senate Bill No. 40, Morris, New Jersey, 45–54.

35. Ibid., 47.

36. David Glovin and John Mooney, "The Pay Gap: Teacher Salaries Differ Dramatically," *Bergen Record* (web page), 24 December 1995, n.p.

37. See the numerous statements at the hearings on 17 July 1996, Public Hearing on

Senate Bill No. 40, Morris, New Jersey; and on 25 July 1996, Public Hearing on Senate Bill No. 40 and Assembly Bill No. 20, Trenton, New Jersey; and on 29 July 1996, Public Hearing on Senate Bill No. 40 and Assembly Bill No. 20, Voorhees, New Jersey.

38. Exchange between Senator MacInnes, a Democrat, and Deputy Commissioner Dipatri, at 17 July 1996 Public Hearing on Senate Bill No. 40, Morris, New Jersey, 9–12.

39. For example, see the comments of the superintendent of Morris Hills Regional High Schools, at the 17 July 1996 Public Hearing on Senate Bill No. 40, Morris, New Jersey, 25–29, or the comments of a parent from a school board from the Livingston School District at the same hearing, 57–62.

40. Colleen O'Dea, "The Price of Parity: Once More Into the Breach," *New Jersey Reporter* ([http://epn.org/njr/mayjun96/school.htm]), 6 of print.

41. Quinnipiac College Poll Institute Press Release, and results, released 3 April 1996. Poll conducted 28 March to 1 April 1996 of 908 New Jersey residents who said they were registered voters.

42. David Glovin, "Revised School Funding Plan Gains Broad Support," *Bergen Record* (web page), 18 December 1996, 1 of print.

43. David Glovin, "School Funding Accord Reached," *Bergen Record* (web page), 17 December 1996, 1–2 of print.

44. Neil MacFarquhar, "Vote in Trenton Sets Standards in Curriculum," *New York Times*, 20 December 1996, A1.

45. Roll call vote on S-40, 19 December 1996.

46. Kelly Richmond, "A Killer Issue: School Funding: Democrats See Advantage," *Bergen County Record* (web page), 22 December 1996, 1–2 of print.

47. David Glovin, "Whitman Signs GOP School Aid Plan," *Bergen County Record* (web page), 21 December 1996, 1 of print; and MacFarquhar, "Vote in Trenton Sets Standards in Curriculum," *New York Times*, 20 December 1996, B6.

48. John Mooney and David Glovin, "Poor School Districts Contest Funding Plan," *Bergen County Record* (web page), 7 January 1997, 1–2 of print.

49. Quinnipiac College Poll, Trend Archive, poll of February 18, 1997. Taken from web page: http://www.quinnipiac.edu/polling/archive.html, "New Jersey State Trends."

50. Address of Governor Christine Todd Whitman to a Joint Session of the New Jersey Legislature concerning the State of the State, Trenton, New Jersey, 14 January 1997. Taken from: http://www.state.nj.us/governor/sos97.adr.html", pp 1 and 3 of print.

51. For a summary of that transition, see E. J. Dionne, *They Only Look Dead* (New York: Touchstone, 1997), 151–230.

52. Jennifer Preston, "Whitman Plans Her Biggest Spending Rise," *New York Times*, 10 February 1997, B5; and Jennifer Preston, "Whitman Sifts Course to Propose Hefty Increase for New Spending," *New York Times*, 11 February 1997, B1.

53. Jennifer Preston, "Trenton Approves Bill Overhauling Welfare System," *New York Times*, 21 February 1997, A1.

54. Jennifer Preston, "Whitman Opens Re-Election Drive Recalling Her Tax Cuts and More," *New York Times*, 15 April 1997, B1.

55. Jennifer Preston, "Whitman, Though Unopposed, Runs TV Ads," *New York Times*, 8 May 1997, B6.

56. Jennifer Preston, "Challengers to Whitman Find Interest Hard to Raise," *New York Times*, 20 May 1997, B1.

57. For background on the issue, see Mary Caffrey, "Breaking the Bank: Whitman's Pension Moves Come up Short," *New Jersey Reporter* 25, no. 6 (March/April 1996); and Jennifer Preston, "Whitman Assailed on Idea of Bonds to Cover Pension," *New York Times*, 24 March 1997, A1.

58. Caffrey, "Breaking the Bank."

59. Jennifer Preston, "New Jersey Is to Scale Back Borrowing for Pension Funds," *New York Times*, 25 February 1997, B8.

60. Jennifer Preston, "Whitman Assailed on Idea of Bonds to Cover Pension," *New York Times*, 24 March 1997, A1; Jennifer Preston, "Union Chief Is Key to Plan by Whitman," *New York Times*, 30 March 1997, 19; Jennifer Preston, "Whitman Plans Late Push for Her Plan on Borrowing," *New York Times*, 19 April 1997, 24; and Melody Petersen, "New Jersey State Workers Worry about Pension Plan," *New York Times*, 21 April 1997, B1.

61. Preston, "Whitman Assailed on Idea of Bonds to Cover Pension," A1.

62. Jennifer Preston, "Whitman Borrowing Plan: Criticism May Not Go Away," *New York Times*, 7 June 1997, 24.

63. Abby Goodnough, "New Jersey's School Financing Is Again Held Unconstitutional," *New York Times*, 15 May 1997, A1.

64. Ibid.

65. Abby Goodnough, "Whitman Vows She'll Track Schools' Use of Extra Money," *New York Times*, 28 May 1997, B7.

66. Jennifer Preston, "Whitman and Legislators Plan $16.8 Billion Budget," *New York Times*, 20 June 1997, B6.

67. Robert Hanley, "Voters Reject Limits on Education in New Jersey," *New York Times*, 17 April 1997, B6.

68. Quinnipiac College Poll, Trend Archive, poll of February 18, 1997. Taken from web page: http://www.quinnipiac.edu/polling/archive.html, "New Jersey State Trends".

69. Melody Petersen, "Whitman Plan to Cut Auto Rates Stymied," *New York Times*, 18 June 1997, B4.

70. Melody Petersen, "Whitman and Lawmakers Back Auto Insurance Bill," *New York Times*, 24 June 1997, B4.

71. · Melody Petersen, "Whitman Gets Auto Plan in Final Trenton Session," *New York Times*, 27 June 1997, B4.

72. Jennifer Preston, "McGreevey Pledges to Roll Back Auto Rates 10%," *New York Times*, 4 September 1997, B1.

73. Quinnipiac College Poll, Trend Archive, poll of February 18, 1997. Taken from web page: http://www.quinnipiac.edu/polling/archive.html, "New Jersey State Trends."

74. "Jennifer Preston, "Whitman Shifts Focus from Car Insurance to Record on Other Issues," *New York Times*, 16 September 1997, B1.

75. Jennifer Preston, "Voters in Poll in New Jersey Fault Whitman on Insurance," *New York Times*, 17 September 1998, A1.

76. Kirk Johnson, "On the Stump, Whitman Touts Record Employment," *New York Times*, 18 October 1997, B4; and Jennifer Preston, "Whitman Stands on Record, but Newer Issues Stir Voters," *New York Times*, 1 November 1997, A1.

77. Melody Petersen, "Taking on Whitman's Good-Times Theme," *New York Times*, 24 September 1997, B5; Brett Pulley, "Rivals for Governor Step Up Campaigning," *New York Times*, 14 October 1997, B4; Jennifer Preston, "Opening Shots: Attack and Contrast in New Jersey," *New York Times*, 19 October 1997, 37; Jennifer Preston, "Whitman and McGreevey Take to Highways and Byways," *New York Times*, 26 October 1997, 35; Jennifer Preston, "McGreevey Offers Plan for Education as His Legacy," *New York Times*, 27 October 1997, A1.

78. Star-Ledger-Eagleton poll released on 11 June 1997. Taken from the web site of the *Bergen County Record,* 'http://www.bergen.com/campaign/njgovpoll.htm'.

79. Herb Jackson, "Poll Shows Whitman, McGreevey in Virtual Tie," *Asbury Park Press*, 31 August 1997, taken from 'http://www.acom/campaign/831polla.htm'; and David M. Halbfinger, "Governor's Race Tightens, 2 Polls Suggest," *New York Times*, 13 October 1997, B4.

80. Jennifer Preston, "New Jersey Poll Finds Volatility among Voters," *New York Times*, 31 October 1997, A1.

81. Ibid., B4. The same results emerge in the Quinnipiac College Poll, Trend Archive, poll of 18 February 1997. Taken from web page: http://www.quinnipiac.edu/polling/archive.html, "New Jersey State Trends."

82. Johnson, "On the Stump," B4.

83. Bruno Tedeschi, "Governor Has Promises to Keep," *Bergen County Record* (web page), 5 November 1997, page 1 of print.

84. Election results for 1997 taken from the Division of Elections, 'http://www.state.nj.us/lps/elections'.

85. Jennifer Preston, "Whitman Holds On by a Razor-Thin Margin," *New York Times*, 5 November 1997, A1; and Marjorie Connelly, "Election '97: A Portrait of New Jersey Voters," *New York Times*, 7 November 1997, sec. 14:6.

86. Melody Petersen, "Legislators Promise Overhaul of New Jersey Car Insurance," *New York Times*, 7 November 1997, B1.

87. Jennifer Preston, "Whitman Restates Pledge on Taxes and Insurance," *New York Times*, 14 January 1998, A1.

88. Jennifer Preston, "Assembly Bill Would End Caps on Rates for City Drivers," *New York Times*, 17 April 1998, B1.

89. Jennifer Preston, "Assembly Passes Plan to Cut Car Premiums," *New York Times*, 21 April 1998, B5; and Jennifer Preston, "New Jersey Legislators Vote to Overhaul Auto Insurance," *New York Times*, 19 May 1998, B1.

90. Property Tax Commission, *Report of Recommendations to Governor Christine Todd Whitman*, Trenton, New Jersey, 16 September 1998, cover letter to the governor.

91. Tax Commission, *Report of Recommendations*, Executive Summary, 2.

92. Pia Sarkar, "Most North Jersey Cities Say Tax Report Isn't Much Help," *Bergen County Record* (web page), 17 September 1998, 1.

93. Herb Jackson, "N.J. Surplus May Go Back to Taxpayers," *Bergen County Record* (web page), 17 September 1998, 1.

94. Office of the Governor, News Release, "Governor Announces $100 Million in Direct Property Tax Relief, Moves Forward with Property Tax Commission Initiatives," Trenton, New Jersey, 16 September 1998.

95. Associated Press (AP), "State Estimate to Fix Schools Is $1.8 Billion," *New York Times*, 18 November 1997, B6.

96. Abby Goodnough, "Urban Schools Do Not Need More Money, the State Argues," *New York Times*, 23 December 1997, B5.

97. Abby Goodnough, "Judge Offers Specific Plans for Schools," *New York Times*, 23 January 1998, B1.

98. Jennifer Preston, "School Spending Debate Returns to Court," *New York Times*, 3 March 1998, B5.

99. Jennifer Preston, "Plan by Whitman on Urban Schools Backed by Court," *New York Times*, 22 May 1998, A1.

100. David M. Halbfinger, "In New Jersey, $12 Billion for Schools," *New York Times*, 14 July 2000, B1.

CHAPTER 10. THE STATE, PARTIES, AND PUBLIC POLICY

1. Joseph Schlesinger, "On the Theory of Party Organizations," *Journal of Politics* 46, no. 2 (May 1984): 383.

2. For a summary of suburbanization changes across the country, see Dennis R. Judd

and Todd Swanstrom, *City Politics: Private Power and Public Policy* (New York: HarperCollins, 1994), 179–270; and Kenneth T. Jackson, *Crabgrass Frontier: The Suburbanization of the United States* (New York: Oxford University Press, 1985).

3. Kenneth Newton, "Feeble Governments and Private Power: Urban Politics and Policies in the United States," in *The New Urban Politics,* ed. Louis H. Masotti and Robert L. Lineberry (Cambridge: Ballinger, 1976), 37–58; and Michael Danielson, *The Politics of Exclusion* (New York: Columbia University Press, 1976).

4. There are numerous summaries of the history of school finance litigation. A good recent summary is Dan A. Lewis and Shadd Maruna, "The Politics of Education," in *Politics in the American States: A Comparative Analysis,* ed. Virginia Gray and Herbert Jacob, 6th ed. (Washington D.C: CQ Press, 1996), 450–60; and Kenneth K. Wong, *Funding Public Schools: Politics and Policies* (Lawrence: University Press of Kansas, 1999).

5. I would argue that this issue has persisted through the 1980s and the 1990s, even though many conservative politicians would like to see it go away, because there is (a) so much evidence of inequality (b) a general commitment to equality of opportunity within our society, and (c) a sense that these unequal conditions really do affect people's opportunities to succeed in society. The depth of commitment to acting about this issue may wax and wane, but the combination of the three conditions just mentioned keeps the issue alive.

6. Key, *Southern Politics,* 307.

7. "The Growth of Suburbs," *New York Times*, 11 September 1990, A20.

8. Michael Barone, William Lilley III, and Laurence J. Defranco, *State Legislative Elections: Voting Patterns and Demographics* (Washington, D.C: Congressional Quarterly, 1998), "Introduction." (unnumbered).

9. Jeffrey M. Stonecash, "Political Cleavage in State Legislative Parties," *Legislative Studies Quarterly* 24, no. 2 (May 1999): 281–302.

10. This was also found by Jennings (1977) in his study comparing Louisiana and Virginia, and in his study (1979) assessing states where parties had different constituencies and alternated in power.

11. Erikson, Wright, and McIver, *Statehouse Democracy,* 78–87.

12. For reviews of how the debate about how much government should do has played out, see Edsall and Edsall, *Chain Reaction;* Greenberg, *Middle-Class Dreams;* Phillips, *Boiling Point;* and Dionne, *They Only Look Dead.*

13. For reviews of the problems Republicans ran into in 1995 when they proposed significant cuts, see Dionne, *They Only Look Dead;* and Maraniss and Weisskopf, *Just Tell Newt to Shut Up..*

14. Erikson, Wright, and McIver, *Statehouse Democracy,* 39–42.

15. Stonecash, "Political Cleavage in State Legislative Houses."

16. Erikson, Wright, and McIver, *Statehouse Democracy,* 14–19, and see the studies on party differences reviewed in chapter 2.

17. Chandler Davidson, *Race and Class in Texas Politics* (Princeton: Princeton University Press, 1990), 18–23.

18. Erikson, Wright, and McIver, *Statehouse Democracy,* 16.

19. Jeffrey M. Stonecash, "The Politics of State-Local Fiscal Relations," in *Governing Partners: State-Local Relations in the United States,* ed. Russell L. Hanson (Boulder, Colo.: Westview Press, 1998), 88.

20. Telephone interview with David Sciarra, executive director, Education Law Center, March 1997.

Bibliography

"The Ad Campaign." *New York Times*, 30 September 1993, B7.

"Address of Governor Christine Todd Whitman to a Joint Session of the New Jersey Legislature concerning the State of the State, Trenton, New Jersey." [cited 14 January 1997]. Available from http://www.state.nj.us/governor/sos97.adr.html".

Advisory Commission on Intergovernmental Relations. *State Limitations on Local Taxes and Expenditures*. Washington, D.C.: U.S. Government Printing Office, 1977.

———. *State Mandating of Local Expenditures*. Washington, D.C.: U.S. Government Printing Office, 1977.

———. *Significant Features of Fiscal Federalism, 1987 Edition*. Washington, D.C., 1987.

Albritton, Robert. "Measuring Public Policy: Impacts of the Supplemental Social Security Income Program." *American Journal of Political Science* 23 (1979): 559.

Alexander, Archibald S. "Just Taxation through Assessment Equalization." *New Jersey Municipalities* 33, no. 1 (1956): 5–7.

Amenta, Edwin, and Bruce G. Carruthers. "The Formative Years of U.S. Spending Policy: Theories of the Welfare State and the American States during the Great Depression." *American Sociological Review* 53 (1988): 661–78.

Amenta, Edwin, et al. "The Political Origins of Unemployment Insurance in Five American States." *Studies in American Political Development* 2 (1987): 137–82.

Annual Report of the Census of Governments. *Governmental Finances*, GF 5. This was issued as a printed report until 1991. Subsequent reports are taken from the web page of the Census of Governments.

Anton, Thomas J.. "The Politics of State Taxation: A Case Study of Decision-Making in the New Jersey Legislature." Dissertation, Princeton University, 1961.

"Arguments Are Heard in School-Aid Case." *New York Times*, 10 January 1973, 86.

Aron, Michael. *Governor's Race*. New Brunswick, N.J.: Rutgers University Press, 1994.

Associated Press. "Byrne Orders Cut of 5% in Jersey's Payroll Costs." *New York Times*, 3 January 1976, Late Jersey Edition, 45.

"Balanced Budget Offered in Jersey." *New York Times*, 14 February 1950, 27.

Barone, Michael, William Lilley III, and Laurence J. Defranco. *State Legislative Elections: Voting Patterns and Demographics*. Washington, D.C: Congressional Quarterly, 1998.

Beadleston, Alfred N. "Equalization and Revaluation at the Local Level." *New Jersey Municipalities* 34, no. 1 (1957): 5–10.

285

Beck, Morris. "Government Finance in New Jersey." In *The Economy of New Jersey*, edited by Solomon J. Fink et al.. New Brunswick, N.J.: Rutgers University Press, 1958.

Berry, Frances Stokes, and William D. Berry. "Tax Innovation in the States: Capitalizing on Political Opportunity." *American Journal of Political Science* 36, no. 3 (1992): 735.

Bowman, Ann and Kearney Bowman. *The Resurgence of the States*. Englewood Cliffs, N.J.: Prentice-Hall.

Brooks, Phil and Bob W. Gassaway. "Improving News Coverage." *State Legislatures*, 1985, 29–31.

Brown, Robert D. "Party Cleavage and Welfare Effort in the American States." *American Political Science Review* 89, no. 1 (1995): 23–33.

Brown, Robert D., and Gerald C. Wright. "Elections and State Party Polarization." *American Politics Quarterly* 20, no. 4 (1992): 411–26

Bureau of Government Research. *1984 New Jersey Legislative District Data Book*. New Brunswick, N.J.: The State University of New Jersey, 1984.

Burns, Nancy. *The Formation of American Local Governments*. New York: Oxford University Press, 1994.

"Byrne Asks July Deadline for School-Aid Legislation." *New York Times*, 26 February 1975, 84.

"Byrne Calls on Teachers to Press for Tax Reform." *New York Times*, 15 November 1975, 59.

"Byrne Cautions Trenton on Schools." *New York Times*, 26 May 1976, 84.

Campbell, Ballard C.. *The Growth of American Government*. Bloomington: Indiana University Press, 1995.

Campbell, Donald T. "'Degrees of Freedom' and the Case Study." *Comparative Political Studies* 8, no. 2 (1975): 178–86.

Churchill, Mary. "Assembly Democrats to Sift State Fiscal Woes." *New York Times*, 27 October 1974.

Clymer, Adam. "A Warning for the G.O.P." *New York Times*, 18 November 1981, B18.

Comments by David Sciarra, Executive Director, Education Law Center, at 17 July 1996 Public Hearing on Senate Bill No. 40, Morris, New Jersey, 45–54.

Comments by Dennis Testa, President, New Jersey Education Association, at 25 July 1996 Public Hearing on Senate Bill No. 40 and Assembly Bill No. 20, 27–31, Trenton, New Jersey.

Comments by Senator Robert J. Martin. July 17, 1996, Public Hearing on Senate Bill No. 40, Morris, New Jersey, 5.

The Commission on State Tax Policy. *The Fifth Report of the Commission on State Tax Policy: Taxation and Public Policy:* Trenton, N.J., 14 April 1950, 34–50.

Connelly, Marjorie. "Election '97: A Portrait of New Jersey Voters." *New York Times*, 7 November 1997, x.

Danielson, Michael. *The Politics of Exclusion*. New York: Columbia University Press, 1976.

Danziger, Sheldon, and Peter Gottschalk. *America Unequal*. Cambridge: Harvard University Press, 1995.

Davidson, Chandler. *Race and Class in Texas Politics*. Princeton: Princeton University Press, 1990.

"Deadlock Foreseen on State Fiscal Woes." *New York Times*, 3 November 1974, 91.

Derthick, Martha. "Intercity Differences in Administration of the Public Assistance Program: The Case of Massachusetts." In *City Politics and Public Policy*, ed. James Q. Wilson. New York: John Wiley, 1968.

———. *The Influence of Federal Grants*. Cambridge: Harvard University Press, 1970.

Dilger, Robert Jay. "The Expansion and Centralization of American Governmental Functions." In *American Intergovernmental Relations Today,* edited by Robert Jay Dilger, 18–22. Englewood Cliffs, N.J.: Prentice-Hall, 1986.

———. *National Intergovernmental Programs*. Englewood Cliffs, N.J.: Prentice-Hall, 1989.

Dionne, E. J. *Why Americans Hate Politics*. New York: Touchstone, 1991.

———. *They Only Look Dead*. New York: Touchstone, 1997.

Division of Taxation, Local Property Branch, State of New Jersey, Department of the Treasury. "Table of Equalized Valuations." Trenton, N.J., 1987.

Doria, Joe. Interview by Jeff Stonecash. 11 July 1996.

Eckstein, Harry. "Case Study and Theory in Political Science." In *Strategies of Inquiry,* edited by Fred Greenstein and Nelson Polsby, 79–137. Reading, Mass.: Addison-Wesley, 1975.

Edsall, Thomas B., and Mary D. Edsall. *Chain Reaction*. New York: Norton, 1991.

Erikson, Robert S., Gerald C. Wright, and John P. McIver. *Statehouse Democracy*. New York: Cambridge University Press, 1993.

Erikson, Robert S., John P. McIver, and Gerald C. Wright. "State Political Culture and Public Opinion." *American Political Science Review* 81, no. 3 (1987): 797–813

"Excerpts from the Debate between Candidates for Governor." *New York Times*, 13 October 1981, B6.

Exchange between Senator MacInnes, a Democrat, and Deputy Commissioner Dipatri, at 17 July 1996 Public Hearing on Senate Bill No. 40, Morris, New Jersey, 9–12.

Felzenberg, Alvin S. "The Impact of Gubernatorial Style on Policy Outcomes: An In-depth Study of Three New Jersey Governors." Dissertation, Princeton University, 1978.

Flanigan, Willaim H., and Nancy H. Zingale. *Political Behavior of the American Electorate*. Washington, D.C.: CQ Press, 1998.

Florio, Jim. Interview by Jeff Stonecash. 16 July 1993.

Frederickson, David C. Nice, and Patricia Frederickson. *The Politics of Intergovernmental Relations*. Chicago: Nelson-Hall, 1995.

Garand, James C. "Explaining Growth in the U.S. States." *American Political Science Review* 82 (1988): 837–49.

George, Alexander L. "Case Studies and Theory Development: The Method of Structured, Focused Comparison." *Diplomacy: New Approaches in History, Theory, and Policy*. New York: Free Press, 1979.

Glovin, David. "Efforts Produce No Measurable Result." *Bergen Record*, 1995.

———. "Salary Guide Pushes Teachers Up the Scale." *Bergen Record*, 1995.

———. "Revised School Funding Plan Gains Broad Support." *Bergen Record*, 1996.

———. "School Funding Accord Reached." *Bergen Record*, 1996.

———. "Whitman Signs GOP School Aid Plan." *Bergen County Record*, 1996.

Glovin, David, and John Mooney. "An Advancing Class: Many Teachers Making $70,000." *Bergen Record*, 1995.

———. "The Pay Gap: Teacher Salaries Differ Dramatically." *Bergen Record*, 1995.

———. "The Teacher Performance Factor." *Bergen Record*, 1995.

Goertz, Margaret E. *Money and Education: Where Did the 400 Million Dollars Go?* Princeton, N.J.: Education Policy Research Institute, Educational Testing Service, 1978.

Goodnough, Abby. "New Jersey's School Financing Is Again Held Unconstitutional." *New York Times*, 15 May 1997, A1.

———. "Whitman Vows She'll Track Schools' Use of Extra Money." *New York Times*, 28 May 1997, B7.

———. "Urban Schools Do Not Need More Money, the State Argues." *New York Times*, 23 December 1997, B5.

———. "Judge Offers Specific Plans for Schools," *New York Times*, 23 January 1998, B1.

Gormley, William T. "Coverage of State Government in the Mass Media." *State Government* 52, no. 2 (1979): 45–51.

Government Finances, the GF-5 series, published by the Bureau of the Census.

Governor's Task Force on Welfare Management. *A State Welfare System for the Poor.* Trenton: State of New Jersey, 2 June 1971.

Gray, Jerry. "Add, Subtract." *New York Times*, 31 January 1992, B4.

———. "Tax Vote Was Easy Part for G.O.P." *New York Times*, 23 May 1992, A29.

———. "G.O.P. Details Sweeping Cuts in New Jersey." *New York Times*, 12 June 1992, B1.

———. "GOP Cuts Florio's Plan on Its Budget." *New York Times*, 19 June 1992, B4.

———. "G.O.P. Votes to Override Budget Veto." *New York Times*, 1 July 1992, B5.

———. "G.O.P. Is Told Not to Alter Constitution." *New York Times*, 14 July 1992, B6.

———. "Whitman's Tax Pledge: A Bold, Risky Surprise." *New York Times*, 20 January 1993, B7.

———. "Florio Gains in Popularity, New Poll Says." *New York Times*, 28 February 1993, 4.

———. "Judge Says Trenton Spending Fails Mandate to Aid Schools." *New York Times*, 1 September 1993, A1.

———. "Florio Attacks Whitman's Tax-Cut Proposal." *New York Times*, 23 September 1993, B1.

———. "Whitman and Florio Issue Hard-Edged Ads." *New York Times*, 30 October 1993, 40.

———. "G.O.P. Plans on Surpluses to Make Up for Tax Cuts." *New York Times*, 1 February 1994, B5.

———. "Whitman's Plan for a 5% Tax Cut Passes in Senate." *New York Times*, 4 March 1994, A1.

———. "Whitman Goal: Cut Taxes without Wounding Voters." *New York Times*, 17 March 1994, B1.

———. "Legislature Agrees to Whitman Budget Request." *New York Times*, 22 June 1994, B7.

———. "Gap Narrowing for Poor School Districts, Study Finds." *New York Times*, 12 October 1994, B6.

Gray, Virginia, and Herbert Jacob, *Politics in the American States: A Comparative Analysis*, 6th ed. Washington, D.C.: CQ Press, 1996.

Greenberg, Stanley B. *Middle-Class Dreams.* New York: Times Books, 1995.

"The Growth of Suburbs." *New York Times*, 11 September 1990, A20.

Halbfinger, David M. "Governor's Race Tightens, 2 Polls Suggest." *New York Times*, 13 October 1997, B4

———. "In New Jersey, $12 Billion for Schools." *New York Times*, 14 July 2000, B1.

Hanley, Robert E. "T and E Problems Persist as New School Year Begins." *New York Times*, 9 September 1979, section 11, 1.

———. "Kean Asks Rise in Consumer Taxes and Fares." *New York Times*, 11 March 1982, A1.

———. "Alter Tax Plan, Democrats Tell Kean." *New York Times*, 12 March 1982, B3.

———. "Democrats Gird to Battle Kean on First Budget." *New York Times*, 14 March 1982, section 11, 1.

———. "Florio Urges Added Aid in City Schools." *New York Times*, 25 May 1990, B1.

———. "The New Math of Rich and Poor." *New York Times*, 10 June 1990, E6.

———. "New School Aid in '91? Toms River Isn't Cheering." *New York Times*, 17 September 1990, B4.

———. "Plan for Property-Tax Relief to Cut Urban School Money." *New York Times*, 25 January 1991, B2.

Hanson, Russell L. *Governing Partners*. Boulder, Colo.: Westview Press, 1998.

Harrington, Michael. *The Other America*. Baltimore: Penguin Books, 1971.

Haytian, Chuck. Interview by Jeff Stonecash. 16 July 1996.

Hedge, David M.. *Governance and the Changing American States*. Boulder, Colo.: Westview Press, 1998.

"How Whitman Sees the Bottom Line." *New York Times*, 22 September 1993, B6.

"Hughes Says G.O.P. Bids for Backlash." *New York Times*, 28 July 1967, 12.

"Imperiale, Withdrawing, Backs Bateman." *New York Times*, 20 September 1977, 87.

Jackson, Herb. "N.J. Surplus May Go Back to Taxpayers." *Bergen County Record*, 17 September 1998, 1.

———. "Poll Shows Whitman, McGreevey in Virtual Tie." Available from 'http://www.app.com/campaign/831polla.htm'.

Jackson, Kenneth T. *Crabgrass Frontier: The Suburbanization of the United States*. New York: Oxford University Press, 1985.

"Jersey Issues Set for Fall Election." *New York Times*, 11 May 1951, 22.

"Jersey May Stay within Revenues." *New York Times*, 28 December 1951, 19.

"Jersey Sales Tax Nearing Reality." *New York Times*, 5 April 1966, 30.

"Jersey's Fund Law Signed by Driscoll." *New York Times*, 20 April 1952, 64.

Johnson, Kirk Johnson. "On the Stump, Whitman Touts Record Employment." *New York Times*, 18 October 1997, B4.

Judd, Dennis R., and Todd Swanstrom. *City Politics*. New York: HarperCollins, 1994.

Kamin, Richard. "A Rational Plan for Needy Cities." *New York Times*, 5 June 1998, section 12, 30.

"Kean and Democrats Agree on Budget Cuts." *New York Times*, 26 June 1982, B4.

Kerr, Peter. "To Cut Local Taxes, Kean Urges Shifting Some Costs to State." *New York Times*, 27 January 1989, B1.

———. "Jersey System of School Aid Is Ruled Fair." *New York Times*, 24 February 1989, B1.

———. "Florio Urges Taxing Rich." *New York Times*, 20 March 1990, B1.

———. "Read His Lips: More Taxes." *New York Times Magazine*, 20 May 1990, 32.

———. "Florio Woos a New Kind of Coalition." *New York Times*, 13 June 1990, B2.

———. "Florio School-Aid Package Gains Final Approval." *New York Times*, 22 June 1990, A1.

———. "As Florio Changes Politics, His Foes Are Overwhelmed and His Allies are Nervous." *New York Times*, 24 June 1990, section 4, 22.

———. "New Jersey Confused Over Taxes." *New York Times*, 27 June 1990, B1.

———. "To Poor, Florio's Plan Is Just Another Promise." *New York Times*, 23 November 1990, A1.

———. "Democrats Urge Big Shift in Florio Plan." *New York Times*, 8 January 1991, B1.

———. "Florio's Gamble." *New York Times*, 9 January 1991, B2.

———. "Florio's Popularity Crashes in Survey." *New York Times*, 15 July 1991, A15.

Kettl, Donald F. *The Regulation of American Federalism*. Baltimore: Johns Hopkins University Press, 1987.

Key, V .O. *Southern Politics*. New York: Knopf, 1949, 307.

King, Wayne. "New Jersey Democrats Wary of Tax Issue." *New York Times*, 28 July 1990, A28.

———. "Threats of Deficit and Tax Revolt Make Trenton Noisy." *New York Times*, 17 September 1991, A1.

———. "G.O.P. Runs Against Florio, Who's Not Running." *New York Times*, 25 September 1991, B2.

———. "Florio Urges Democrats to Fight Back." *New York Times*, 24 October 1991, B1.

———. "With Anti-Florio Voting Wave, Republicans Win the Legislature." *New York Times*, 6 November 1991, A1.

———. "New Jersey G.O.P. Vows to Roll Back Millions in Taxes." *New York Times*, 6 November 1991, A1.

———. "All Is Scarce in Trenton Except Republicans." *New York Times*, 15 January 1992, B4.

———. "Another in a Series: New Jersey Republicans Propose a Revised School Aid Plan." *New York Times*, 13 March 1992, B5.

———. "Sales Tax Cut a Step Closer in Trenton." *New York Times*, 24 March 1992, B4.

———. "Trenton May Dance a Two-Step Tax Shuffle." *New York Times*, 27 March 1992, 28.

———. "Legislature in New Jersey Cuts Sales Tax." *New York Times*, 3 April 1992, B1.

———. "Democrats Stalk Out of Budget Hearing." *New York Times*, 29 April 1992, B6.

———. "Florio Vetoes 1-Cent Cut in Sales Tax." *New York Times*, 19 May 1992, B1.

———. "Some Back Florio on Tax; Others Side with G.O.P.." *New York Times*, 20 May 1992, B6.

———. "Homestead Rebate Cuts Won't Include Elderly." *New York Times*, 19 June 1992, B4.

———. "Errors Cited for Budget in New Jersey." *New York Times*, 24 June 1992, B1.

———. "Senate in Trenton Passes Budget with Sharp Reductions." *New York Times*, 26 June 1992, B5.

———. "G.O.P. Vows Budget Fight with Florio." *New York Times*, 28 June 1992, A23.

———. "Shift in School Fund Gains in Trenton." *New York Times*, 30 June 1992, B4.

———. "Quality Education Act Reconsidered." *New York Times*, 21 July 1992, B6.

———. "Trenton G.O.P. Shifting School Aid to Suburbs." *New York Times*, 28 August 1992, 40.

———. "Florio Seeks $15.6 Billion in New Budget." *New York Times*, 9 February 1993, B1.

Kirp, David L., John P. Dwyer, and Larry A. Rosenthal. *Our Town: Race, Housing, and the Soul of Suburbia*. New Brunswick, N.J.: Rutgers University Press, 1995.

Klagholz, Leo. *Core Curriculum Content Standards: The New Jersey Department of Education*. Trenton, New Jersey, 1996.

Kozol, Jonathan. *Savage Inequalities*. New York: Crown, 1991.

"Leaders in Jersey Oppose New Taxes." *New York Times*. 11 January 1950, 30.

Lehne, Richard. *The Quest for Justice*. New York: Longman, 1978.

Lehne, Richard, and Alan Rosenthal, eds. *Politics in New Jersey*. New Brunswick, N.J.: Eagleton Institute of Politics, 1979.

Leone, Richard C. "The Politics of Gubernatorial Leadership: Tax and Education Reform in New Jersey." Dissertation, Princeton University, 1969.

———. Interview by Jeff Stonecash. 16 July 1997.

Levy, Clifford J. "In a Wealthy District, Opposition to Whitman's Cuts in School Aid." *New York Times*, 3 February 1995, A1.

Levy, Frank. *Dollars and Dreams: The Changing American Income Distribution*. New York: W.W. Norton, 1988.

Lijphart, Arend. "The Comparable-Cases Strategy in Comparative Research." *Comparative Political Studies* 8, no. 2 (1975): 159–61.

Liner, Blaine E. "Sorting Out State–Local Relations." In *Decade of Devolution: Persepectives on State–Local Issues,* edited by E. Blaine Liner, 21–22. Washington, D.C: Urban Institute Press, 1989.

MacFarquhar, Neil. "Vote in Trenton Sets Standards in Curriculum." *New York Times*, 20 December 1996, A1.

Massey, Douglas S., and Nancy A. Denton. *American Apartheid*. Cambridge: Harvard University Press, 1993.

Maurer, Alvin. "The Pattern of Politics in Jersey Is Crazy Quilt." *New York Times,* 24 April 1977, section 4, 53.

Mayhew, David R. *Placing Parties in American Politics*. Princeton: Princeton University Press, 1986.

McCormick, Richard P. "An Historical Overview." In *Politics in New Jersey*, ed. Richard Lehne and Alan Rosenthal. New Brunswick, N.J.: Eagleton Institute of Politics, 1979.

McLarin, Kimberly J. "Tax-Cut Temptation." *New York Times*, 8 October 1993, B6.

———. "Trenton Committee Snags on School Spending Plans." *New York Times*, 31 March 1994, B6.

———. "Financing of Poor Schools Back in New Jersey Court." *New York Times*, 10 May 1994, B5.

———. "Budget's Losers Display a Touch of Resignation." *New York Times*, 24 January 1995, B5.

———. "Whitman Plans Change in School-Fund Formula." *New York Times*, 17 February 1995, B4.

Meislin, Richard J. "Jersey Economy Dominates Second Florio-Kean Debate." *New York Times*, 2 October 1981, B2.

———. "Jersey Poll Indicates Voters' Background Overshadows Issues." *New York Times*, 21 October 1981, A1.

———. "Poll Finds It's Still a Kean-Florio Toss-Up." *New York Times*, 25 October 1981, section 11, 1.

———. "Taxes Are a Crucial Question in Race for Governor in New Jersey." *New York Times*, 27 October 1981, section 2, 1.

———. "Kean: G.O.P. Candidate with Liberal Tendency." *New York Times*, 28 October 1981, B1.

Moakley, Maureen. "New Jersey." In *The Political Life of the American States*. New York: Praeger, 1984.

———. "Political Parties." In *The Political State of New Jersey*, edited by Gerald Pomper. New Brunswick, N.J.: Rutgers University Press, 1986.

Moakley, Maureen, and Gerald Pomper. "Party Organizations." In *Politics in New Jersey*, ed. Richard Lehne and Alan Rosenthal, 88–93. New Brunswick, N.J.: Eagleton Institute of Politics, 1979.

"Money Measures Voted." *New York Times,* 27 March 1951, 30.

Mooney, John. "Evaluation of Teachers Inconsistent in New Jersey." *Bergen Record*: 31 December 1995.

———. "Finding a Way to Better Schools." *Bergen Record,* 8 December 1996.

Mooney, John, and David Glovin. "Poor School Districts Contest Funding Plan." *Bergen County Record*, 7 January 1997.

Morgan, David. *The Capitol Press Corps*. Westport, Conn.: Greenwood Press, 1978.

Moscow, Warren. "Driscoll Attacks Federal Spending." *New York Times,* 18 January 1950, 1.

Moscow, Warren. "Economies in Jersey Hailed by Driscoll." *New York Times,* 19 April 1953, 73.

Murray, Charles. *Losing Ground*. New York: Basic Books, 1984.

Naravaez, Alfonso A. "Jersey Assembly, Ending Deadlock, Votes Income Tax." *New York Times*, 8 July 1976, 1.

———. "Jersey Senate Approves 1.5% State Income Tax." *New York Times*, 18 June 1976, 1.

———. "Jersey's Assembly Rejects Income Tax." *New York Times*, 22 June 1976, 73.

———. "2 Candidates for Governor Clash on Education and Are Booed." *New York Times*, 28 October 1977, part 2, 17.

———. "Jersey Assembly Votes Death-Penalty Bill, 54–19." *New York Times,* 22 June 1982, B2.

New Jersey Department of Education. *Comprehensive Plan for Educational Improvement and Financing*. Trenton, N.J., 1996.

New Jersey Statutes Annotated, 54A:2–1. 1996 pocket.

"New Tobacco Tax Advances in Jersey." *New York Times*, 25 May 1982, B1.

Newton, Kenneth. "Feeble Governments and Private Power: Urban Politics and Policies in the United States." *The New Urban Politics*. Cambridge, Mass.: Ballinger, 1976.

"1997 election results taken from the Division of Elections." Available from http://www.state.nj.us/lps/elections.

Odden, Allan R. and Lawrence O. *School Finance: A Policy Perspective*. New York: McGraw-Hill, 1992.

O'Dea, Colleen. "The Price of Parity: Once More Into the Breach." *New Jersey Reporter*. Available from: http://epn.org/njr/mayjun96/school.htm.

Office of the Governor. "Governor Announces $100 Million in Direct Property Tax Relief, Moves Forward with Property Tax Commission Initiatives." Trenton, N.J., 16 September 1998.

Orfield, Gary. *The Closing Door.* Cambridge: Harvard University Press, 205–34.

Patterson, James T. *America's Struggle against Poverty.* Cambridge: Harvard University Press, 1994.

Paterniti, Thomas. Interview by Jeff Stonecash. 10 July 1996.

Petersen, Melody. "New Jersey State Workers Worry About Pension Plan." *New York Times,* 21 April 1997, B1.

———. "Whitman Plan to Cut Auto Rates Stymied." *New York Times,* 18 June 1997, B4.

———. "Whitman and Lawmakers Back Auto Insurance Bill." *New York Times,* 24 June 1997, B4.

———. "Whitman Gets Auto Plan in Final Trenton Session." *New York Times,* 27 June 1997, B4.

———. "Taking on Whitman's Good-Times Theme." *New York Times,* 24 September 1997, B5.

———. "Legislators Promise Overhaul of New Jersey Car Insurance." *New York Times,* 7 November 1997, B1.

Peterson, Iver. "Poll Indicates Florio Is Winning Approval of 1990 Tax Increases." *New York Times,* 28 September 1993, A1.

———. "Whitman Pledges to Cut Taxes by Next Budget." *New York Times,* 4 November 1993, A1.

———. "State Aid and Whitman Tax Plan." *New York Times,* 30 November 1993, B6.

———. "As Whitman Nears Inaugural, Debt Complicates Tax-Cut Pledge." *New York Times,* 16 January 1994, A1.

———. "Inaugural Surprise: Whitman Wants Tax Cut Now." *New York Times,* 19 January 1994, A1.

———. "Whitman Challenges the Teachers." *New York Times,* 6 February 1994, 39.

———. "Whitman Calls for Tax Cut Aimed at the Middle Class." *New York Times,* 16 March 1994, B1.

———. "Trenton Panel Offers Plan on School Aid." *New York Times,* 8 April 1994, B1.

———. "Commission Urges Curbing Pay in New Jersey Schools." *New York Times,* 9 April 1994, 23.

———. "New Jersey Teachers Flex Muscles, but Carefully." *New York Times,* 19 April 1994, B1.

———. "Schools Are Target of Budget Ire After Cuts by Trenton." *New York Times,* 21 April 1994, B7.

———. "Huge Protest by State Unions Threatens Whitman Budget." *New York Times,* 13 June 1994, B1.

———. "Court's Decision Gives a Grateful Whitman Some Breathing Space." *New York Times,* 13 July 1994, B6.

———. "Whitman Pledges Early Completion of 30% Tax Cut." *New York Times,* 24 January 1995, A1.

———. "Overspending School Districts Facing $11 Million Penalty." *New York Times,* 22 February 1995, B5.

———. "In Rare Accord, Leaders in Both Parties Say Public Employees' Salaries Are Rising Too Fast." *New York Times*, 24 February 1995, B6.

———. "Whitman Puts Standards Above Money for Schools." *New York Times*, 12 January 1996, B3.

Phillips, Kevin. *The Politics of Rich and Poor*. New York: Random House, 1991.

Pittenger, John C. "The Courts." In *The Political State of New Jersey*, edited by Gerald M. Pomper. New Brunswick, N.J.: Rutgers University Press, 1985.

Pole, J. R. *The Pursuit of Equality in American History*. Berkeley: University of California Press, 1978.

Pomper, Gerald. "Political Parties." In *The Political State of New Jersey*, edited by Gerald Pomper. New Brunswick, N.J.: Rutgers University Press, 1986.

"A Portrait of New Jersey Voters." *New York Times*, 4 November 1993, B9.

Preston, Jennifer. "Whitman Plans Her Biggest Spending Rise." *New York Times*, 10 February 1997, B5.

———. "Whitman Sifts Course to Propose Hefty Increase for New Spending." *New York Times*, 11 February 1997, B1.

———. "Trenton Approves Bill Overhauling Welfare System." *New York Times*, 21 February 1997, A1.

———. "New Jersey Is to Scale Back Borrowing for Pension Funds." *New York Times*, 25 February 1997, B8.

———. "Whitman Assailed on Idea of Bonds to Cover Pension." *New York Times*, 24 March 1997, A1.

———. "Union Chief is Key to Plan by Whitman." *New York Times*, 30 March 1997, 19.

———. "Whitman Opens Re-Election Drive Recalling Her Tax Cuts and More." *New York Times*, 15 April 1997, B1.

———. "Whitman Plans Late Push for Her Plan on Borrowing." *New York Times*, 19 April 1997, 24.

———. "Whitman, Though Unopposed, Runs TV Ads." *New York Times*, 8 May 1997, B6.

———. "Challengers to Whitman Find Interest Hard to Raise." *New York Times*, 20 May 1997, B1.

———. "Whitman Borrowing Plan: Criticism May Not Go Away." *New York Times*, 7 June 1997, 24.

———. "Whitman and Legislators Plan $16.8 Billion Budget." *New York Times*, 20 June 1997, B6.

———. "McGreevey Pledges to Roll Back Auto Rates 10%." *New York Times*, 4 September 1997, B1.

———. "Whitman Shifts Focus from Car Insurance to Record on Other Issues." *New York Times*, 16 September 1997: B1.

———. "Opening Shots: Attack and Contrast in New Jersey." *New York Times*, 19 October 1997, 37.

———. "Whitman and McGreevey Take to Highways and Byways." *New York Times*, 26 October 1997, 35.

———. "McGreevey Offers Plan for Education as His Legacy." *New York Times*, 27 October 1997, A1.

———. "New Jersey Poll Finds Volatility Among Voters." *New York Times*, 31 October 1997, A1.

———. "Whitman Holds on by a Razor-Thin Margin." *New York Times*, 5 November 1997, A1.

———. "Whitman Restates Pledge on Taxes and Insurance." *New York Times*, 14 January 1998, A1.

———. "School Spending Debate Returns to Court." *New York Times*, 3 March 1998, B5.

———. "Assembly Bill Would End Caps on Rates for City Drivers." *New York Times*, 17 April 1998, B1.

———. "Assembly Passes Plan to Cut Car Premiums." *New York Times*, 21 April 1998, B5.

———. "New Jersey Legislators Vote to Overhaul Auto Insurance." *New York Times*, 19 May 1998, B1.

———. "Plan by Whitman on Urban Schools Backed by Court." *New York Times*, 22 May 1998, A1.

———. "Voters in Poll in New Jersey Fault Whitman on Insurance." *New York Times*, 17 September 1998, A1.

Property Tax Commission. *Report of Recommendations to Governor Christine Todd Whitman*. Trenton, N.J., 16 September 1998.

Pulley, Brett. "Parity in Schools." *New York Times*, 15 May 1997, B6.

———. "Rivals for Governor Step Up Campaigning." *New York Times*, 14 October 1997, B4.

Purdum, Todd S. "Whitman Concedes Chance of Higher Property Taxes." *New York Times*, 22 January 1994, 27.

Quinnipiac College Poll, Trend Archive, poll of 18 February 1997. Available from: http://www.quinnipiac.edu/polling/archive.html, "New Jersey State Trends."

Quinnipiac College Poll Institute Press Release, and results, released 3 April 1996. Poll conducted 28 March to 1 April 1 1996, of 908 New Jersey residents who said they were registered voters.

Reeher, Grant. *Narratives of Justice*. Ann Arbor: University of Michigan Press, 1996.

Remington, Richard S. "Kean Gives Final Approval to Income, Sales Tax Hikes." *Star-Ledger*, 1 January 1983, 1.

Richmond, Kelly. "A Killer Issue: School Funding: Democrats See Advantage." *Bergen County Record*, 22 December 1996.

Rivlin, Alice M. *Reviving the American Dream*. Washington, D.C.: Brookings Institution, 1992.

Robinson v. Cahill 287 Atlantic Reporter, 2d 187, p. 198

Roll call vote on S-40, 19 December 1996.

Ronan, Thomas. "Governor Hails Aid Idea but Asks More U.S. Funds." *New York Times,* 24 January 1971, 1.

Rosenthal, Alan. *The Decline of Representative Democracy*. Washington, D.C.: CQ Press, 1997.

Rudvolt, Harold J. "The Right to Learn." *New Jersey State Bar Journal,* 1970.

Salmore, Barbara, and Stephen Salmore. *Candidates, Parties, and Campaigns*. Washington, D.C: Congressional Quarterly Press, 1989.

———. *New Jersey Politics and Government: Suburban Politics Comes of Age*. Lincoln: University of Nebraska Press, 1993.

Salmon, Edward H. "Public School Finance Reform in New Jersey." Diss., University of Delaware, 1991.

Sarkar, Pia. "Most North Jersey Cities Say Tax Report Isn't Much Help." *Bergen County Record*, 17 September 1998, 1.

Schlesinger, Joseph. "On the Theory of Party Organizations." *Journal of Politics* 46, no. 2 (1984): 383.

Sciarra, David. Interview by Jeff Stonecash. March 1997.

Senate Bill No. 40, Introduced 27 June 1996, pages 1 and 2.

"Senate Passes a Measure Guaranteeing 'Thorough and Efficient' Education." *New York Times,* 28 May 1975, 87.

Smothers, Ronald. "Mt. Laurel Votes to Build Homes for Poor." *New York Times*, 12 April 1997, B1.

"State Estimate to Fix Schools is $1.8 Billion." *New York Times*, 18 November 1997, B6.

Star-Ledger-Eagleton poll released on June 11, 1997. Available from the web site of the *Bergen County Record,* 'http://www.bergen.com/campaign/njgovpoll.htm'.

State of New Jersey. *The General Property Tax in New Jersey: A Century of Inequities: Sixth Report of the Commission on State Tax Policy.* Trenton, N.J., 1953.

Stephens, G. Ross. "Fiscal Centralization in the States." *Journal of Politics* 36 (1974): 52–66.

Stevens, Robert, and Rosemary Stevens. *Welfare Medicine in America: A Case Study of Medicaid.* New York: Free Press, 1974.

Stockman, Gerald. Interview by Jeff Stonecash. 17 July 1996.

Stonecash, Jeffrey M. "State Policies Regarding Local Resource Acquisition." *American Politics Quarterly* 9, no. 4 (1981): 401–25.

———. "Fiscal Centralization in the American States: Similarity and Diversity." *Publius* 13, no. 4 (1983): 123–37.

———. "Incremental and Abrupt Change in Fiscal Centralization in the American States, 1957–1983." In *The Politics of Intergovernmental Relations,* ed. David R. Morgan and J. Edward Benton. Westport, Conn.: Greenwood Press, 1986.

——— "Inter-Party Competition, Political Dialogue, and Public Policy: A Critical Review." *Policy Studies Journal* 16, no. 2 (1987–88): 243–62.

——— "State Responses to Declining National Support: Behavior in the Post 1978 Era." *Policy Studies Journal* 18, no. 3 (1990): 214–26.

——— "'Split' Constituencies and the Impact of Party Control." *Social Science History* 16, no. 3 (1992): 455–78.

——— *American State and Local Politics.* New York: Harcourt and Brace, 1995.

——— "The State Politics Literature: Moving Beyond Covariation Studies and Pursuing Politics." *Polity* 28, no. 4 (1996): 561–81.

——— "The Politics of State-Local Fiscal Relations." *Governing Partners: State-Local Relations in the United States.* Boulder, Colo.: Westview Press, 1998.

——— "Political Cleavage in State Legislative Parties." *Legislative Studies Quarterly* 24, no. 2 (1999): 281–302.

——— *Class and Party in American Politics.* Boulder, Colo.: Westview, 2000.

Sugrue, Thomas J. *The Origins of the Urban Crisis.* Princeton: Princeton University Press, 1996.

Sullivan, Joseph F. "Plan Reached to Finance Schools Till End of Year." *New York Times*, 16 July 1975, 79.

———. "School Closings in Jersey Jeopardize the Handicapped." *New York Times*, 7 July 1976, 37.

———. "Bateman is Routed: Govenor Sweeps Bergan, Key G.O.P. Area–Gets Big Blue Collar Vote. " *New York Times*, 9 November 1977, 1.

———. "Census Dramatizes Changes in Jersey Life During the 1970s." *New York Times*, 26 January 1981, 3.

———. "Kramer and Kean: A Shift in Emphasis." *New York Times*, 1 February 1981, section 2, 8.

———. "Jersey Race to Test President's Policies." *New York Times*, 7 June 1981, 1.

———. "Florio and Kean Get the Race into High Gear." *New York Times*, 30 August 1981, section 11, 1.

———. "Kean and Florio Evaluate Education." *New York Times*, 23 October 1981, B2.

———. "Kean Gives Vow He Won't Raise Tax on Income." *New York Times*, 2 December 1981, B1.

———. "Legislature Survives a Stormy Session." *New York Times*, 1 August 1982, section 11, 1.

———. "Tomorrow Is a Big Day for the Budget." *New York Times*, 12 December 1982, section 11, 1.

———. "Kean Rejects Income-Tax Rise." *New York Times*, 16 December 1982, B3.

———. "Jersey Democrats to Seek a Compromise on Taxes." *New York Times*, 17 December 1982, B4.

———. "Showdown on Budget Is Set by Karcher." *New York Times*, 19 December 1982, section 11, 1.

———. "Jersey Lawmakers Approve Tax Rise, but Kean Vetoes It." *New York Times*, 21 December 1982, B1.

———. "Tax Rises Proposed in Jersey; Kean to Work for Both Bills." *New York Times*, 28 December 1982, B3.

———. "Jersey Considers Tax Compromise to Raise Funds." *New York Times*, 31 December 1982, B2.

———. "Taxes Resolved, Kean Addresses Other Problems." *New York Times*, 9 January 1983, section 11, 1.

———. "2 Bills Facing Vetoes Pressed by Democrats." *New York Times*, 25 March 1984, section 11, 1.

———. "Jersey Assembly Votes Income Tax Relief." *New York Times*, 4 January 1985, B2.

———. "Kean Will Propose $8.8 Billion Budget, Including Tax Relief." *New York Times*, 27 January 1985, A1.

———. "Kean Proposes Income Tax Cut of 10% for 1985." *New York Times*, 10 May 1985, B2.

———. "Kean Signs Bill Providing Cuts on Income Tax." *New York Times*, 27 August 1985, B2.

———. "Aid to Cities Splits Kean and G.O.P. in Assembly." *New York Times*, 1 March 1987, section 11, 1.

———. "Hardwick and Kean Split on Aid to Localities." *New York Times,* 10 April 1988, section 12, 1.

———. "Jersey's Funds for Schools Found Flawed." *New York Times*, 26 August 1988, B1.

———. "Leaders of New Jersey Tax Rebellion Take Aim at Legislature." *New York Times*, 23 November 1990, B6.

———. "Florio Calls for Election to be a Referendum on Bush." *New York Times*, 30 October 1991, B1.

———. "Fight on Trenton Aid to Poor School Districts Goes to Court, Again." *New York Times*, 9 July 1992, B1.

———. "'90 Tax Rise Overshadows Trenton Races." *New York Times*, 18 October 1993, B1.

———. "Legislature Divided over Kean Budget." *New York Times*, 31 January 1994, B2.

———. "Battered Democrats Try a New Direction." *New York Times*, 6 February 1994, 44.

Sullivan, Joseph F. "Whitman Asks for Time to Solve School Aid Gap." *New York Times*, 25 May 1994, B6.

———. "Learning the Power of Tax Cuts." *New York Times*, 20 June 1994, B5.

———. "Top New Jersey Court Orders New Plan for School Funds." *New York Times*, 13 July 1994, 1.

———. "Kean Shift to the Left Sets Stage for Race." *New York Times*, 3 February 1995, section 11, 1.

———. "For Whitman and Senate, Agreement on School Aid." *New York Times*, 19 May 1995, B5.

Sullivan, Ronald. "Hughes Calls Victory a Mandate for Program Equaling Johnson's." *New York Times*, 4 November 1965, 51:2.

———. "Jersey Sales Tax Signed by Hughes." *New York Times*, 28 April 1966, 1.

———. "A New Tax Needed, Hughes Asserts." *New York Times*, 11 January 1967, 23.

———. "Jersey's Budget Is Near $1 Billion." *New York Times*, 15 February 1967, 24.

———. "Hughes Says G.O.P. Is Injecting Racial Issue into Its Campaign." *New York Times*, 28 October 1967, 31.

———. "Busing of Pupils a Top Jersey Issue." *New York Times*, 29 October 1967, 72.

———. "Hughes and Case Take to Stump as Jersey Campaign Nears End." *New York Times*, 6 November 1967, 25.

———. "A Hughes Setback." *New York Times*, 8 November 1967, 1–6.

———. "Hughes Is Warned of Tax Increase." *New York Times*, 14 January 1968, 16.

———. "Hughes Says Urban Need May Dictate Budget Rise." *New York Times*, 16 February 1968, 1.

———. "Hughes Asks Rise in Tax to Aid Cities." *New York Times*, 23 April 1968, 1.

———. "Hughes Asks Income Tax." *New York Times*, 26 April 1968, 1.

———. "Jersey Spending of $2 Billion Asked." *New York Times*, 28 April 1968, 38.

———. "Jersey 'Very Ill,' Hughes Declares." *New York Times*, 5 May 1968, 17.

———. "Republicans Cut Hughes Program." *New York Times*, 23 May 1968, 38.

———. "Hughes Says G.O.P. Aid Cuts 'Could Provoke Civil Disorder.'" *New York Times*, 24 May 1968, 24.

———. "Republicans Revolt in Jersey: Lean to Hughes on Urban Aid." *New York Times*, 28 May 1968, 1.

———. "Hughes Appeals for Aid to Cities." *New York Times*, 16 June 1968, 41.

———. "Jersey Senate Backs a Budget of $1.15 Billion." *New York Times*, 18 June 1968, 27.

———. "Hughes Vetoes 32 Bills in Jersey; G.O.P. to Fight for Aid Plans." *New York Times*, 10 September 1968, 43.

———. "Hughes Defeated on Aid Programs." *New York Times*, 14 September 1968.

———. "Hughes' Budget Asks $1.36 Billion." *New York Times*, 11 February 1969, 1.

———. "Cahill and Meyner Clash in Angry Debate." *New York Times*, 20 October 1969, 1.

———. "Cahill Proposes a 5% Sales Levy in Budget Crisis." *New York Times*, 13 January 1970, 1.

———. "Now Cahill Inherits a Few Disasters." *New York Times*, 18 January 1970, section 4, 6.

———. "$50 Million Newark Aid Plan Is Voted By New Jersey Legislature." *The New York Time*, 19 December 1970, 20.

———. "Cahill Presents Austerity Budget." *New York Times*, 17 February 1971, 26.

———. "High Court Refuses to Hear Plea by Jersey Defending School Tax." *New York Times*, 24 October 1973, 97.

———. "Byrne Tax Proposal Appears in Trouble; G.O.P. Is Opposed." *New York Times*, 14 June 1974, 69 and 71.

———. "Byrne's Tax Defeat." *New York Times*, 29 July 1974, 51.

———. "New Jersey Had 18 Months, and Still No School Plan." *New York Times*, 12 January 1975, section 4, 6.

———. "66 Million Withheld from Jersey Budget." *New York Times*, 17 January 1975, 1.

———. "Byrne to Seek Income Tax and Cut in the Sales Levy." *New York Times*, 28 January 1975, 1.

———. "Byrne Takes Tax Fight to the People." *New York Times*, 27 June 1975, 75.

———. "Legislature to Give All 'Efficient Schooling.'" *New York Times*, 23 September 1975, 79.

———. " Byrne Says Defeat of Bond Proposals Creates New Crisis." *New York Times*, 6 November 1975, 1.

———. "Byrne Says an Income Tax Is Now Up to Legislature." *New York Times*, 14 November 1975, 79.

———. "Byrne to Ask High Court to Order New School Plan." *New York Times*, 27 November 1975, 71.

Tedeschi, Bruno. "Governor Has Promises to Keep." *Bergen County Record*, 5 November 1997.

"Text of Governor Meyner's Inaugural Address in Trenton." *New York Times*, 20 January 1954, 12.

Thomas, Clive S., and Ronald J. Hrebenaer. "Interest Groups in the States." In *Politics in the American States: A Comparative Analysis,* edited by Virginia Gray, Russell L. Hanson, and Herbert Jacob, 113–43. Washington, D.C.: CQ Press, 1999.

"28 in Black Patrol Walking the Troubled Streets." *New York Times*, 9 July 1970, 1.

U.S. Department of Commerce, U.S. Bureau of the Census. *City and County Data Book.* Washington, D.C.: Government Printing Office, 1957 and 1992.

"Using His Right, Florio Moves from Dead to Dead Heat." *New York Times*, 30 September 1993, A1.

Van Tassel, Priscilla. "Poor Districts Gain in Battle on School Funds." *New York Times*, 27 May 1984, section 11, 1.

———. "School Financing Challenged at Trial." *New York Times*, 5 October 1986, section 11, 1.

Waggoner, Walter H. "Jersey Passes Districting Plan; Senate Will Have 29 Members." *New York Times*, 13 April 1965, 41.

———. "Republican Rule Ended in Jersey." *New York Times*, 3 November 1965, 31.

———. "Trenton Session Reopening Today." *New York Times*, 2 July 1969, 43.

———. "Jersey Approves Anticrime Bills." *New York Times*, 3 July 1969, 1.

———. "Cahill Says Rising Relief Costs May Bring Need for New Taxes." *New York Times*, 2 November 1970, 82.

———. "Cahill Says Rising Relief Costs May Bring Need for New Taxes." *New York Times*, 20 November 1970, 82.

———. "Cahill Sees Ruling as Proving the Need to Find A New Way to Pay for Schools." *New York Times*, 4 April 1973, 91.

———. "Byrne Presses Late Drive for a Jersey School Tax." *New York Times*, 24 December 1974, 43.

———. "Senate Bids Court Rehear Tax Case." *New York Times*, 14 January 1975, 72.

Waldron, Martin. "School Equality Upheld in New Jersey." *New York Times*, 31 January 1976, 1.

———. "New School Taxes Unlikely in New Jersey." *New York Times*, 3 February 1976, 65.

———. "Byrne's Tax Plan Draws Union Fire." *New York Times*, 6 February 1976, 61.

———. "Jersey Assembly Passes an Income Tax Measure." *New York Times*, 16 March 1976, 1.

———. "Schools in Jersey Face July Closing." *New York Times*, 14 May 1976, 19.

———. "Income Tax Fails as Issue in Legislative Primaries, Dugan and Mrs. Ammond Defeated in Senate Race." *New York Times*, 9 June 1977.

———. "High Court Lets Stand the Order That Could Close State Schools July 1." *New York Times*, 11 June 1976, 23.

———. "Income Tax Fails to Help State's Cities." *New York Times*, 16 October 1977, section 11, 1.

Walker, David B. *The Rebirth of Federalism*. Chatham, N.J.: Chatham House, 1995.

Walters, Jonathan. "The Whitman Squeeze." *Governing,* November 1995, 18–25.

Wattenberg, Martin. *The Decline of American Political Parties, 1952–1994*. Cambridge: Harvard University Press, 1996.

Weiher, Gregory R., and Jon Lawrence. "Growth in State Government Employment: A Time Series Analysis." *Western Political Quarterly* 44 (1991): 373–88.

Weisberg, Jacob. *In Defense of Government: The Fall and Rise of Public Trust*. New York: Scribner, 1996.

Weisbrot, Robert. *Freedom Bound: A History of the Civil Rights Movement*. New York: Penguin, 1991.

Weischadle, David E. "T and E: Is the Act An Asset or Not?" *New York Times*, 12 December 1978, section 11, 46.

Weissman, Art. *Christine Todd Whitman*. New York: Birch Lane Press, 1996.

Welch, Susan, and Kay Thompson. "The Impact of Federal Incentives on State Policy Innovation." *American Journal of Political Science* 24, no. 4 (1980): 715–29.

Wright, George C. "Jersey Leadership Taken by Meyner." *New York Times*, 15 May 1953, 1.

———. "$89,500,000 Levy for New Jersey Seen." *New York Times*, 2 April 1954, 50.

———. "Meyner's Budget Averts Tax Rises." *New York Times*, 1 February 1955, 6.

———. "Budget in Jersey Asks $315,452,130." *New York Times*, 7 February 1956, 7.

———. "Meyner Appeals to Legislature." *New York Times*, 16 September 1956, 54.

———. "Meyner to Offer a Record Budget." *New York Times*, 4 January 1957, 13.

———. "342 Million Budget Sets Jersey Record; Tax Rises Averted." *New York Times*, 19 February 1957, 1.

———. "Meyner Wins in Jersey, Takes Assembly." *New York Times*, 6 November 1957, 1.

———. "Meyner Asks Rise of 1C in 'Gas' Tax to Finance Roads." *New York Times* 15 January 1958, 1.

———. "Meyner Budget Sets 399 Million Mark; Seeks New Taxes." *New York Times*, 18 February 1958, 1.

———. "Jersey Advances Business Tax Bill." *New York Times*, 22 April 1958, 45.

———. "GOP Acts to Cut Meyner's Budget." *New York Times*, 6 May 1958, 37.

———. "Meyner and Legislative Chiefs Agree on Record Jersey Budget." *New York Times*, 27 May 1958, 33.

Wright, Gerald C., Robert C. Erikson, and John P. McIver. "Measuring State Partisanship and Ideology with Survey Data." *Journal of Politics* 47 (1985): 469–89.

———. "Public Opinion and Policy Liberalism in the American States." *American Journal of Political Science* 31, no. 4 (1987): 980–1001.

Wuthnow, Robert. *The Consciousness Reformation.* Berkeley: University of California Press, 1976.

Yin, Robert K. *Case Study Research: Design and Methods.* Thousand Oaks, Calif.: Sage, 1994.

Zarate, Vincent R. "Kean Backs Sales Tax Hike as Alternative to Gas Levy." *Star-Ledger*, 8 December 1982, 1.

———. "Legislators to Vote on Income Tax Hike for 'Rich'." *Star-Ledger*, 16 December 1982, 22.

———. "Dems Ready to Defy Kean on Income Tax Hike Vote." *Star-Ledger*, 19 December 1982, 1.

———. "Governor Vetoes Boost in the State Income Tax." *Star-Ledger*, 21 December 1982, 1.

———. "Kean Says Tax Increases Will Balance Books Till '84." *Star-Ledger*, 2 January 1983, 1, 10–11.

Index